The Way of the House Husband

KOUSUKE OONO

3

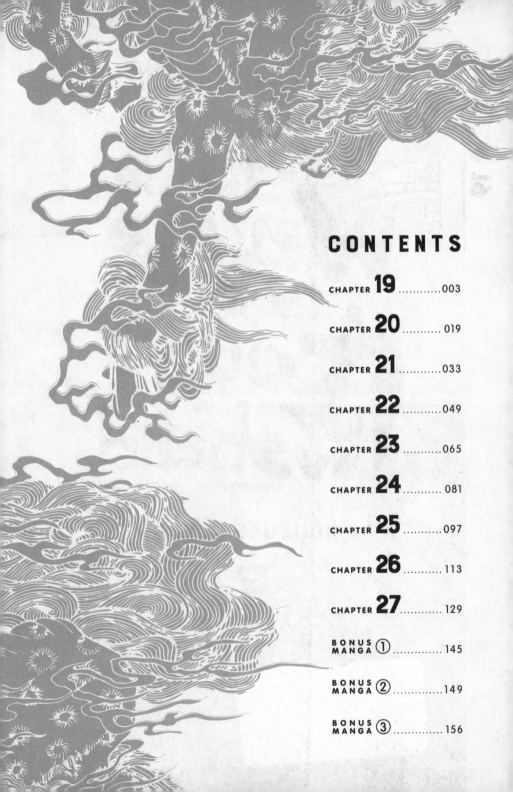

CONTENTS

CHAPTER **19** 003

CHAPTER **20** 019

CHAPTER **21** 033

CHAPTER **22** 049

CHAPTER **23** 065

CHAPTER **24** 081

CHAPTER **25** 097

CHAPTER **26** 113

CHAPTER **27** 129

BONUS MANGA ① 145

BONUS MANGA ② 149

BONUS MANGA ③ 156

CHAPTER 19

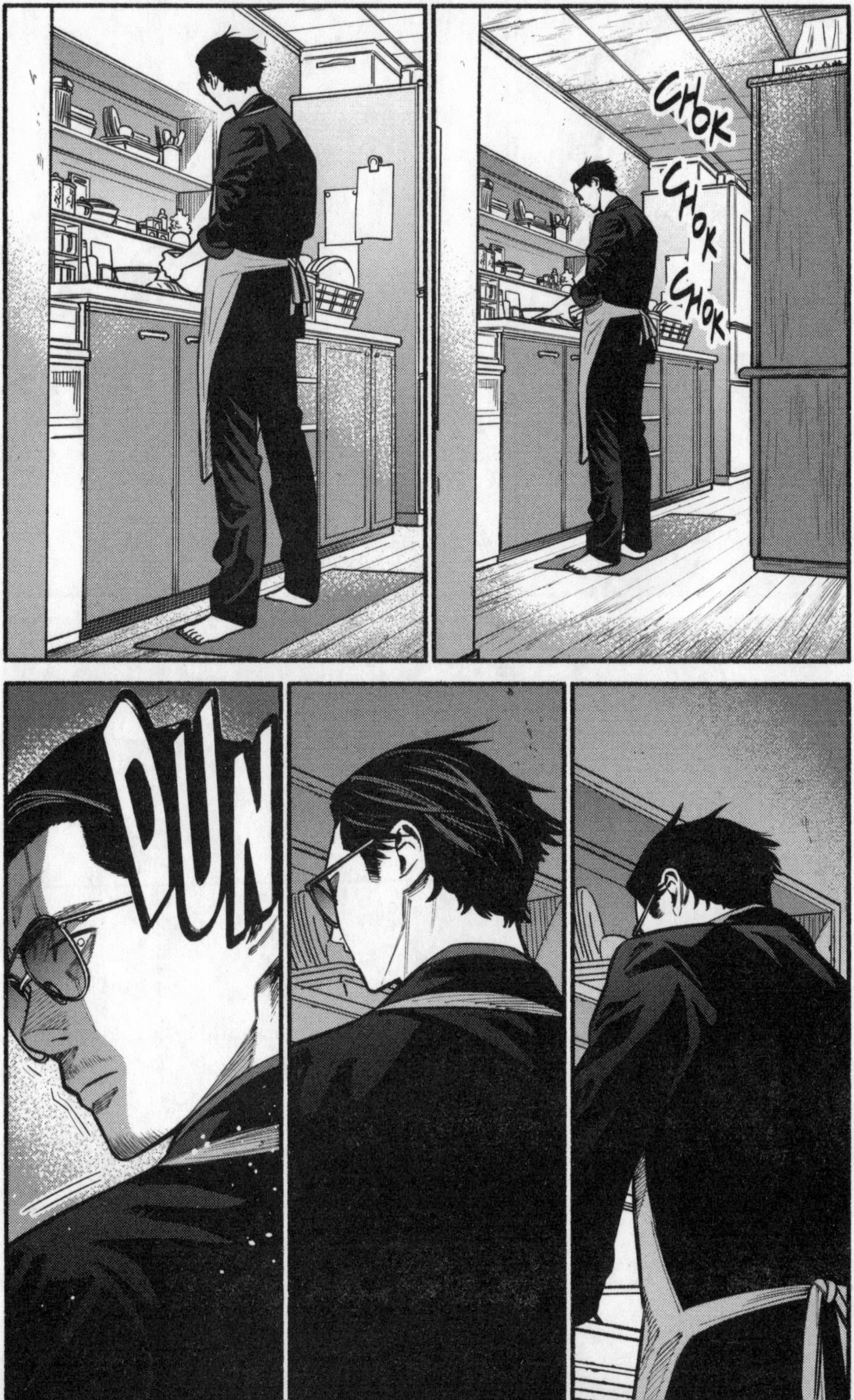
CHOK
CHOK
CHOK
CHOK
DUN

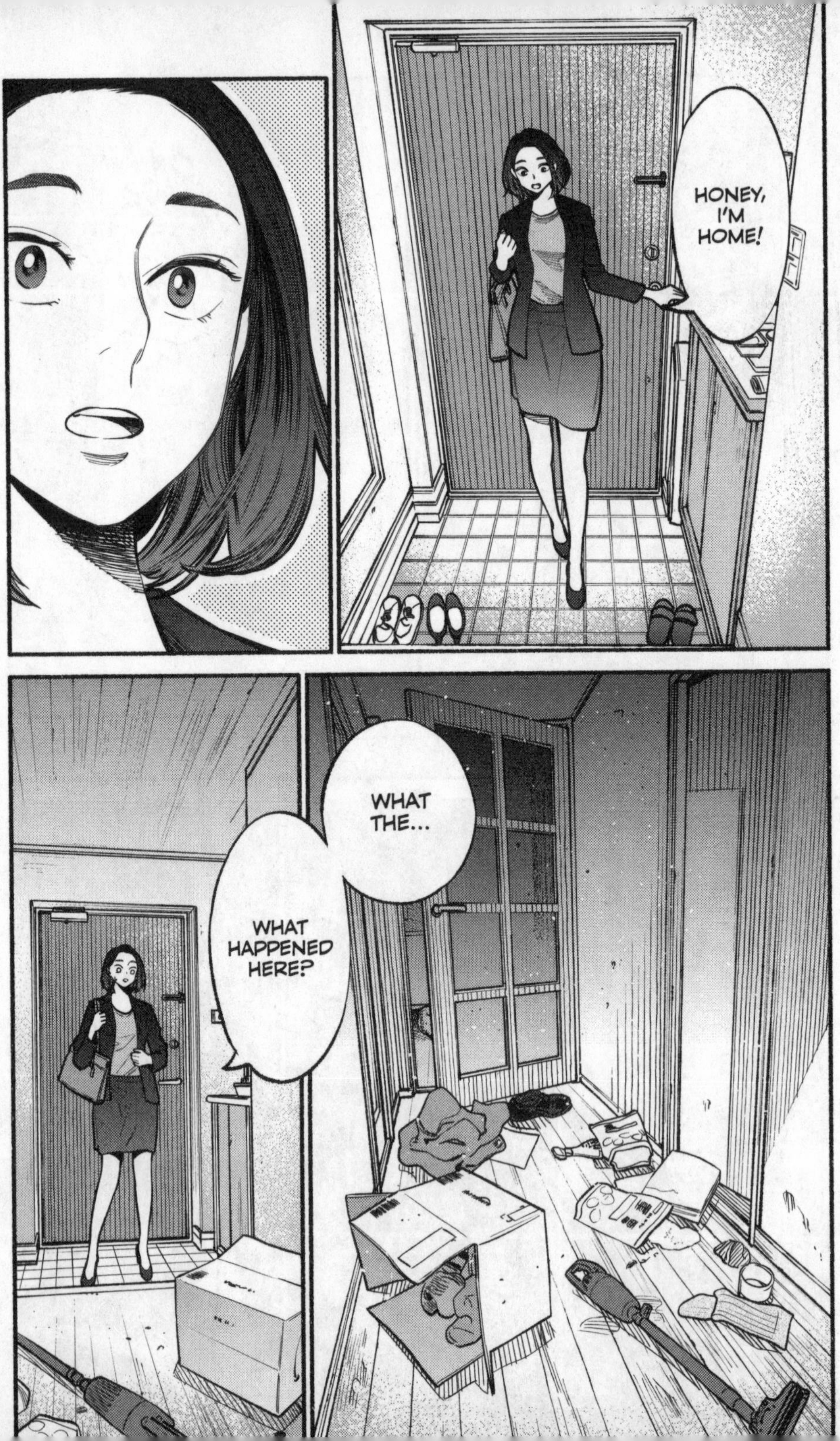
HONEY, I'M HOME!
WHAT THE...
WHAT HAPPENED HERE?

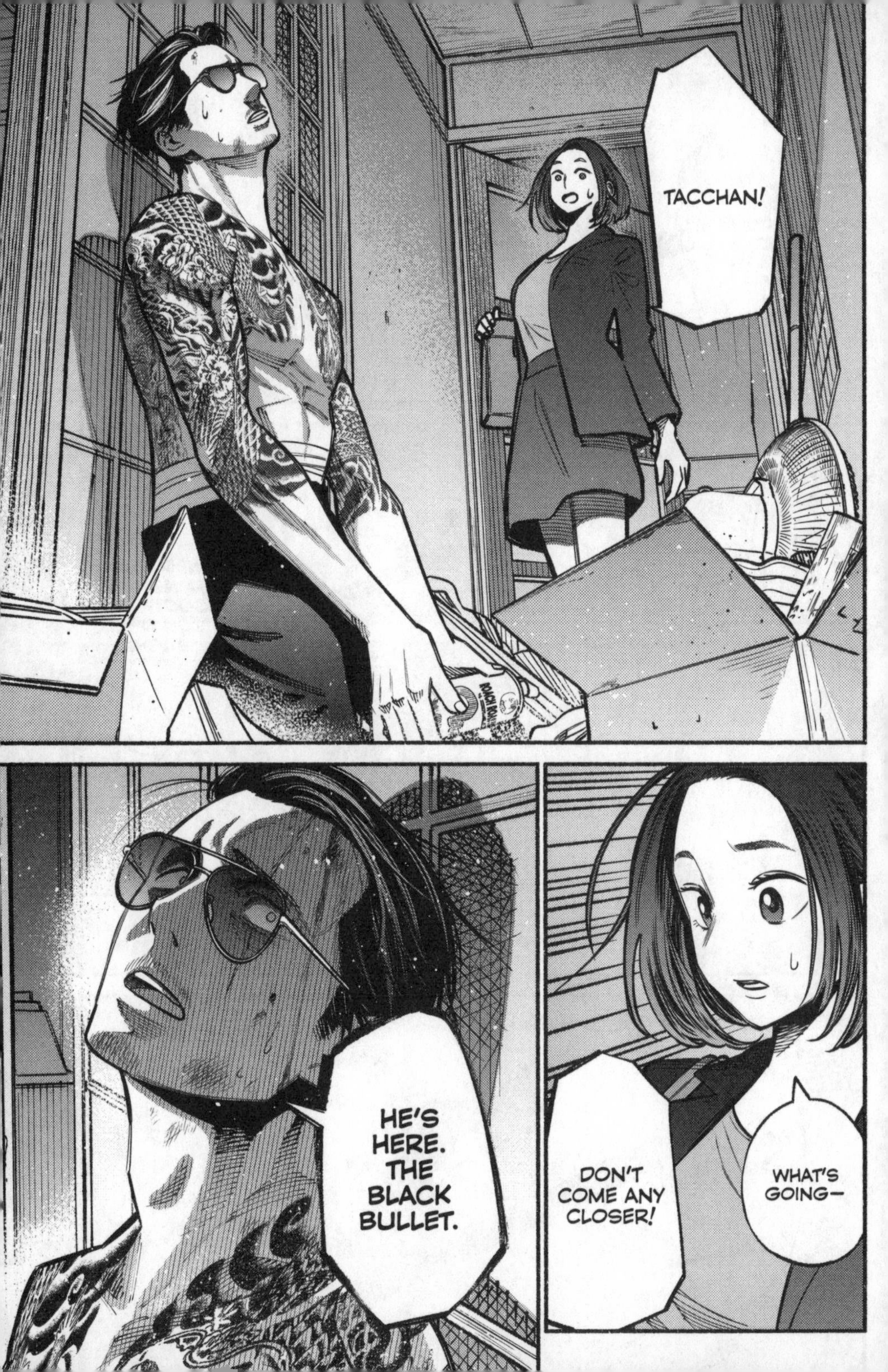
TACCHAN!
WHAT'S GOING—
DON'T COME ANY CLOSER!
HE'S HERE. THE BLACK BULLET.

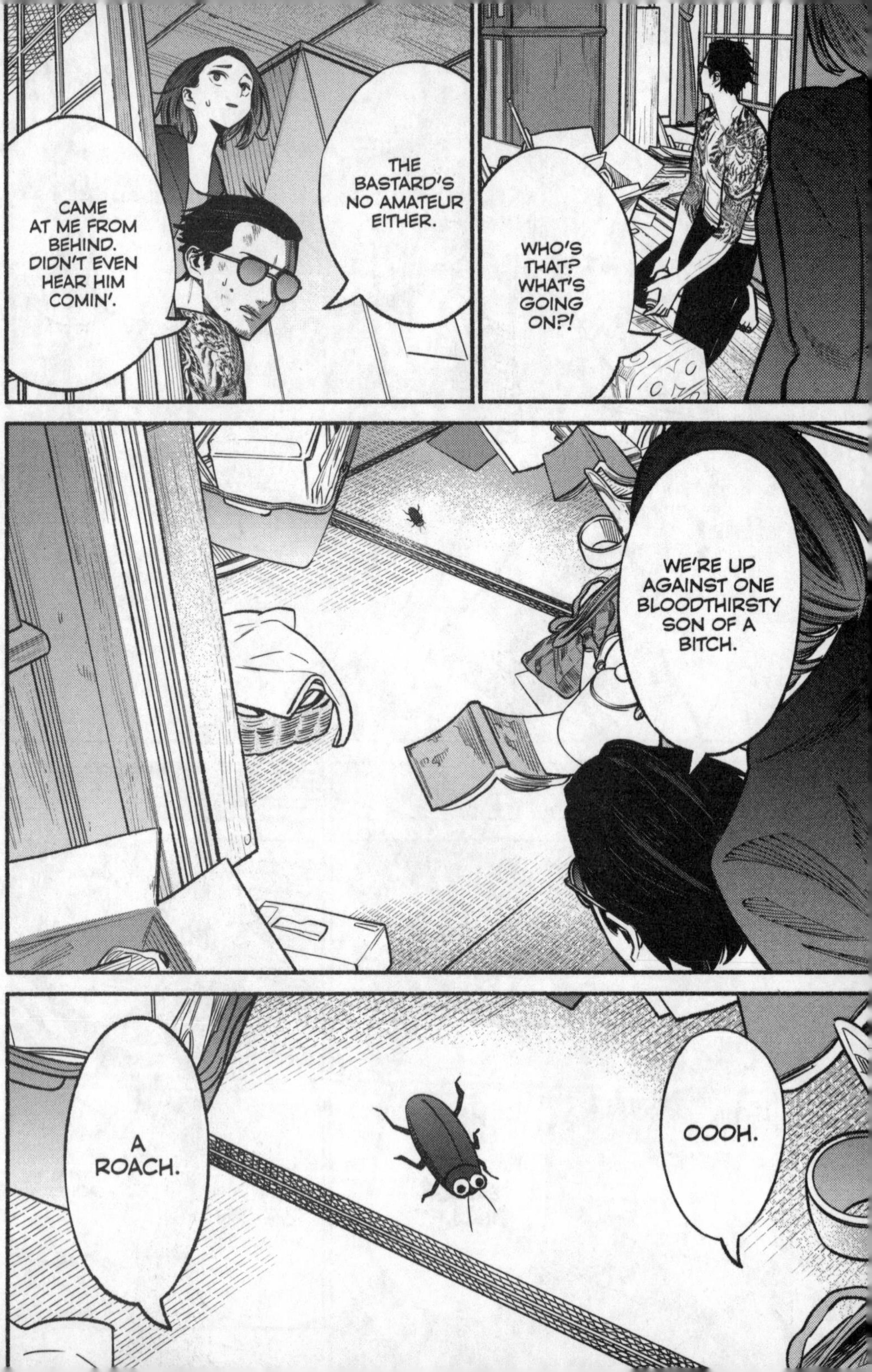
WHO'S THAT? WHAT'S GOING ON?!
THE BASTARD'S NO AMATEUR EITHER.
CAME AT ME FROM BEHIND. DIDN'T EVEN HEAR HIM COMIN'.
WE'RE UP AGAINST ONE BLOODTHIRSTY SON OF A BITCH.
OOOH.
A ROACH.

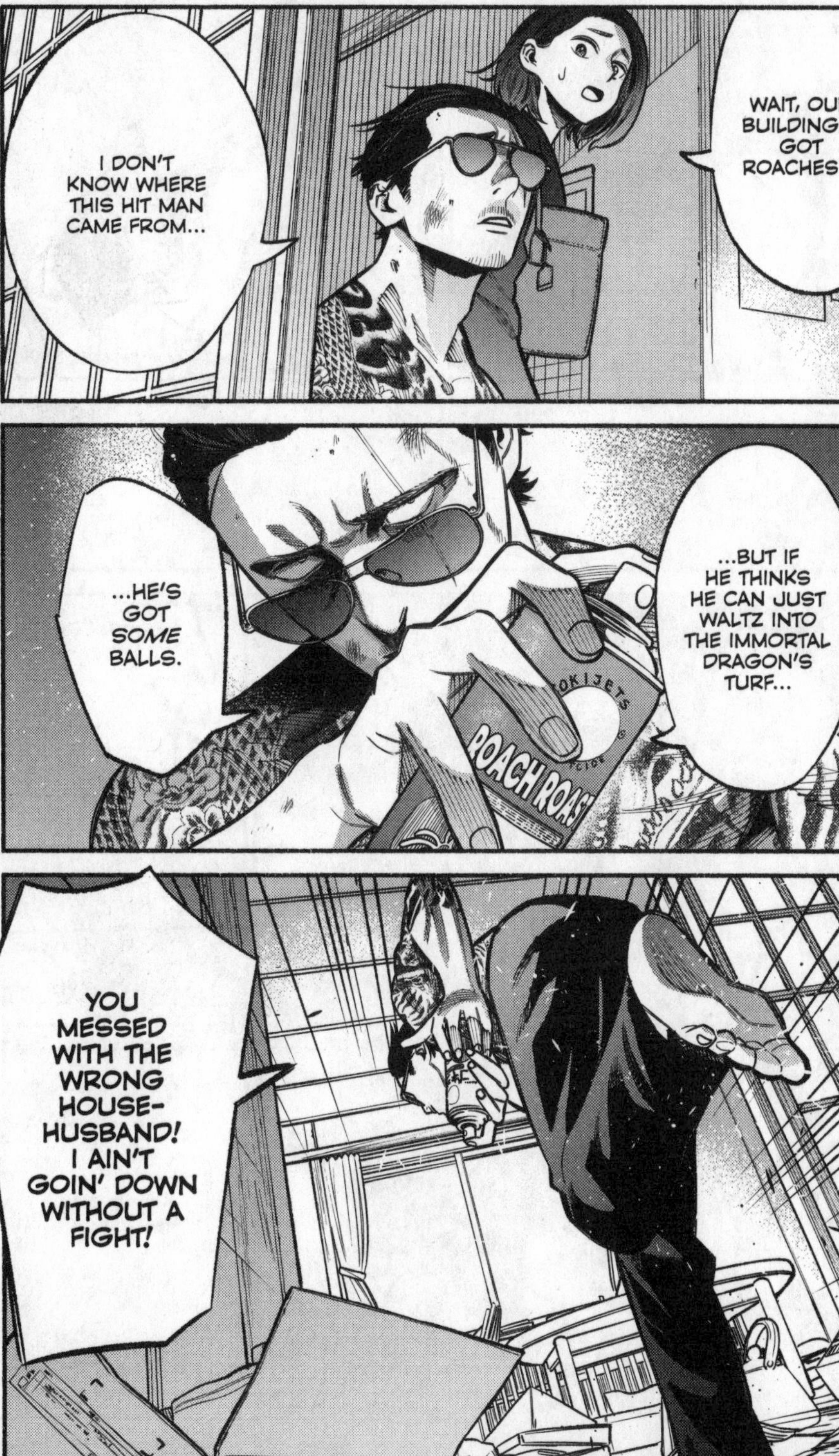
WAIT, OUR BUILDING'S GOT ROACHES?!
I DON'T KNOW WHERE THIS HIT MAN CAME FROM...
...BUT IF HE THINKS HE CAN JUST WALTZ INTO THE IMMORTAL DRAGON'S TURF...
...HE'S GOT *SOME* BALLS.
YOU MESSED WITH THE WRONG HOUSE-HUSBAND! I AIN'T GOIN' DOWN WITHOUT A FIGHT!

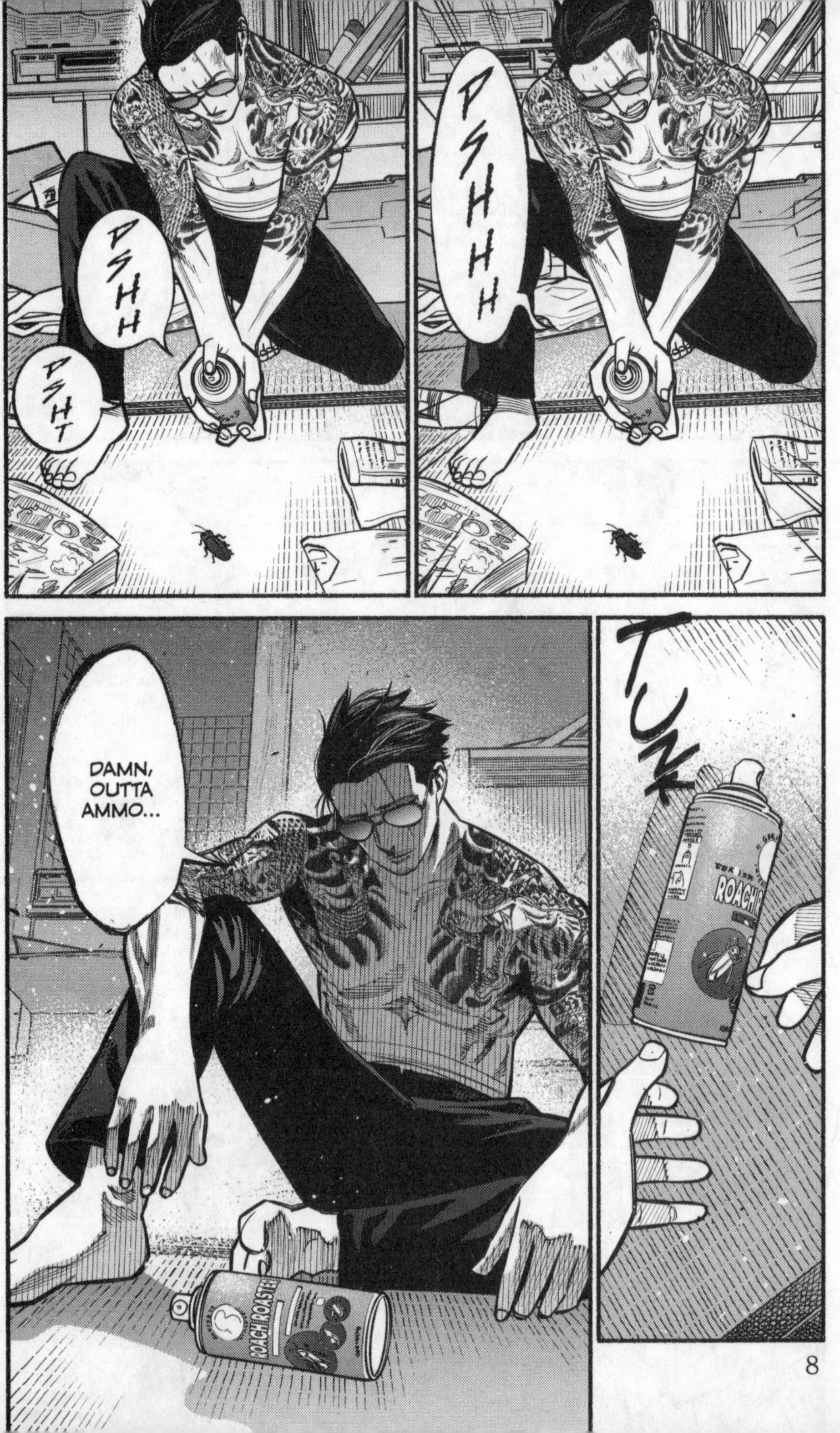
PSHHHH
PSHH
PSHT
TUNK
ROACH
DAMN, OUTTA AMMO...
ROACH ROASTER

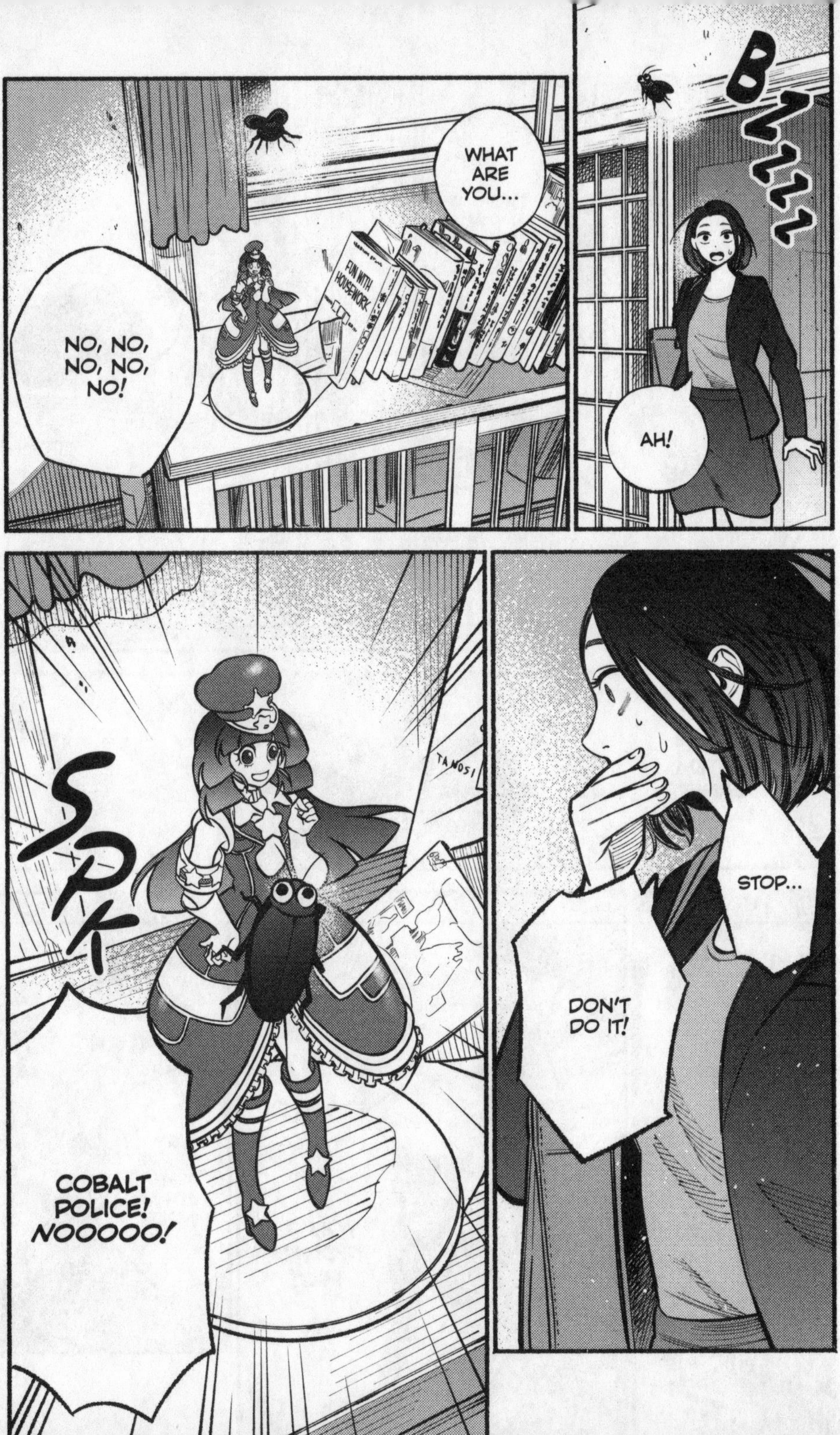
BZZZZ
AH!
WHAT ARE YOU...
FUN WITH HOUSEWORK
NO, NO, NO, NO, NO!
STOP...
DON'T DO IT!
TANOSI
SPK
COBALT POLICE! NOOOOO!

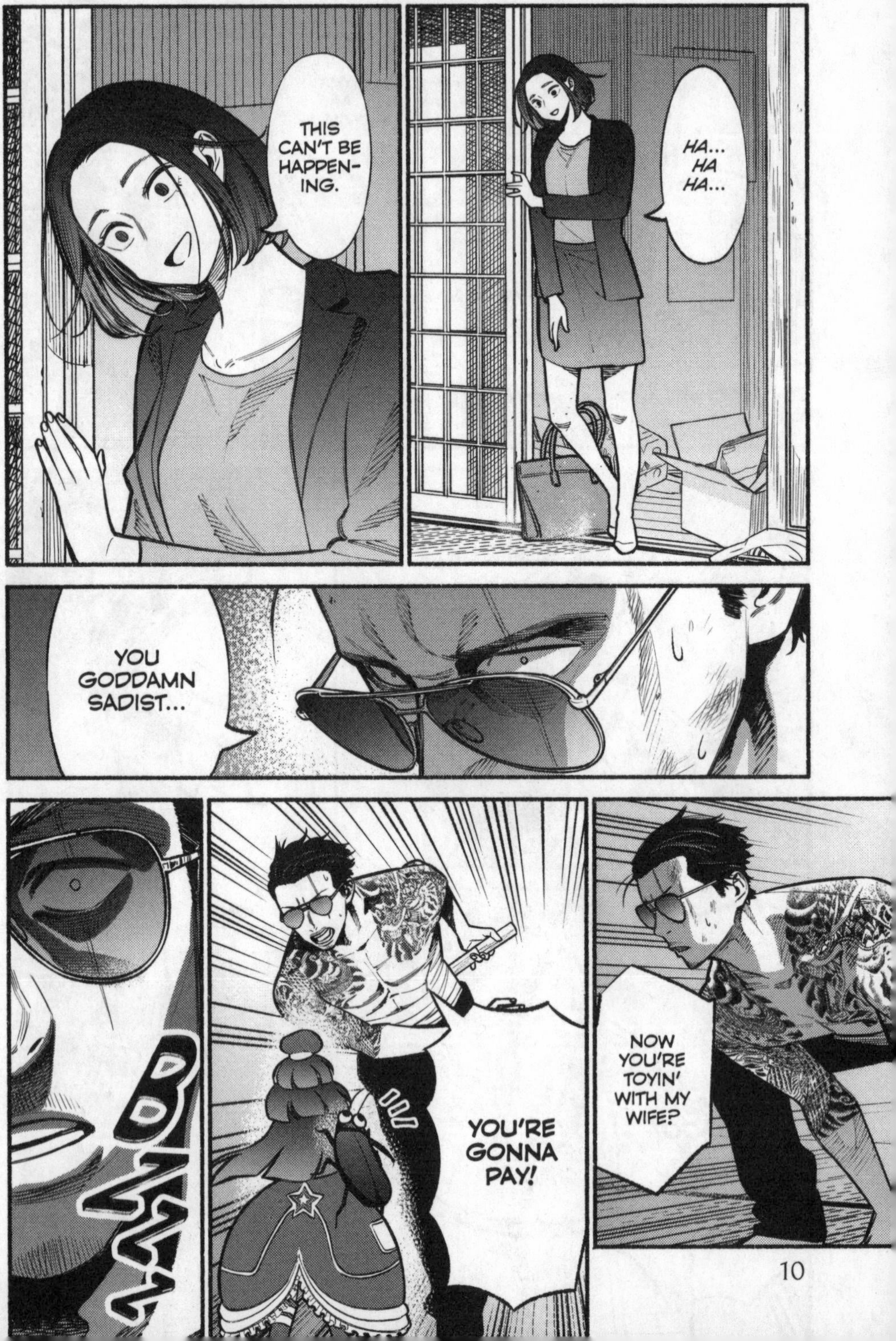
HA... HA HA...
THIS CAN'T BE HAPPEN-ING.
YOU GODDAMN SADIST...
NOW YOU'RE TOYIN' WITH MY WIFE?
YOU'RE GONNA PAY!

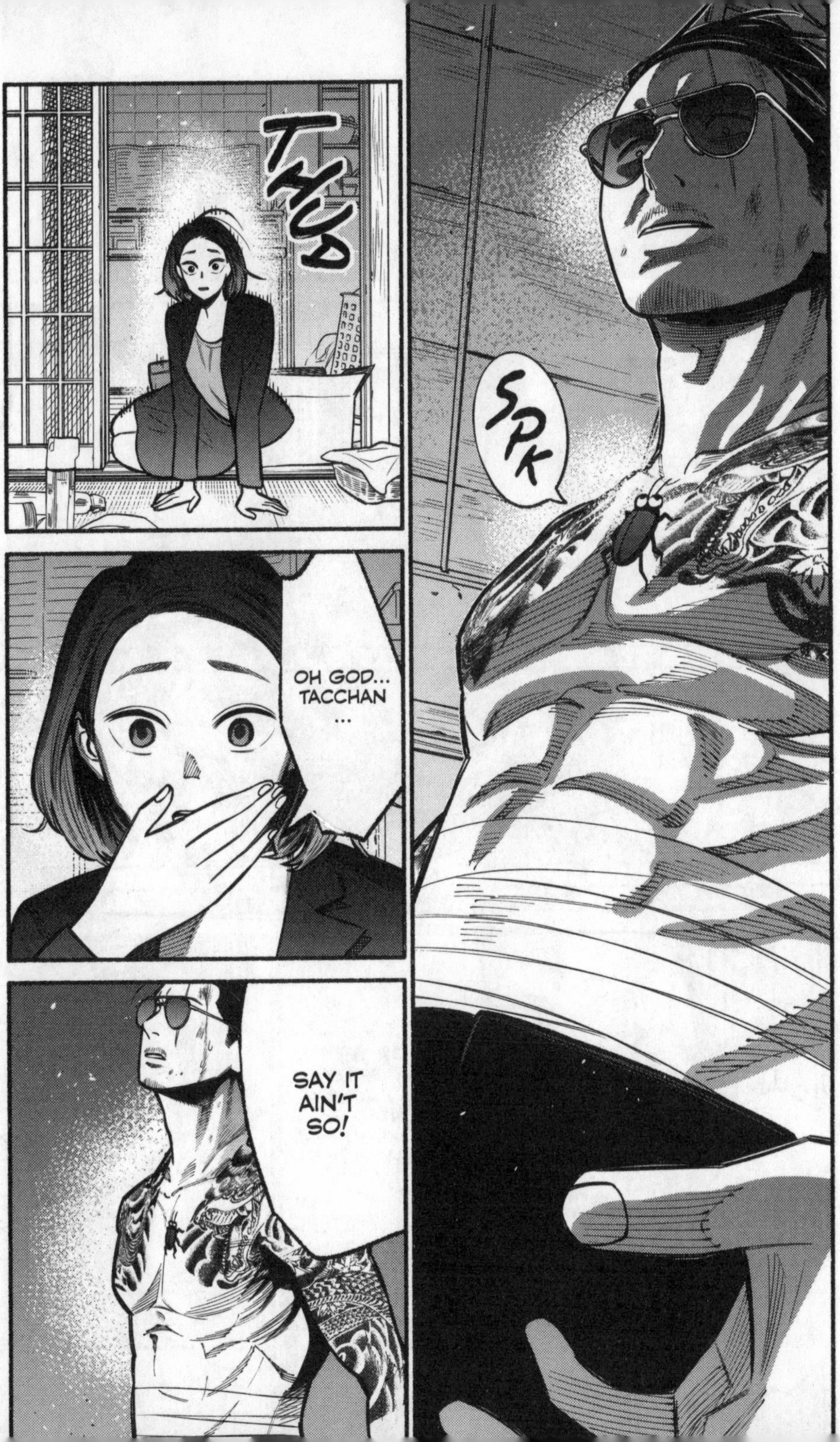
SPK
THUD
OH GOD... TACCHAN ...
SAY IT AIN'T SO!

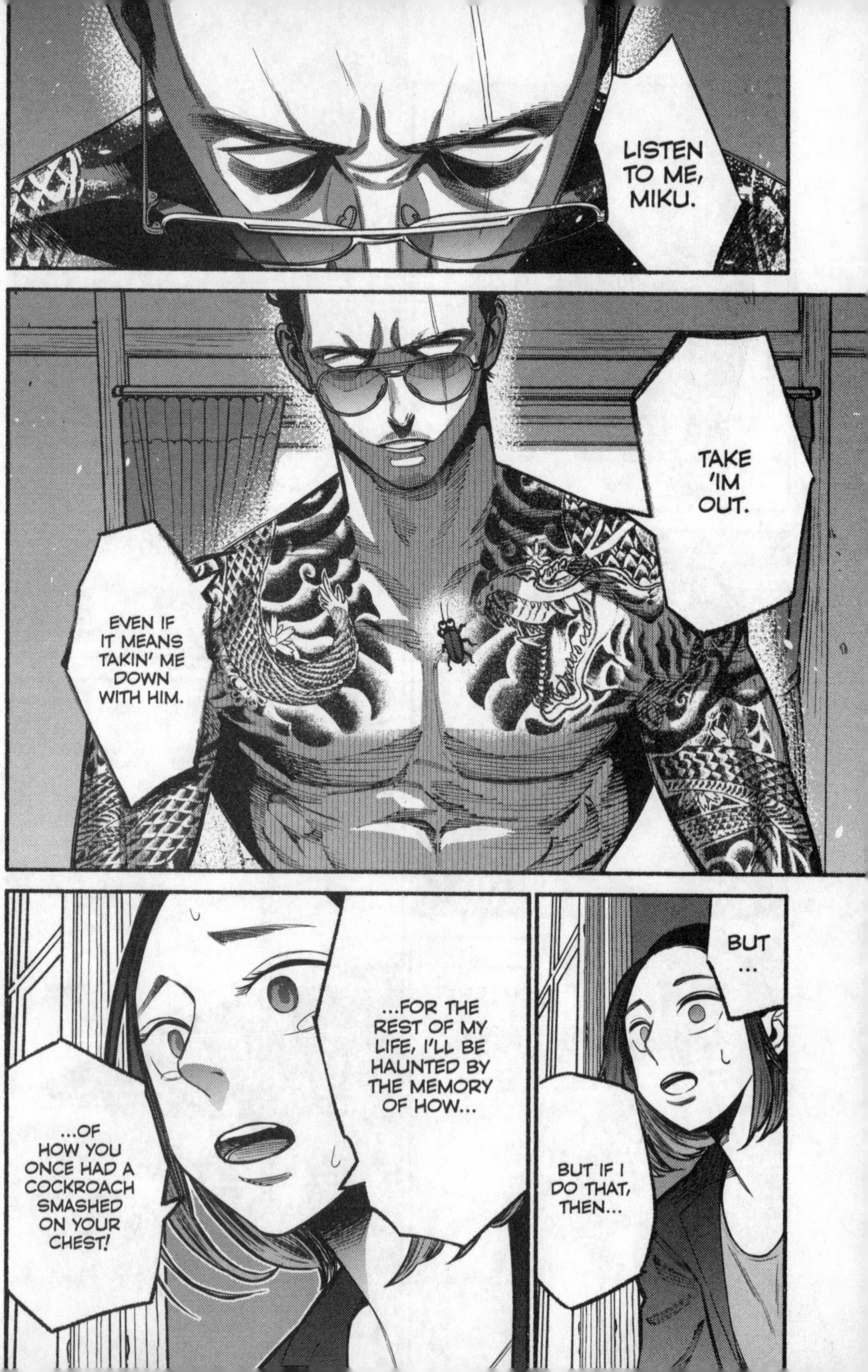
LISTEN TO ME, MIKU.
TAKE 'IM OUT.
EVEN IF IT MEANS TAKIN' ME DOWN WITH HIM.
BUT...
BUT IF I DO THAT, THEN...
...FOR THE REST OF MY LIFE, I'LL BE HAUNTED BY THE MEMORY OF HOW...
...OF HOW YOU ONCE HAD A COCKROACH SMASHED ON YOUR CHEST!

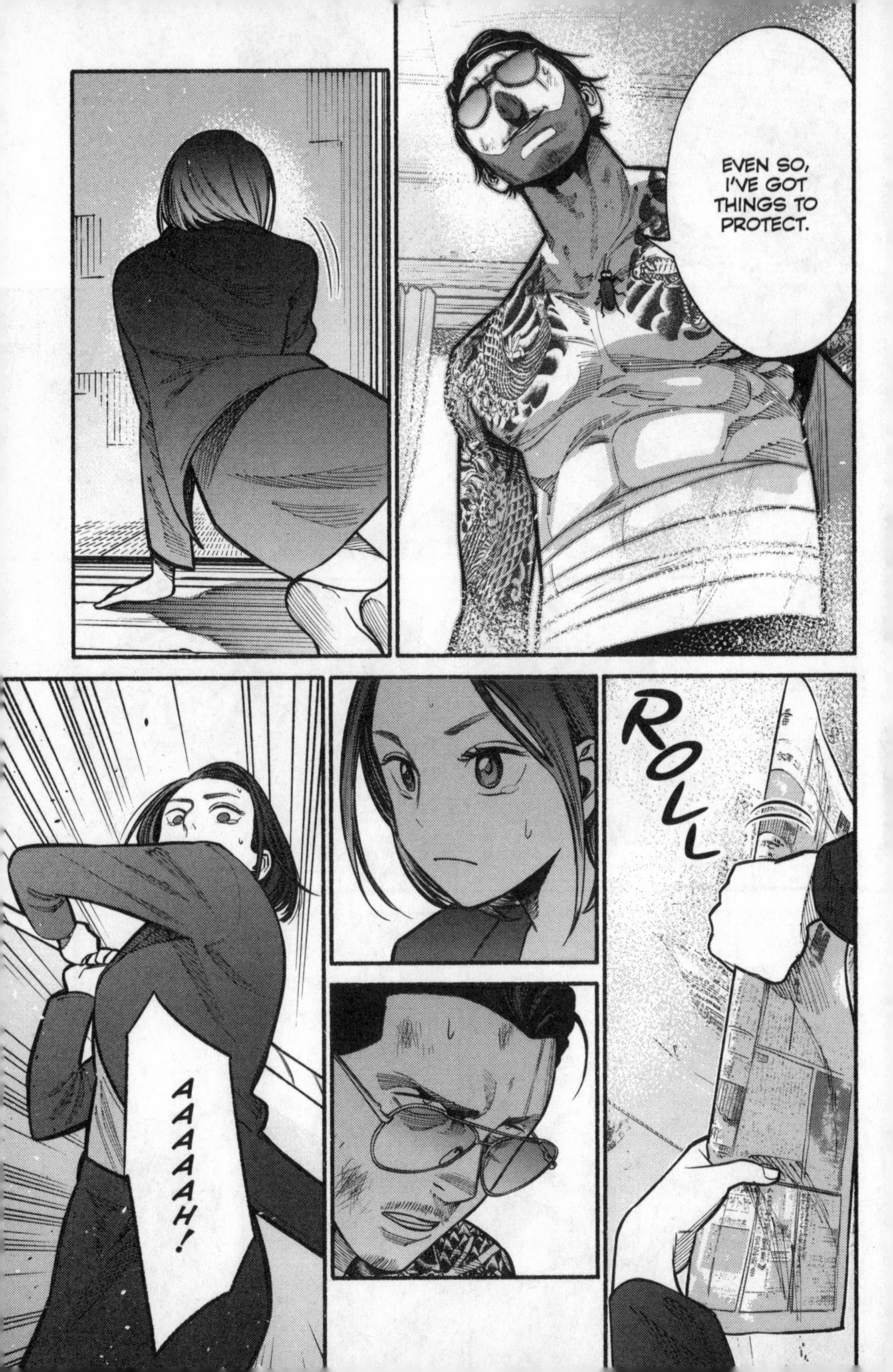
EVEN SO, I'VE GOT THINGS TO PROTECT.
ROLL
AAAAAH!

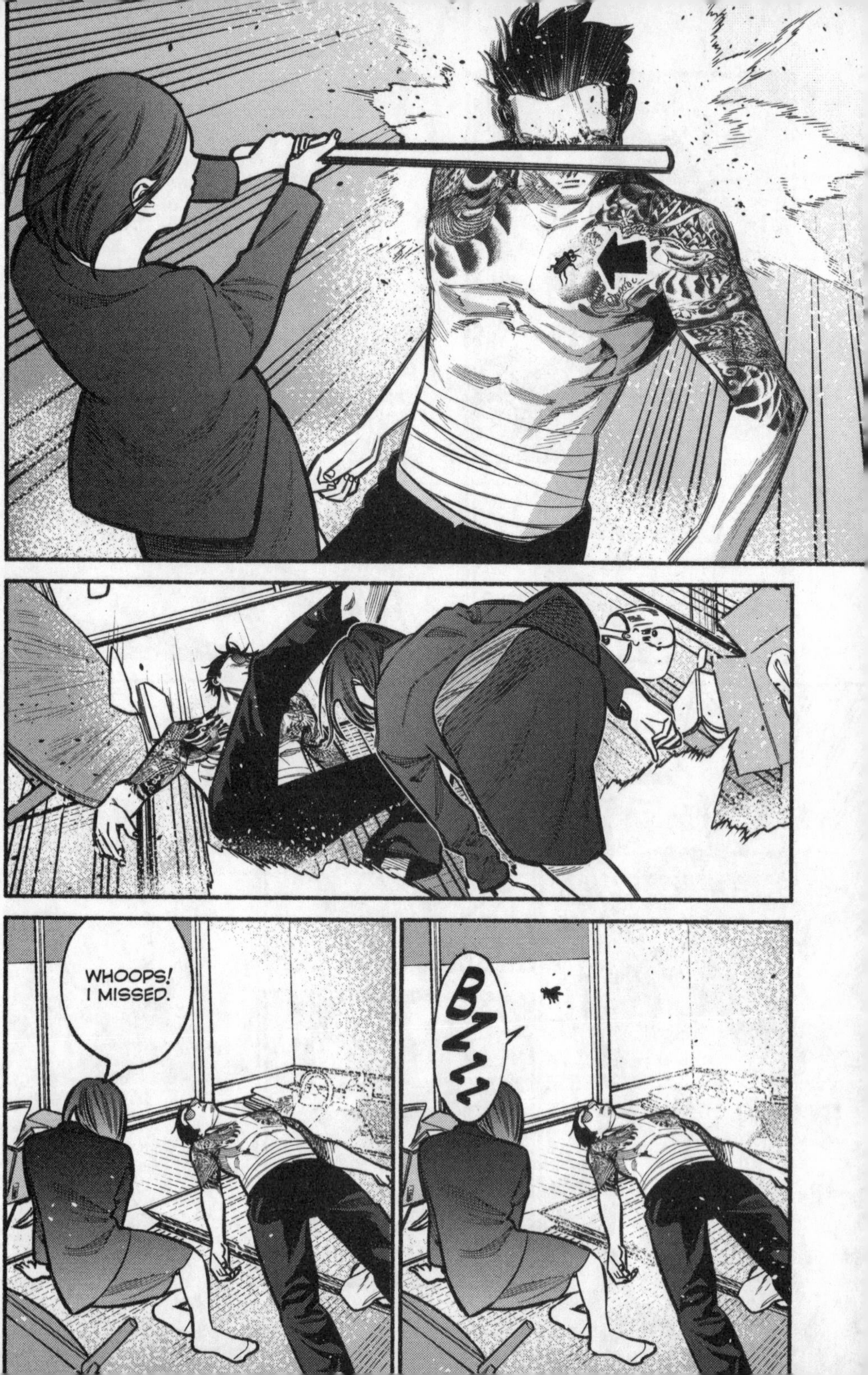
BZZZ
WHOOPS! I MISSED.

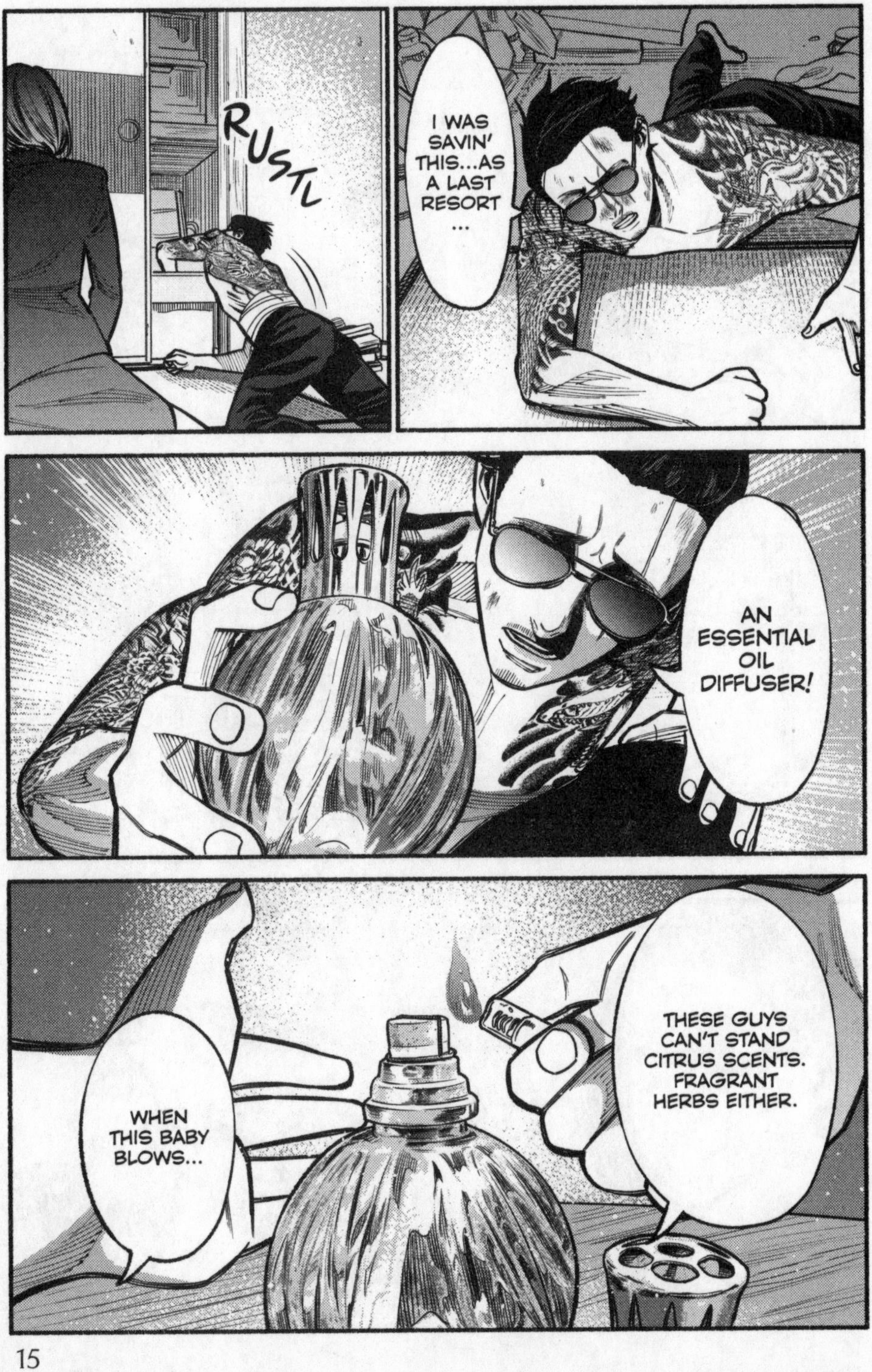
I WAS SAVIN' THIS...AS A LAST RESORT...
RUSTL
AN ESSENTIAL OIL DIFFUSER!
THESE GUYS CAN'T STAND CITRUS SCENTS. FRAGRANT HERBS EITHER.
WHEN THIS BABY BLOWS...

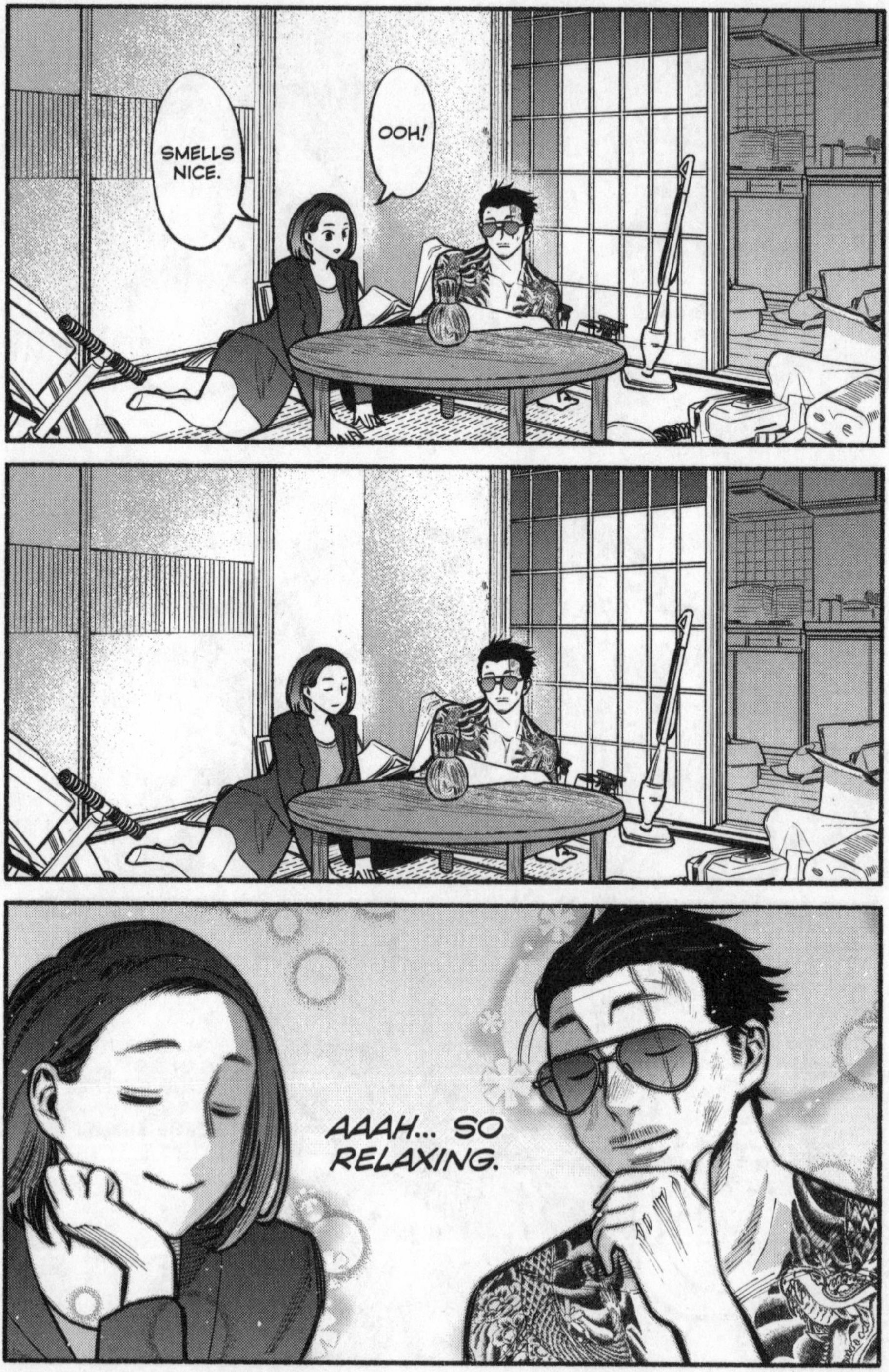
OOH!
SMELLS NICE.
AAAH... SO RELAXING.

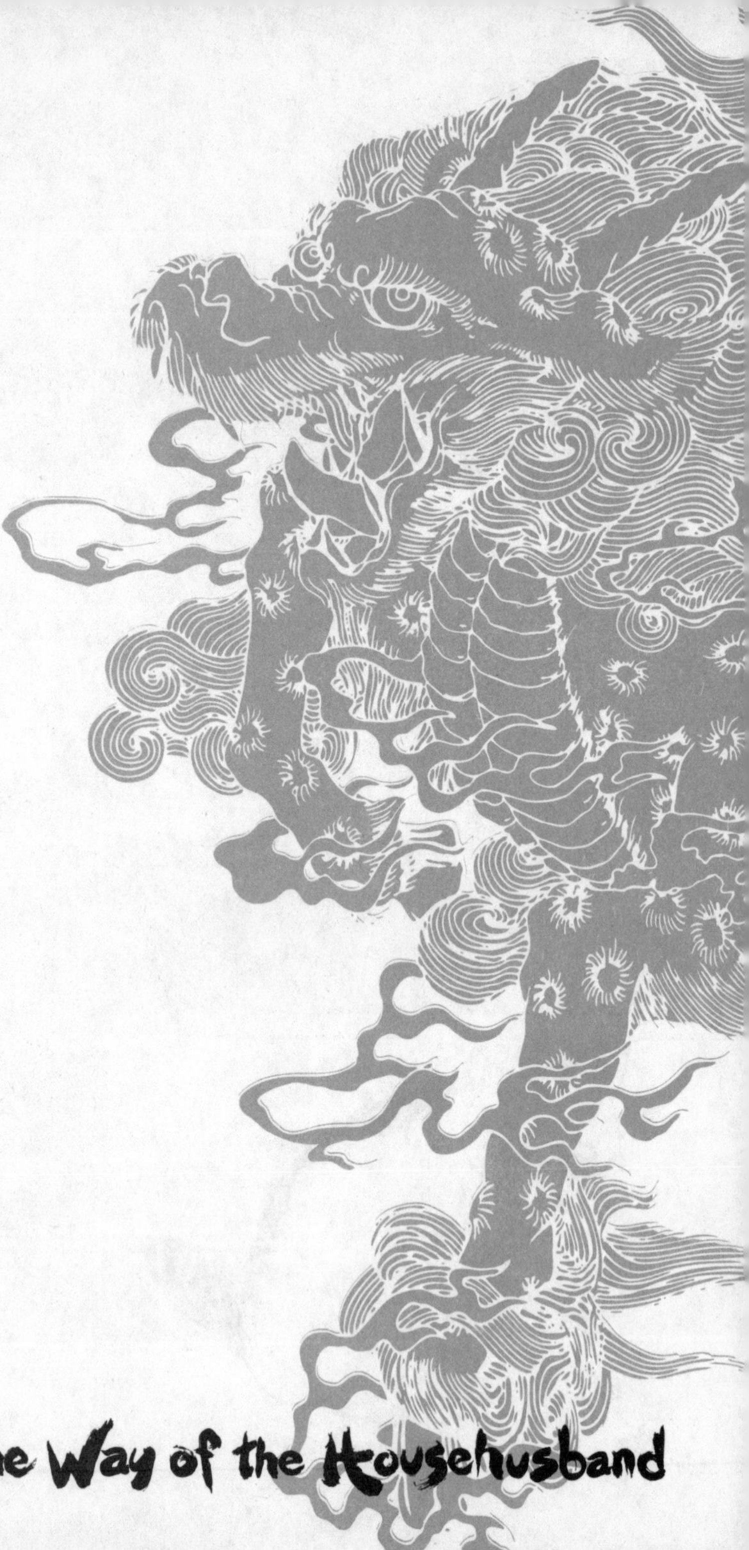

The Way of the Househusband

CHAPTER 20

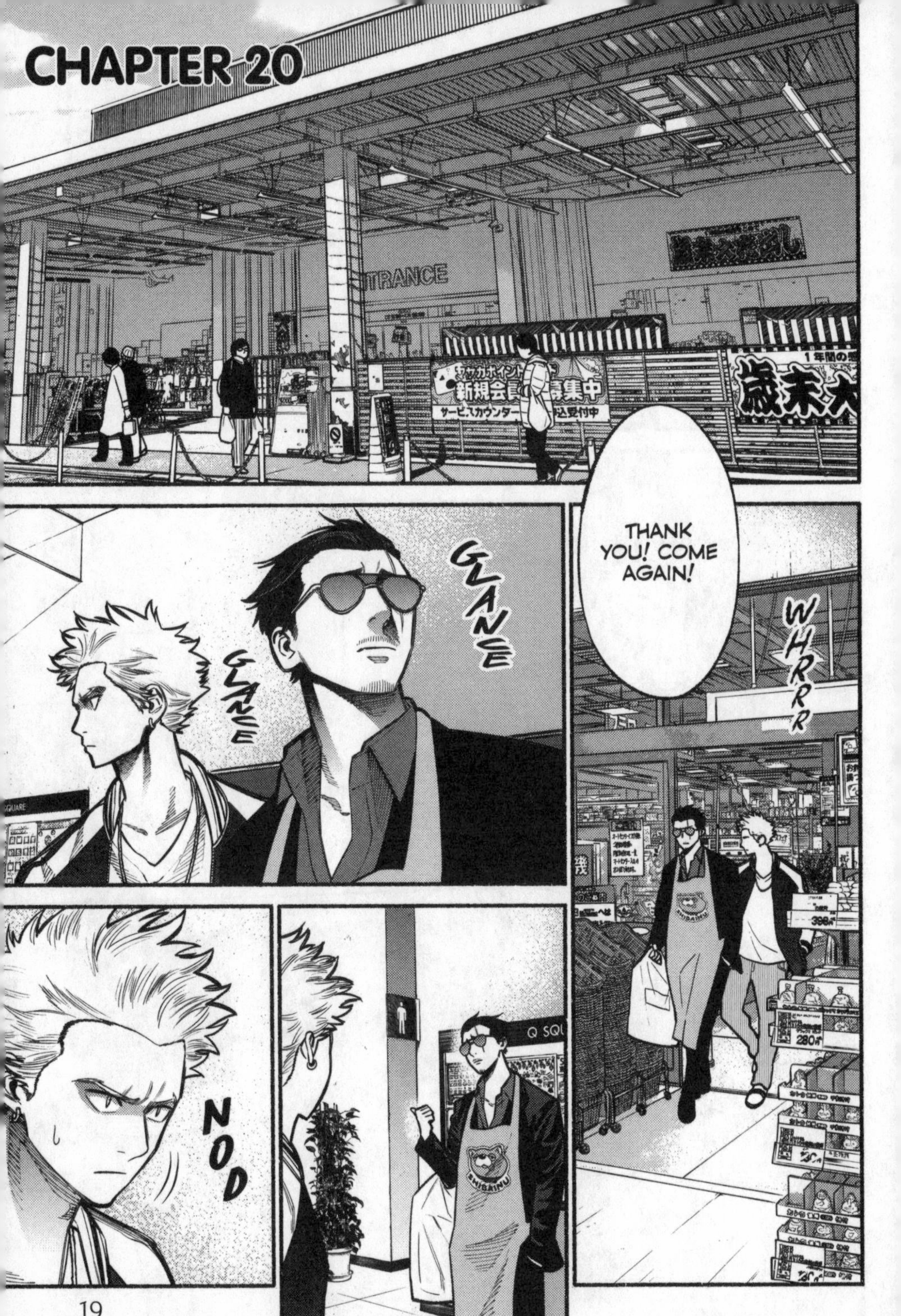
THANK YOU! COME AGAIN!
WHRRR
GLANCE
GLANCE
NOD

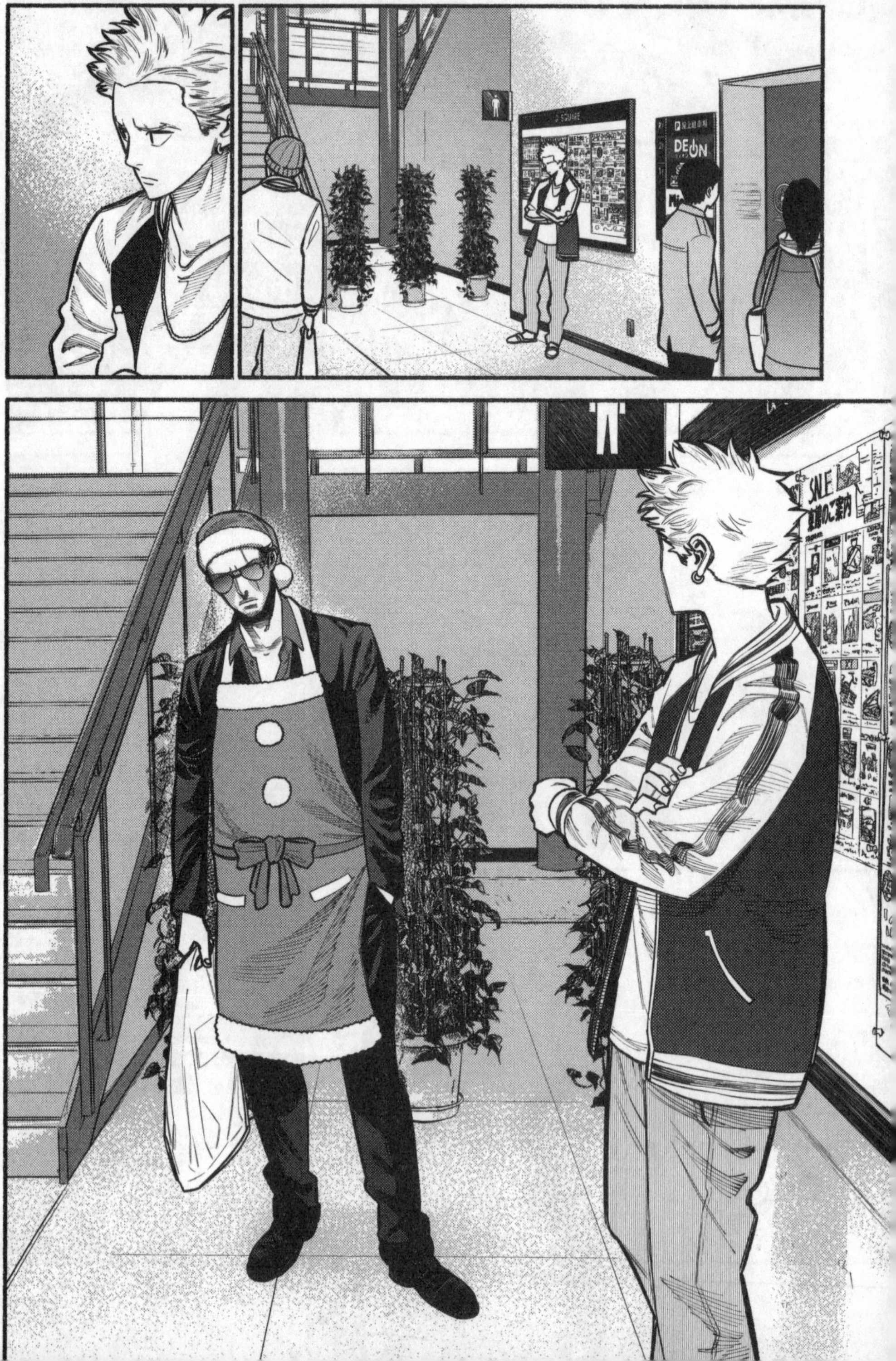
SALE

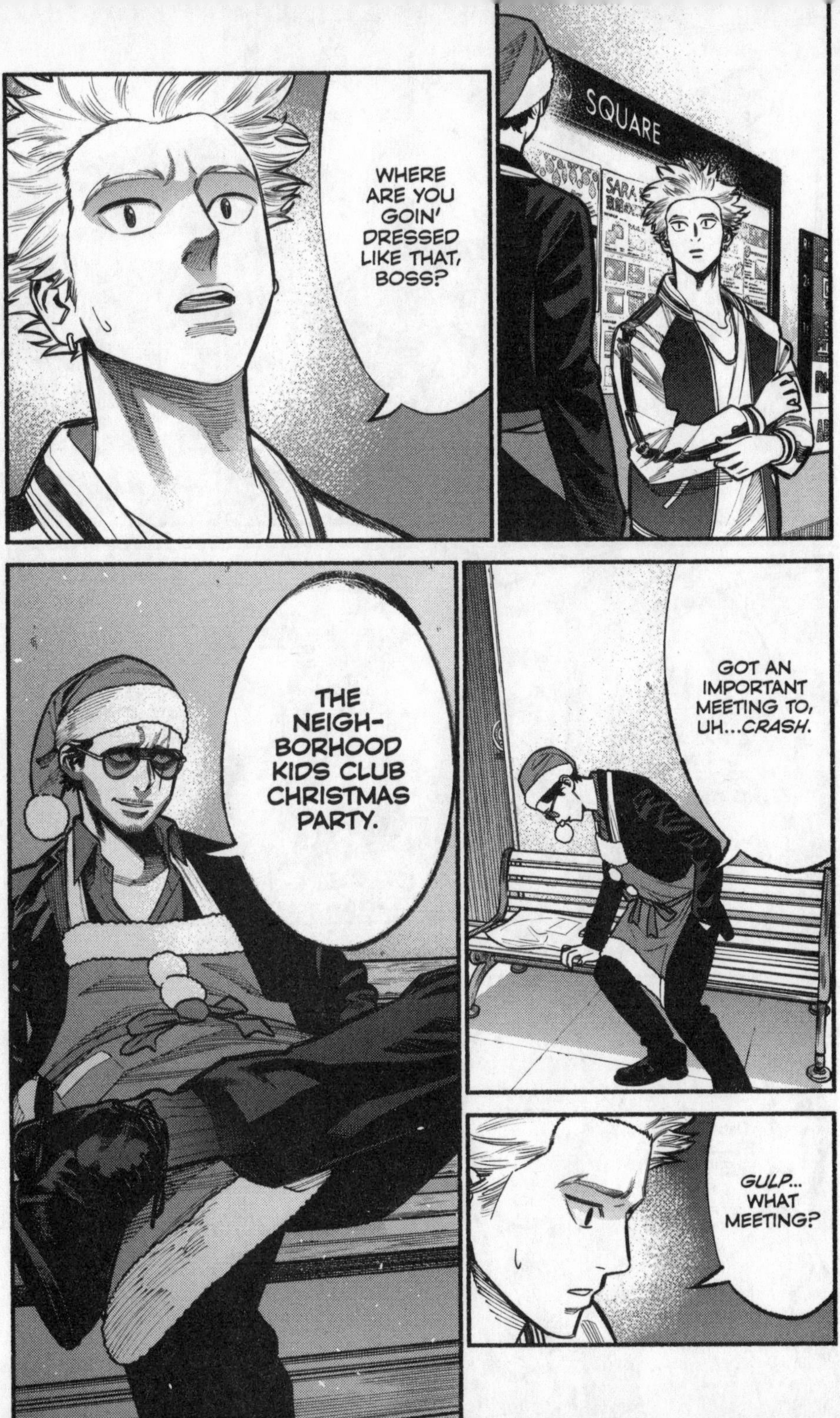
SQUARE
SARA
WHERE ARE YOU GOIN' DRESSED LIKE THAT, BOSS?
GOT AN IMPORTANT MEETING TO, UH...*CRASH*.
GULP... WHAT MEETING?
THE NEIGH-BORHOOD KIDS CLUB CHRISTMAS PARTY.

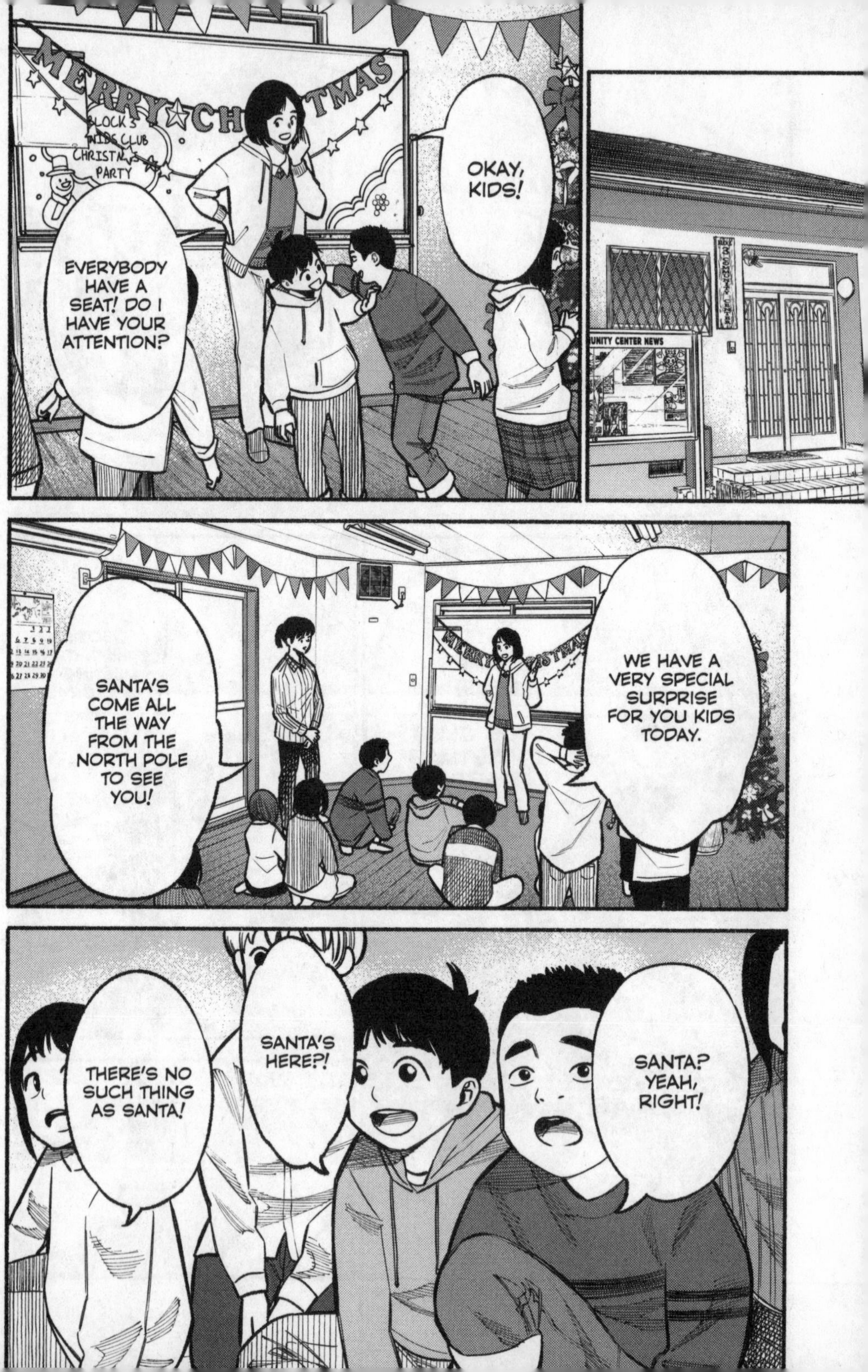
UNITY CENTER NEWS
OKAY, KIDS!
EVERYBODY HAVE A SEAT! DO I HAVE YOUR ATTENTION?
WE HAVE A VERY SPECIAL SURPRISE FOR YOU KIDS TODAY.
SANTA'S COME ALL THE WAY FROM THE NORTH POLE TO SEE YOU!
SANTA? YEAH, RIGHT!
SANTA'S HERE?!
THERE'S NO SUCH THING AS SANTA!

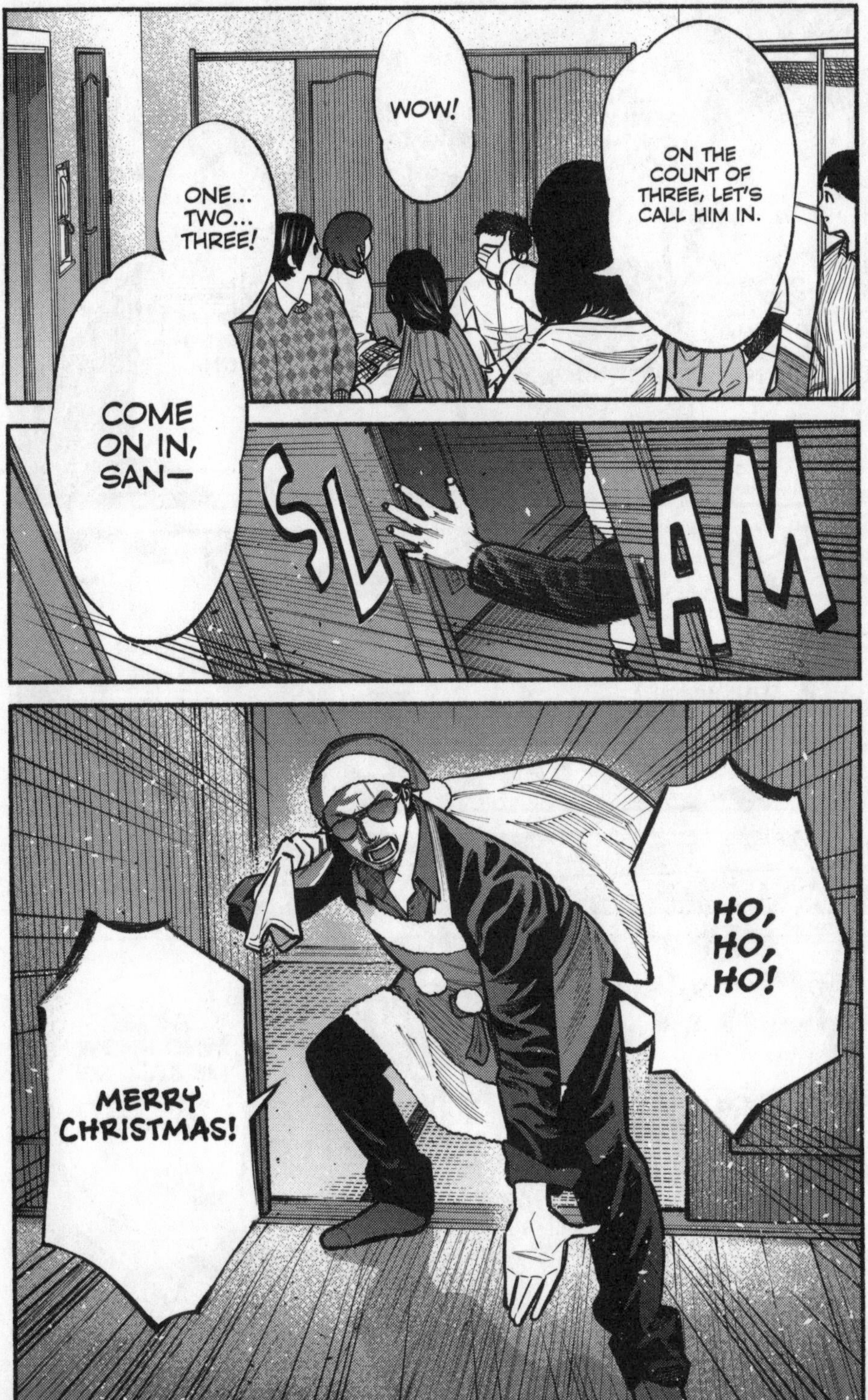
ON THE COUNT OF THREE, LET'S CALL HIM IN.
WOW!
ONE... TWO... THREE!
COME ON IN, SAN—
SLAM
HO, HO, HO!
MERRY CHRISTMAS!

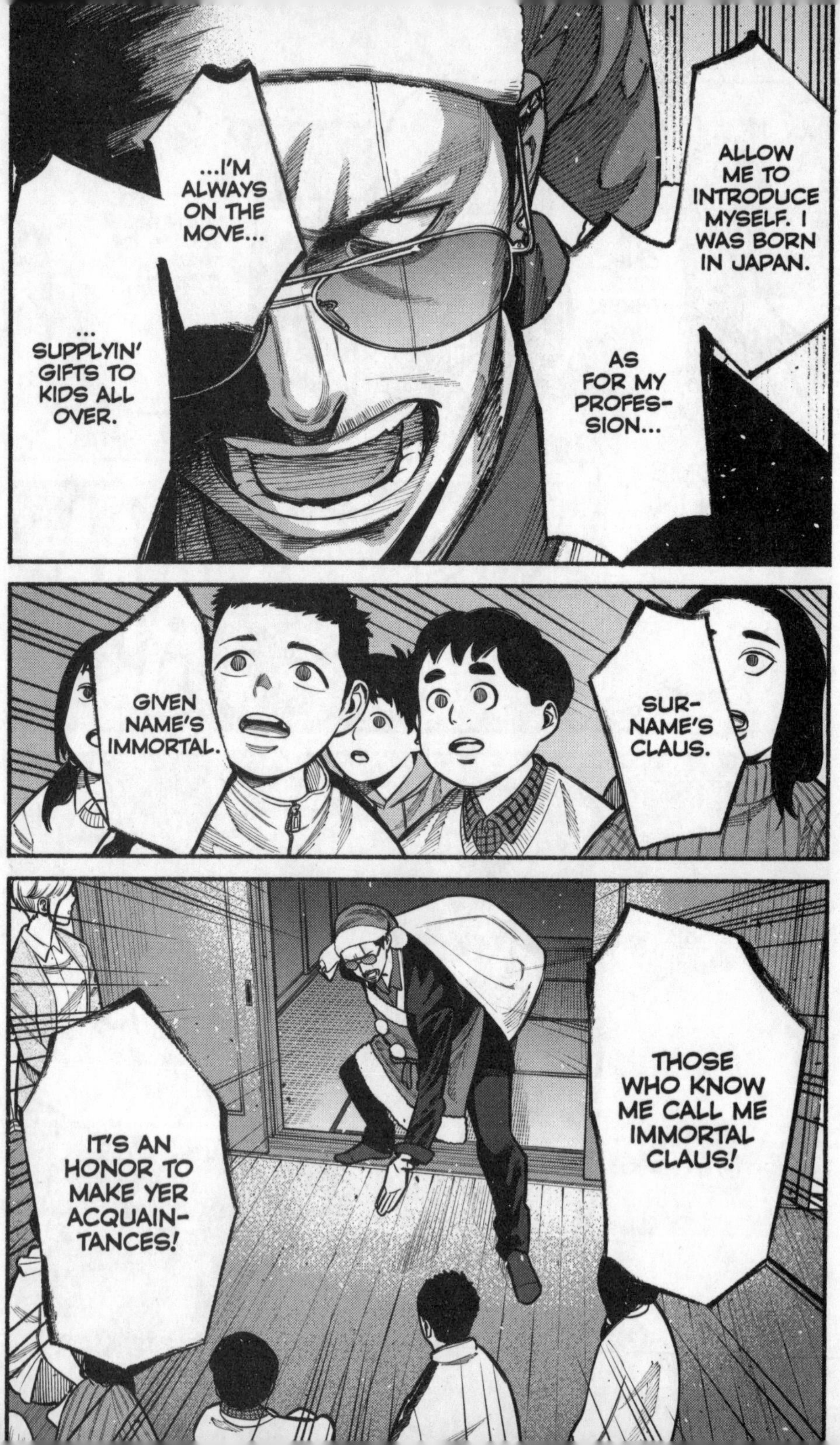
ALLOW ME TO INTRODUCE MYSELF. I WAS BORN IN JAPAN.
...I'M ALWAYS ON THE MOVE...
AS FOR MY PROFESSION...
...SUPPLYIN' GIFTS TO KIDS ALL OVER.
SURNAME'S CLAUS.
GIVEN NAME'S IMMORTAL.
THOSE WHO KNOW ME CALL ME IMMORTAL CLAUS!
IT'S AN HONOR TO MAKE YER ACQUAINTANCES!

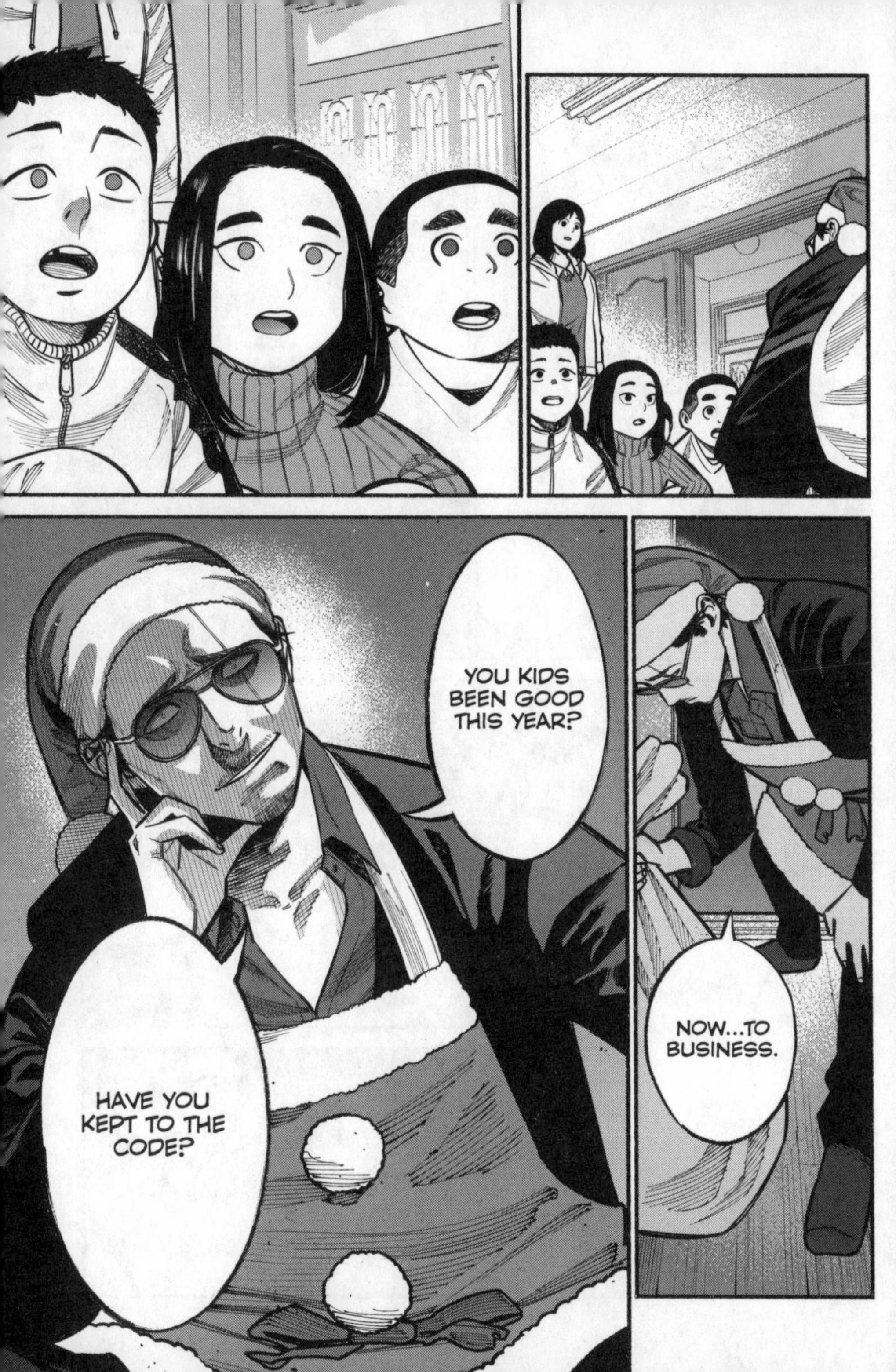
NOW...TO BUSINESS.
YOU KIDS BEEN GOOD THIS YEAR?
HAVE YOU KEPT TO THE CODE?

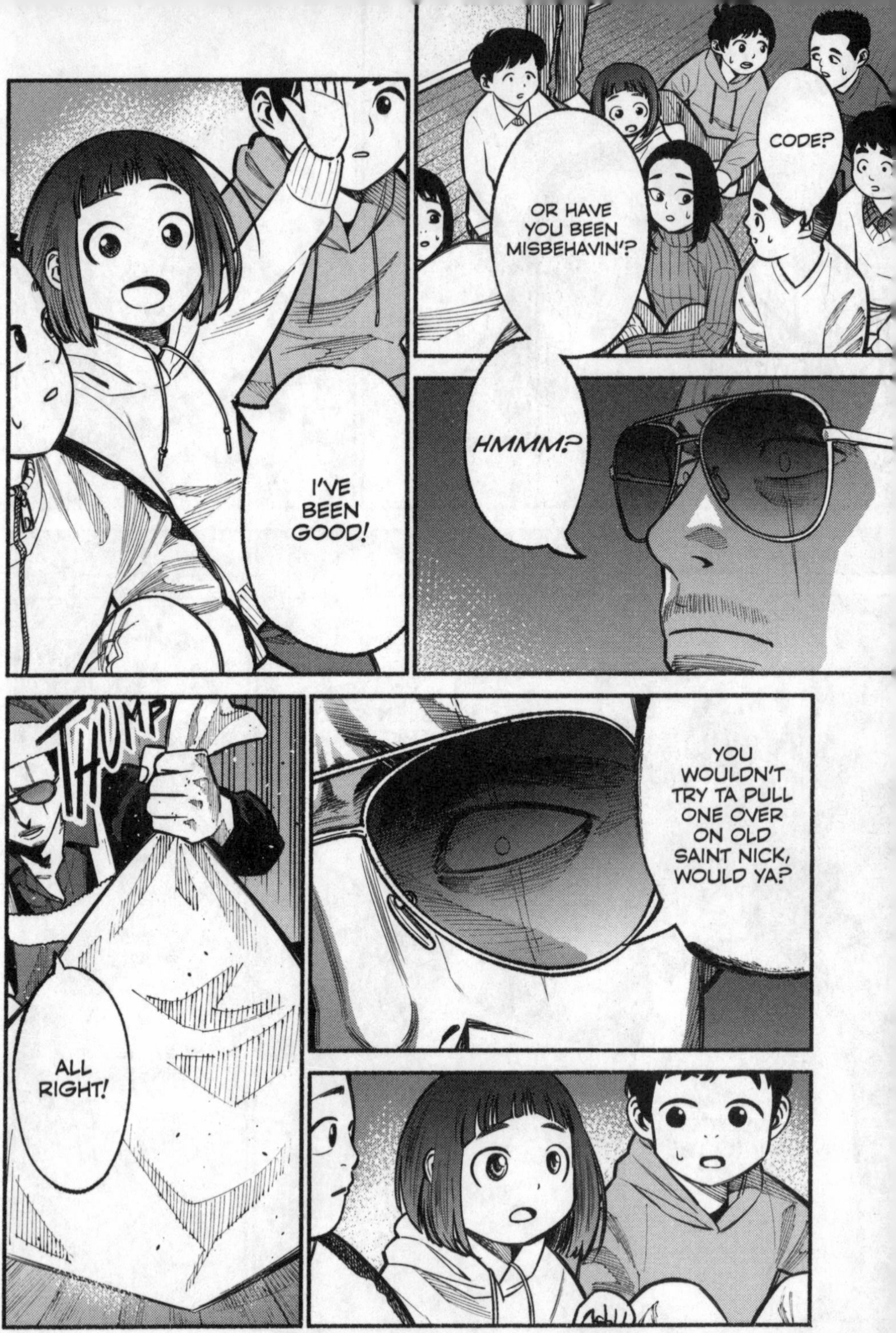
CODE?
OR HAVE YOU BEEN MISBEHAVIN'?
HMMM?
I'VE BEEN GOOD!
YOU WOULDN'T TRY TA PULL ONE OVER ON OLD SAINT NICK, WOULD YA?
THUMP
ALL RIGHT!

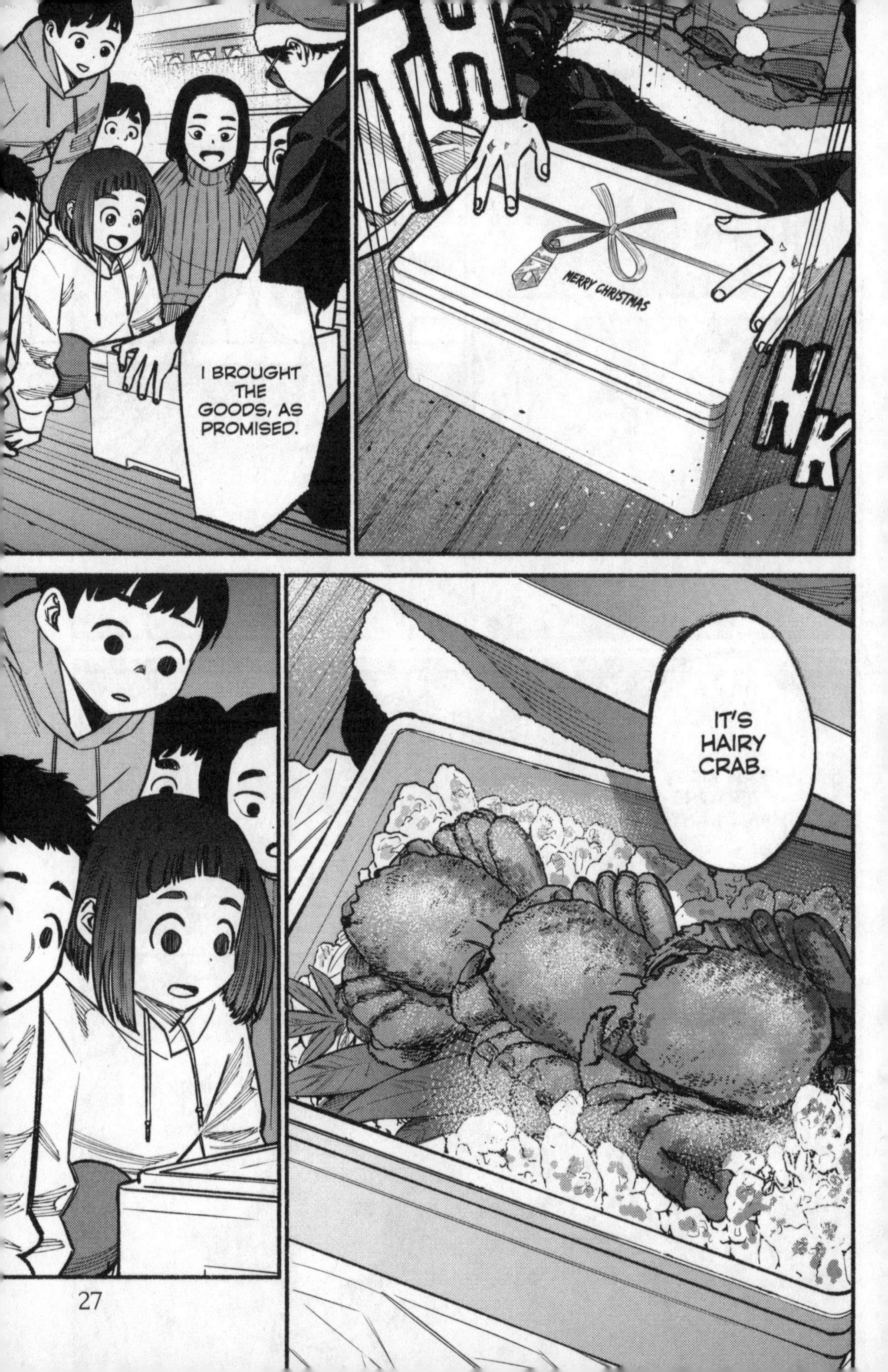
MERRY CHRISTMAS
I BROUGHT THE GOODS, AS PROMISED.
IT'S HAIRY CRAB.

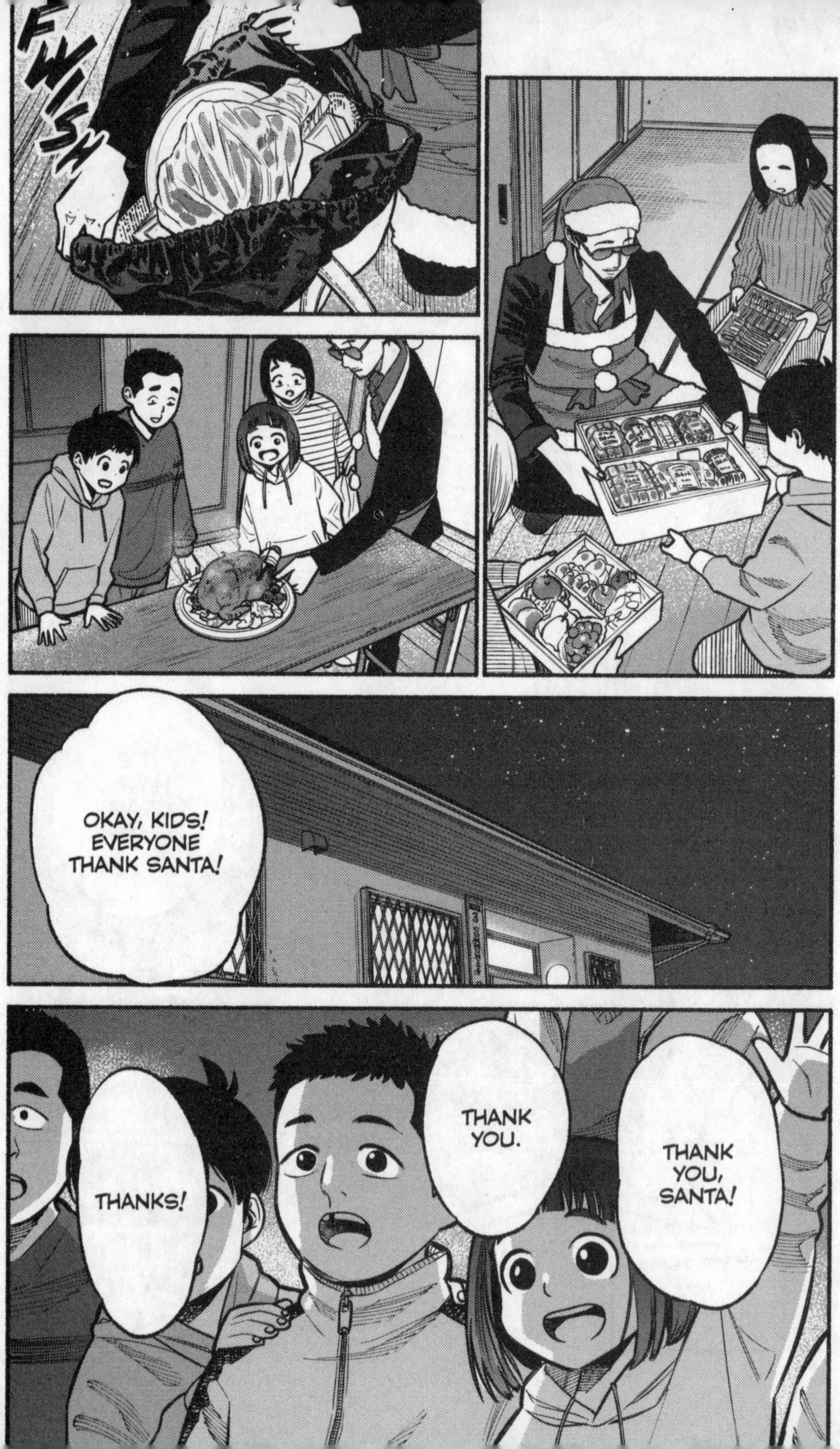
FWISH
OKAY, KIDS! EVERYONE THANK SANTA!
THANK YOU, SANTA!
THANK YOU.
THANKS!

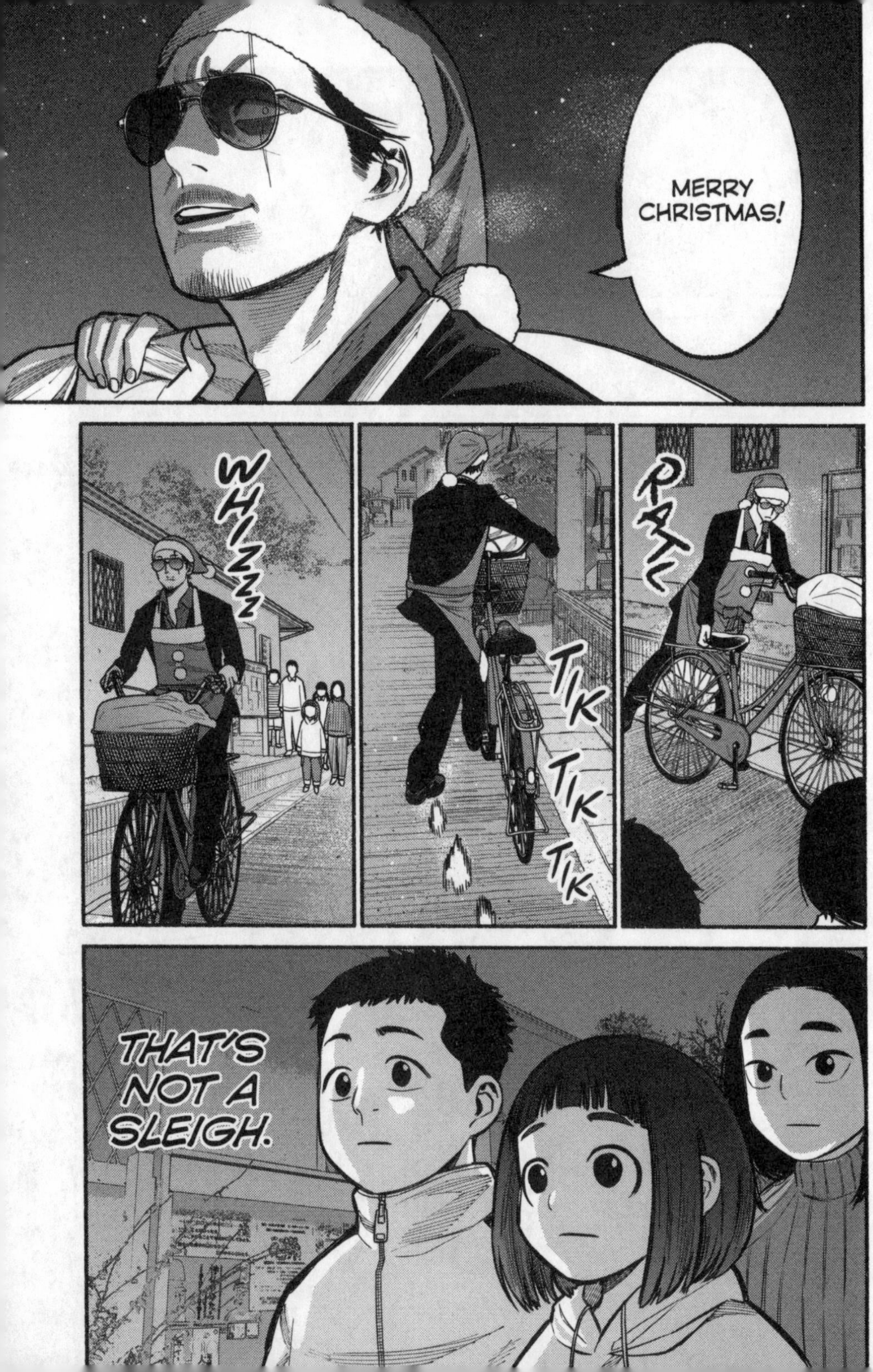
MERRY CHRISTMAS!
RATL
TIK TIK TIK TIK
WHIZZZ
THAT'S NOT A SLEIGH.

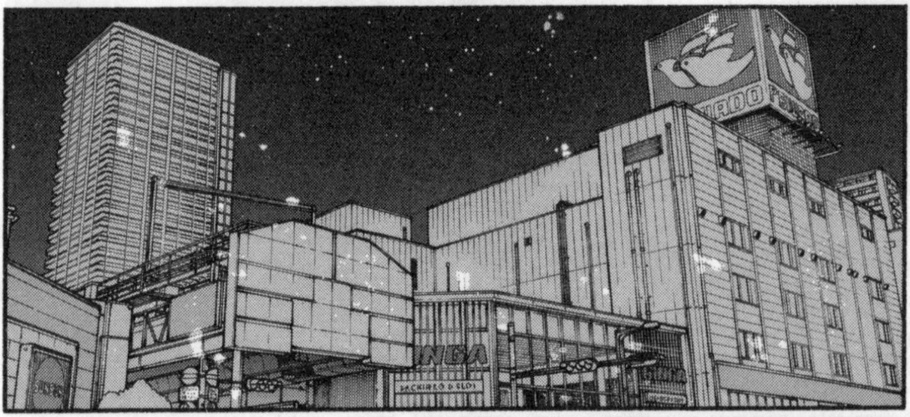
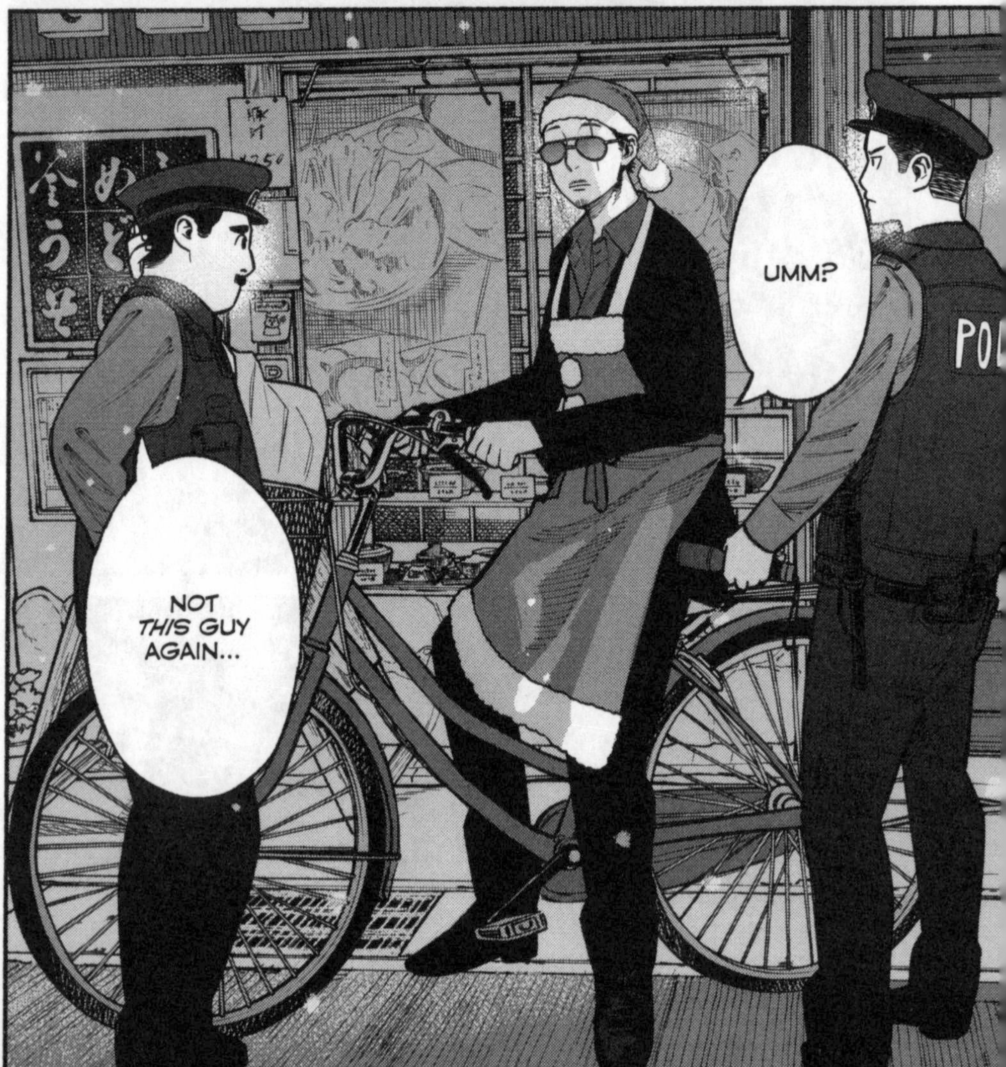
UMM?
NOT *THIS* GUY AGAIN...

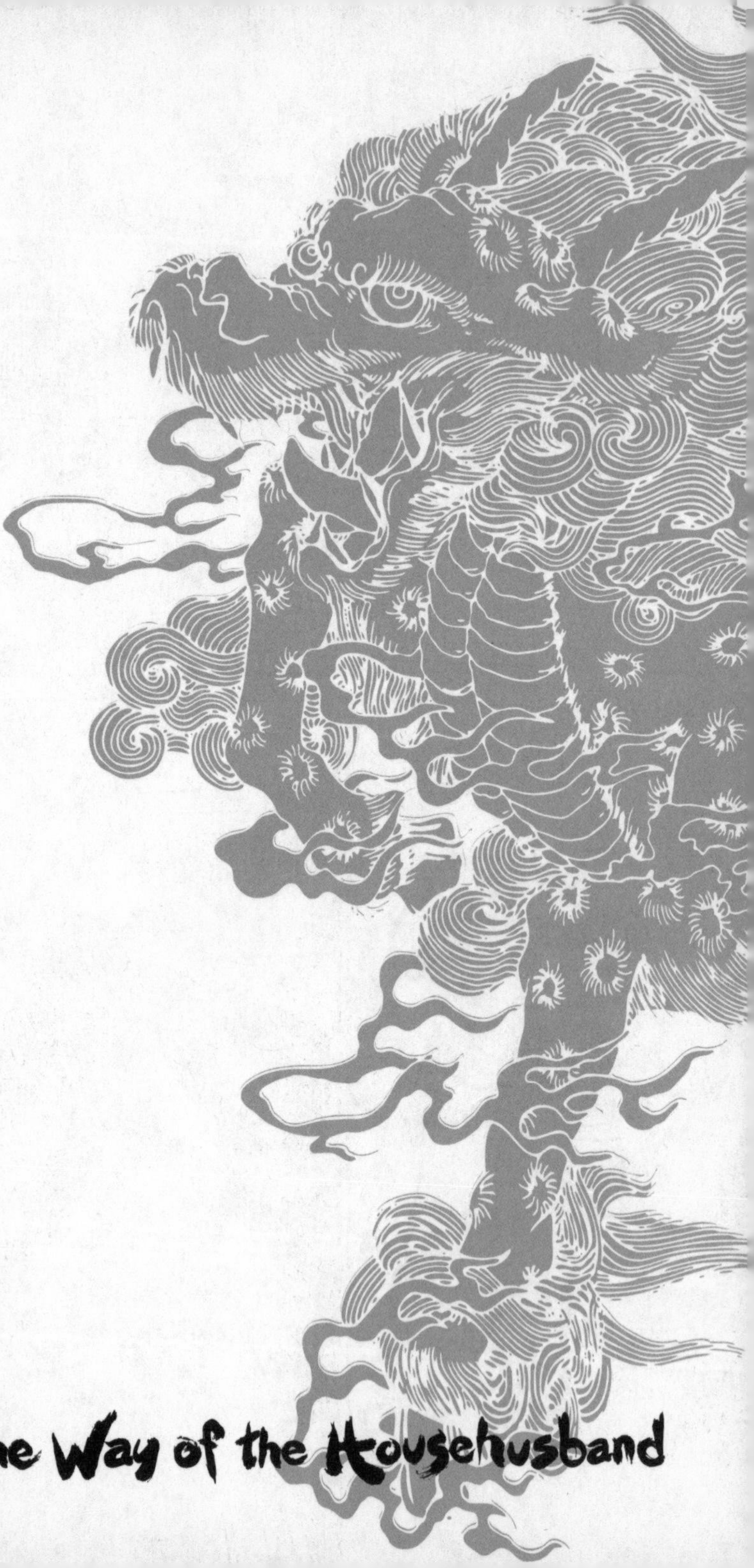

The Way of the Househusband

CHAPTER 21

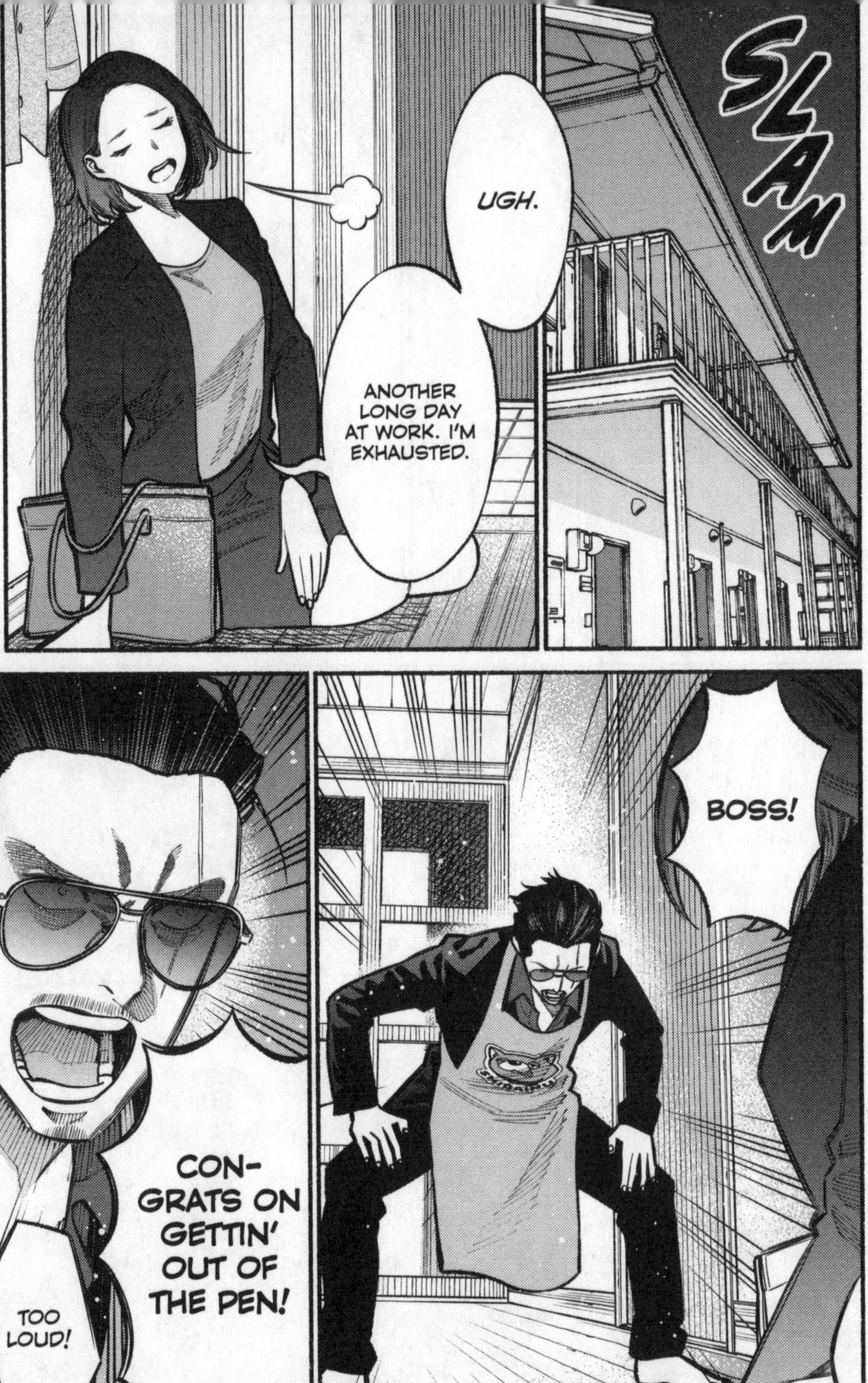
SLAM
UGH.
ANOTHER LONG DAY AT WORK. I'M EXHAUSTED.
BOSS!
CON-GRATS ON GETTIN' OUT OF THE PEN!
TOO LOUD!

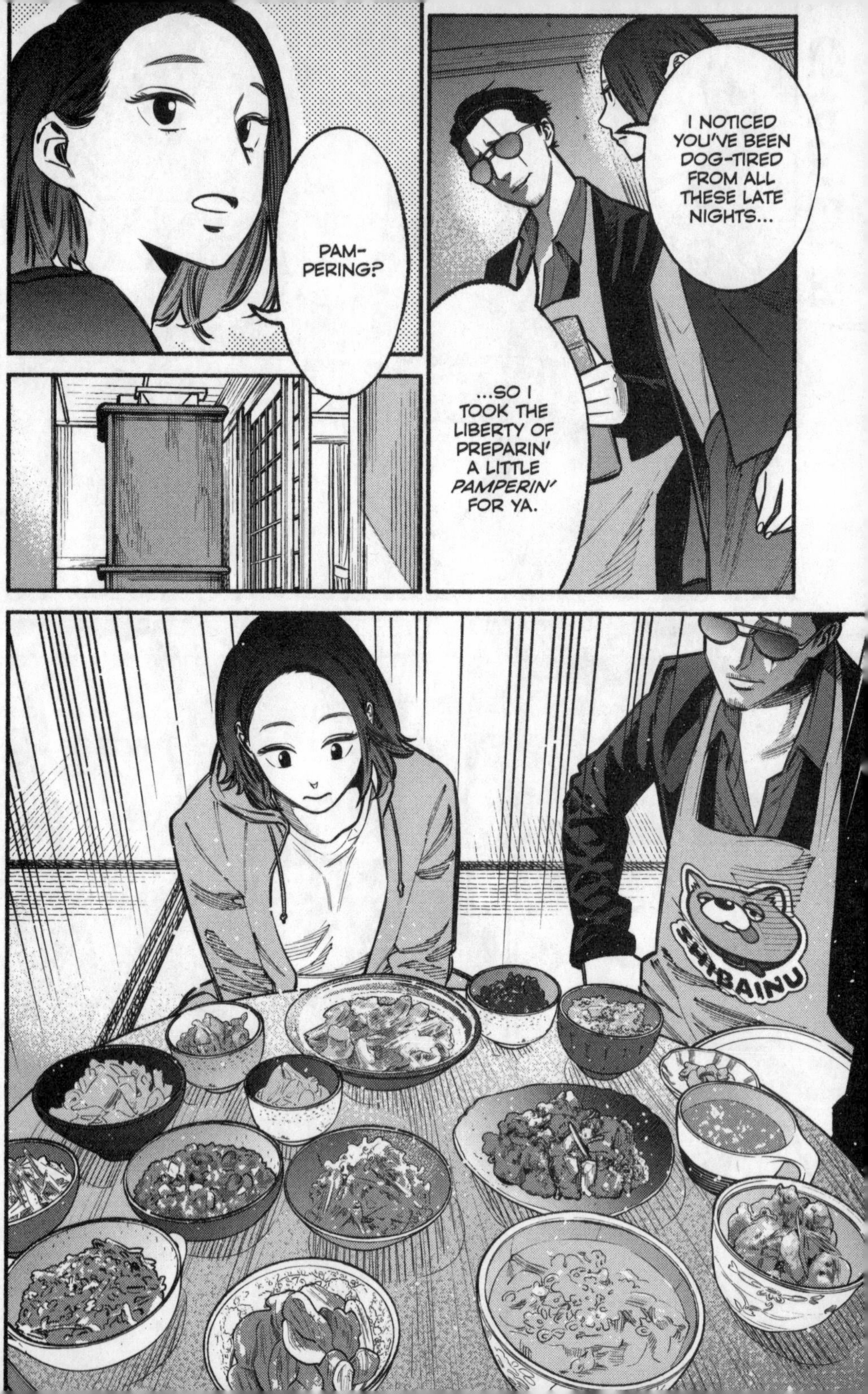
I NOTICED YOU'VE BEEN DOG-TIRED FROM ALL THESE LATE NIGHTS...
...SO I TOOK THE LIBERTY OF PREPARIN' A LITTLE *PAMPERIN'* FOR YA.
PAM-PERING?
SHIBAINU

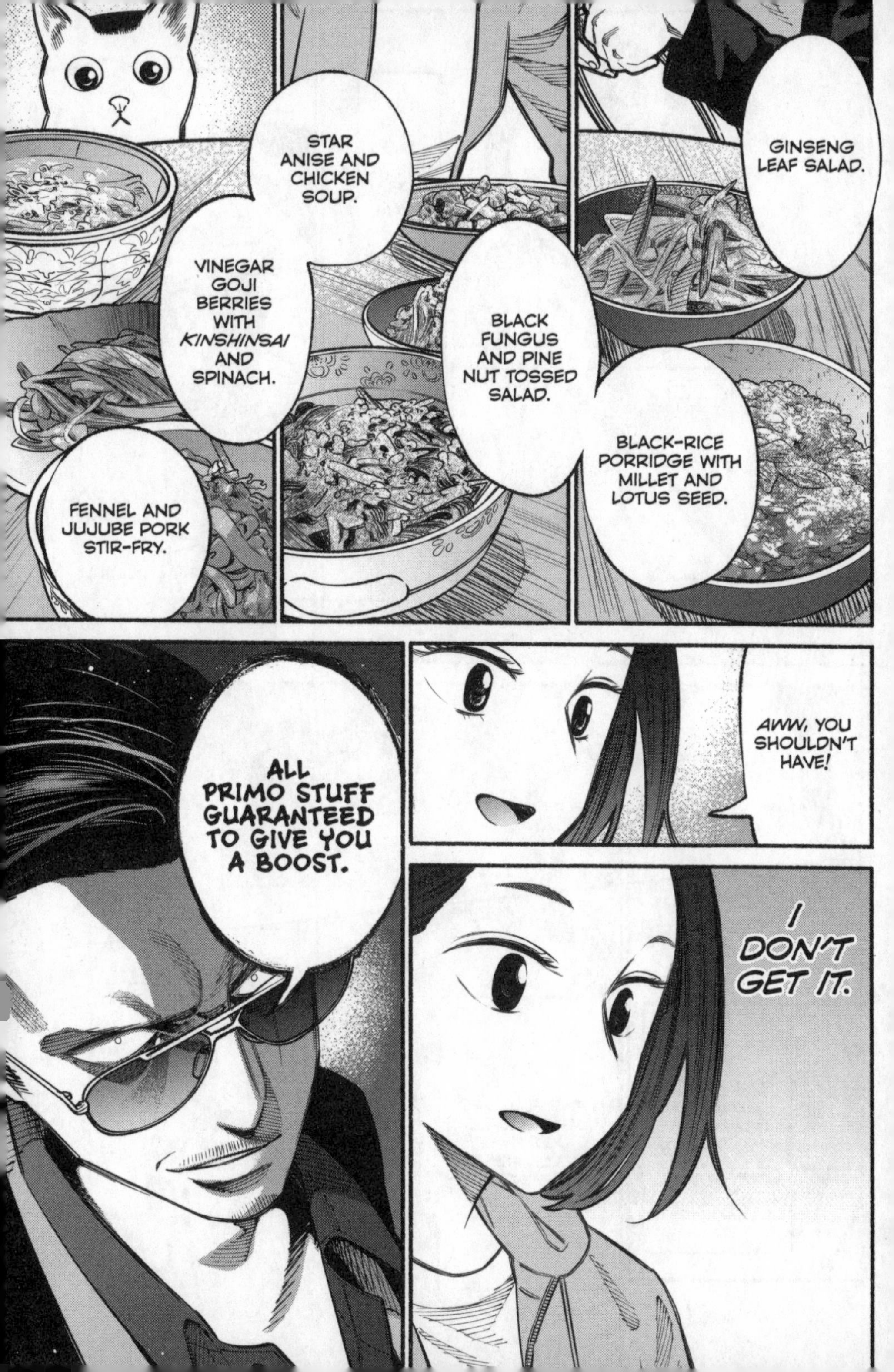
GINSENG LEAF SALAD.
BLACK-RICE PORRIDGE WITH MILLET AND LOTUS SEED.
BLACK FUNGUS AND PINE NUT TOSSED SALAD.
STAR ANISE AND CHICKEN SOUP.
VINEGAR GOJI BERRIES WITH *KINSHINSAI* AND SPINACH.
FENNEL AND JUJUBE PORK STIR-FRY.
AWW, YOU SHOULDN'T HAVE!
I DON'T GET IT.
ALL PRIMO STUFF GUARANTEED TO GIVE YOU A BOOST.

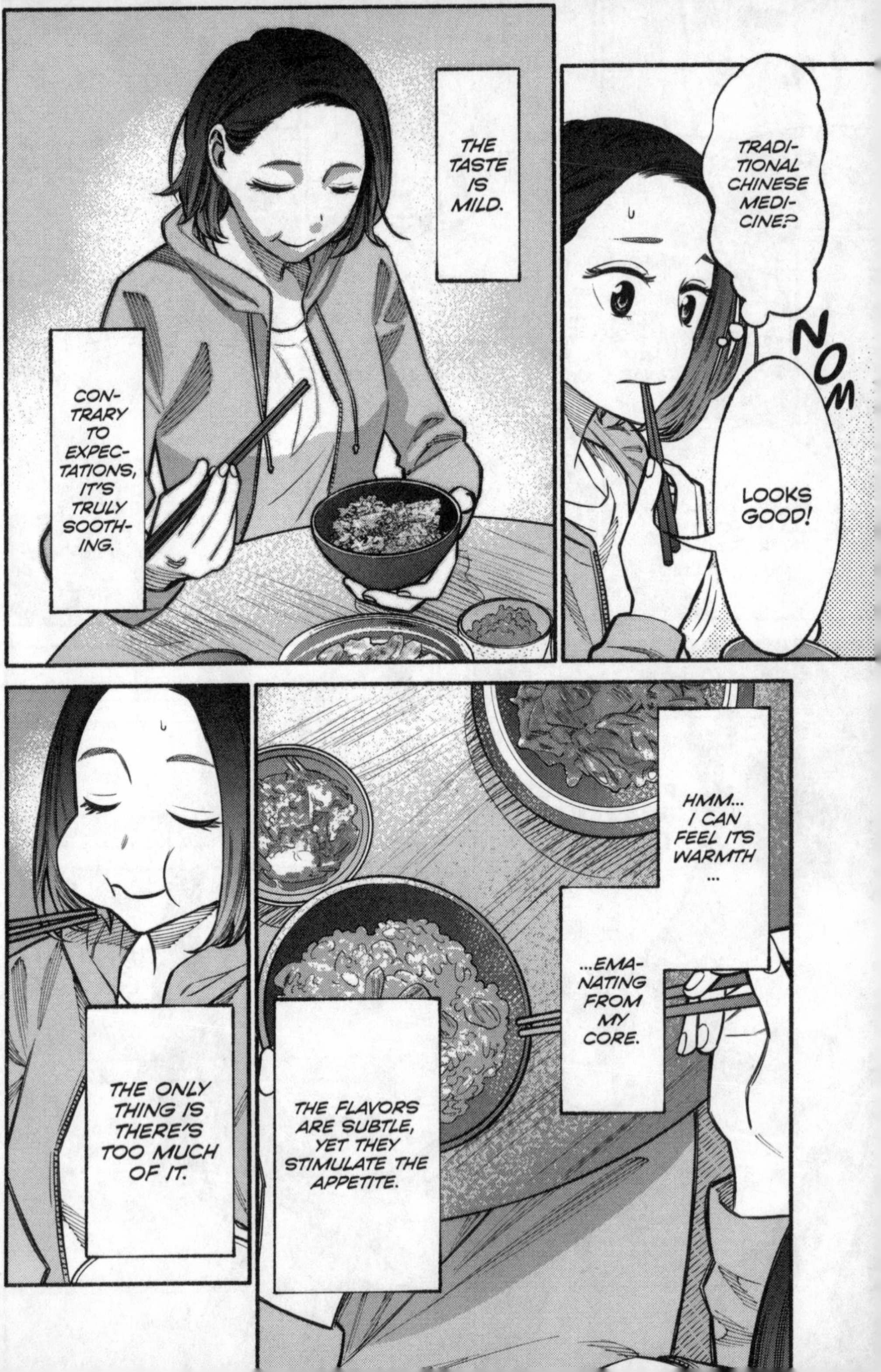
TRADI-TIONAL CHINESE MEDI-CINE?
NOM
LOOKS GOOD!
THE TASTE IS MILD.
CON-TRARY TO EXPEC-TATIONS, IT'S TRULY SOOTH-ING.
HMM... I CAN FEEL ITS WARMTH ...
...EMA-NATING FROM MY CORE.
THE FLAVORS ARE SUBTLE, YET THEY STIMULATE THE APPETITE.
THE ONLY THING IS THERE'S TOO MUCH OF IT.

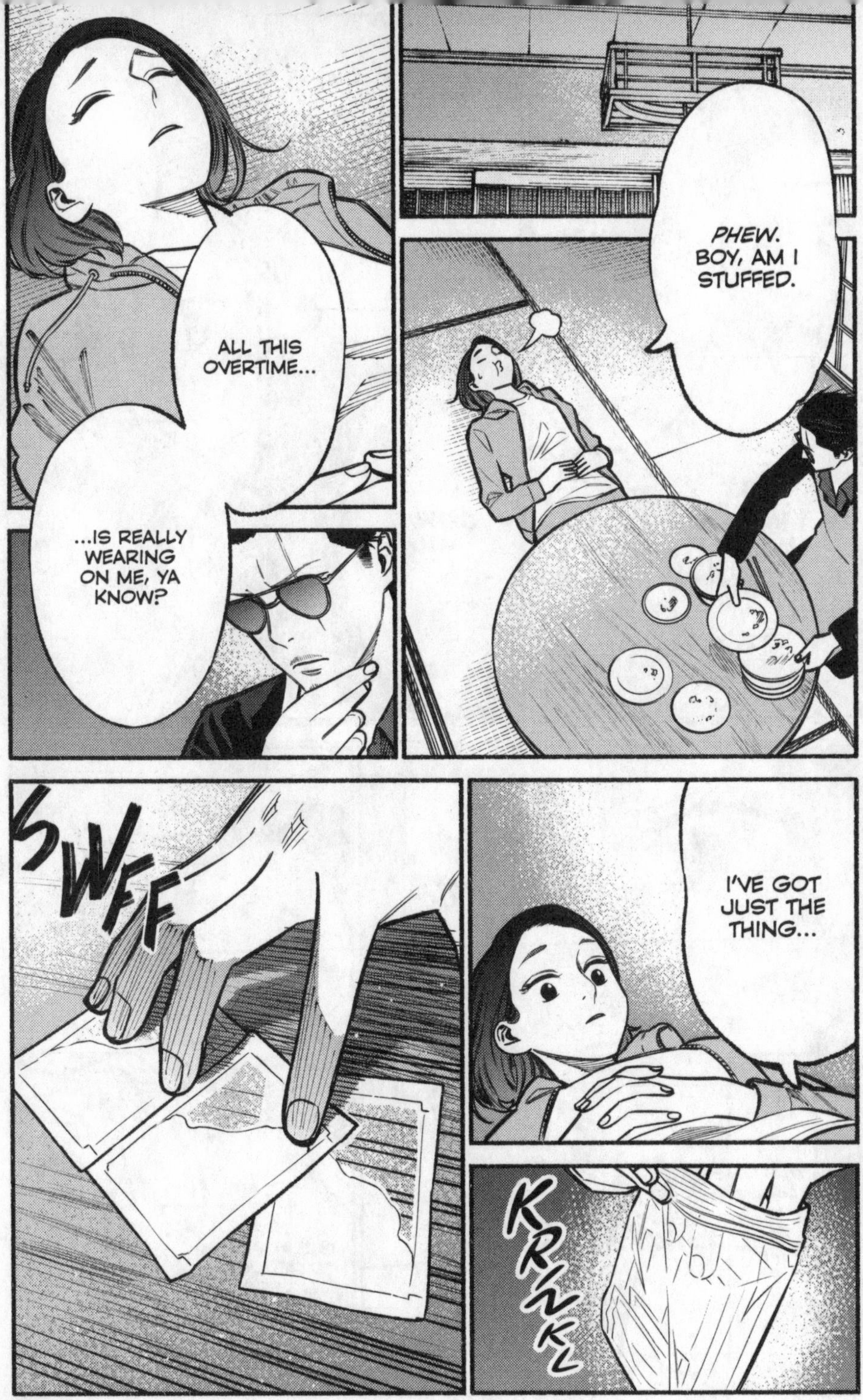
PHEW. BOY, AM I STUFFED.
ALL THIS OVERTIME...
...IS REALLY WEARING ON ME, YA KNOW?
I'VE GOT JUST THE THING...
KRNKL
SWFF

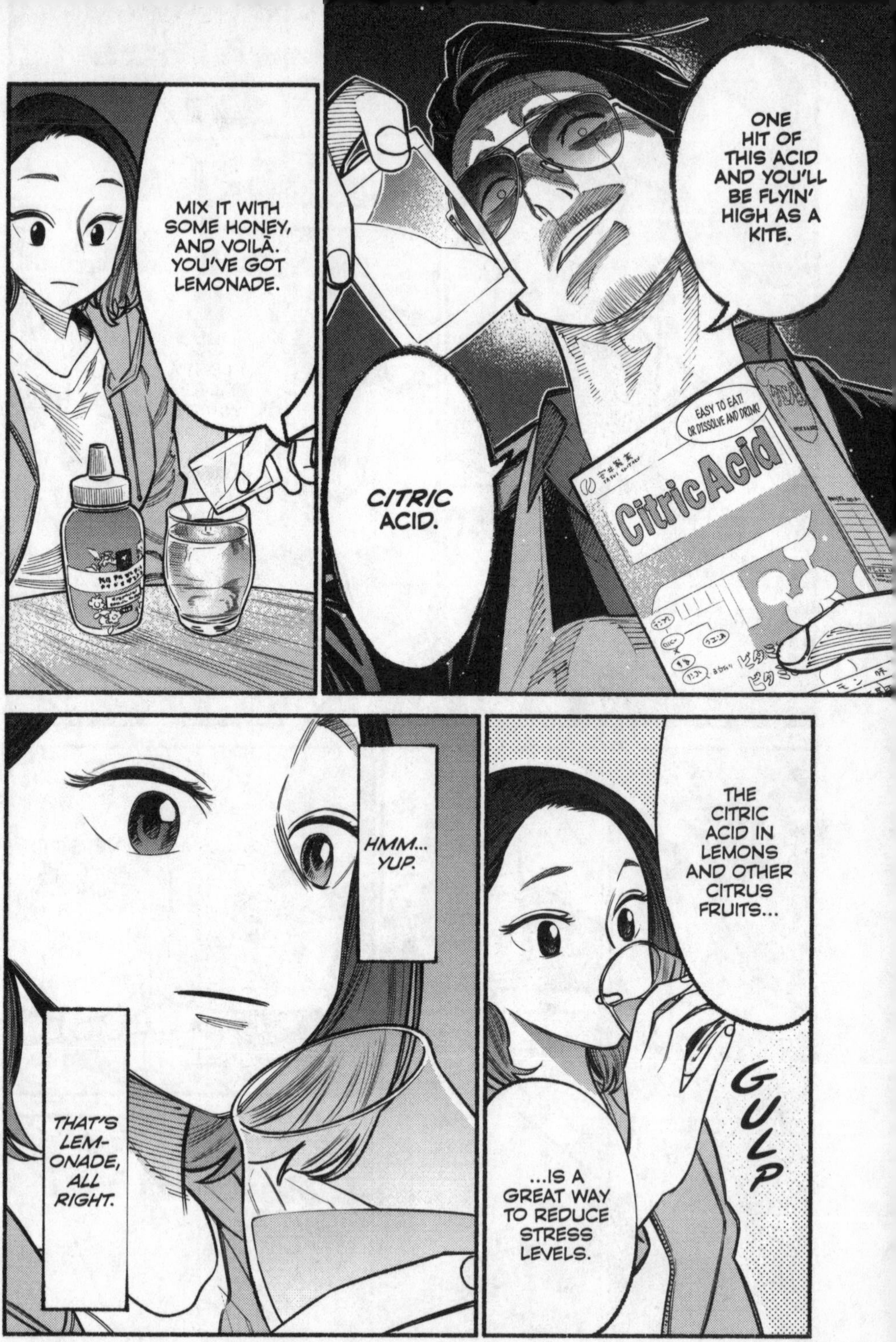
ONE HIT OF THIS ACID AND YOU'LL BE FLYIN' HIGH AS A KITE.
EASY TO EAT! OR DISSOLVE AND DRINK!
CitricAcid
CITRIC ACID.
MIX IT WITH SOME HONEY, AND VOILÀ. YOU'VE GOT LEMONADE.
THE CITRIC ACID IN LEMONS AND OTHER CITRUS FRUITS...
GULP
...IS A GREAT WAY TO REDUCE STRESS LEVELS.
HMM... YUP.
THAT'S LEM-ONADE, ALL RIGHT.

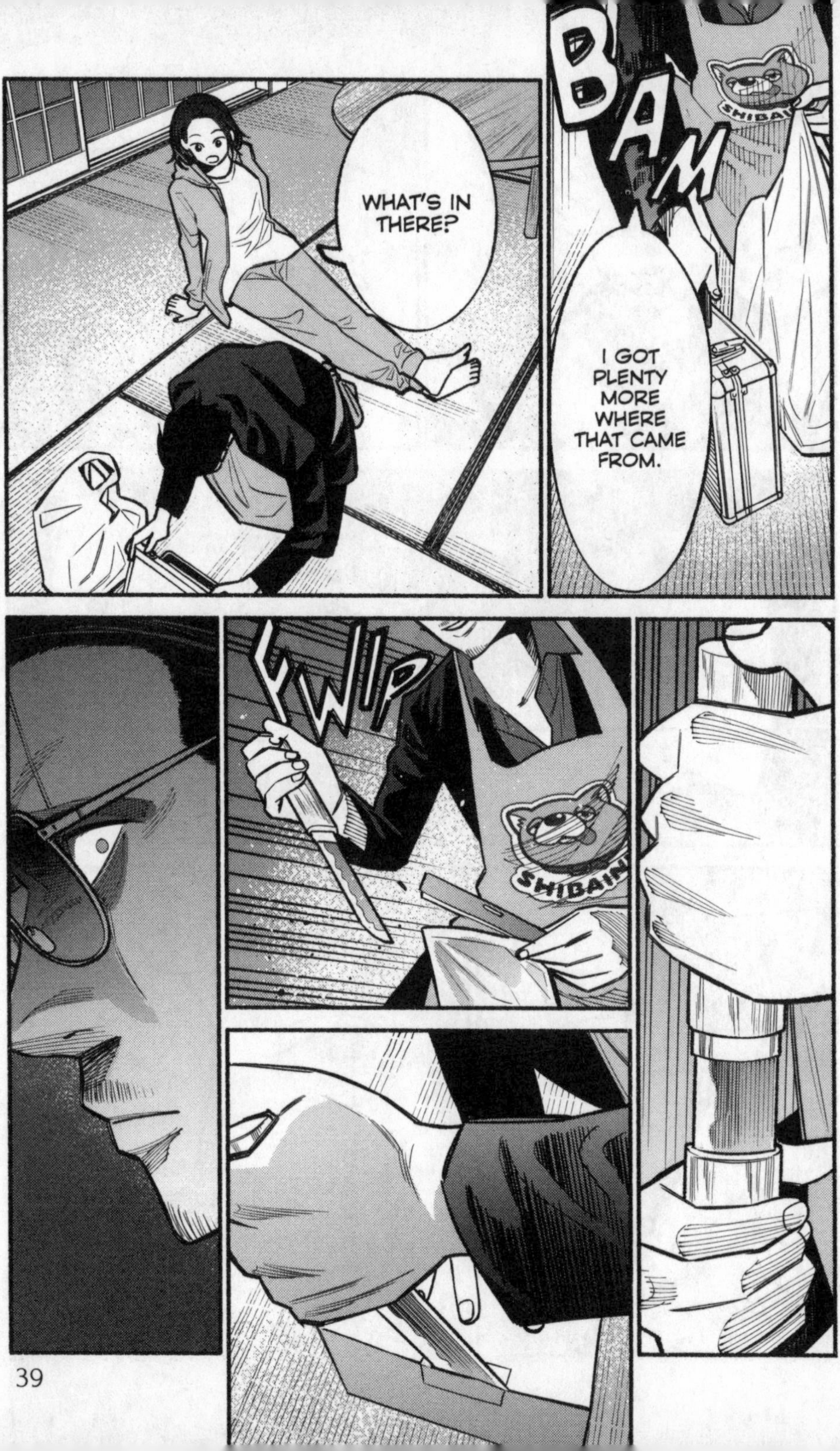
BAM
I GOT PLENTY MORE WHERE THAT CAME FROM.
WHAT'S IN THERE?
WHIP

WHAT'S THIS FOR?
HEY!
I CAN'T SEE!
STOP!
QUIT STRUG-GLIN'!
SHHH...

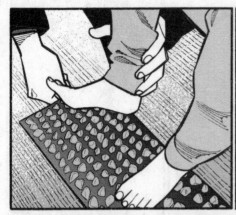

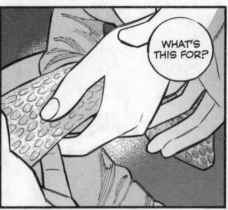

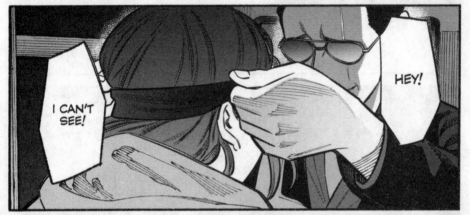

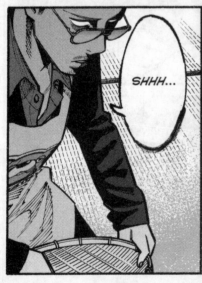

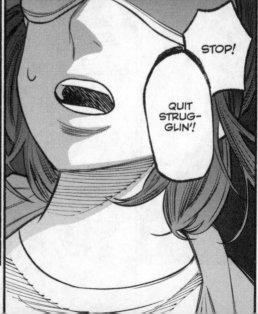

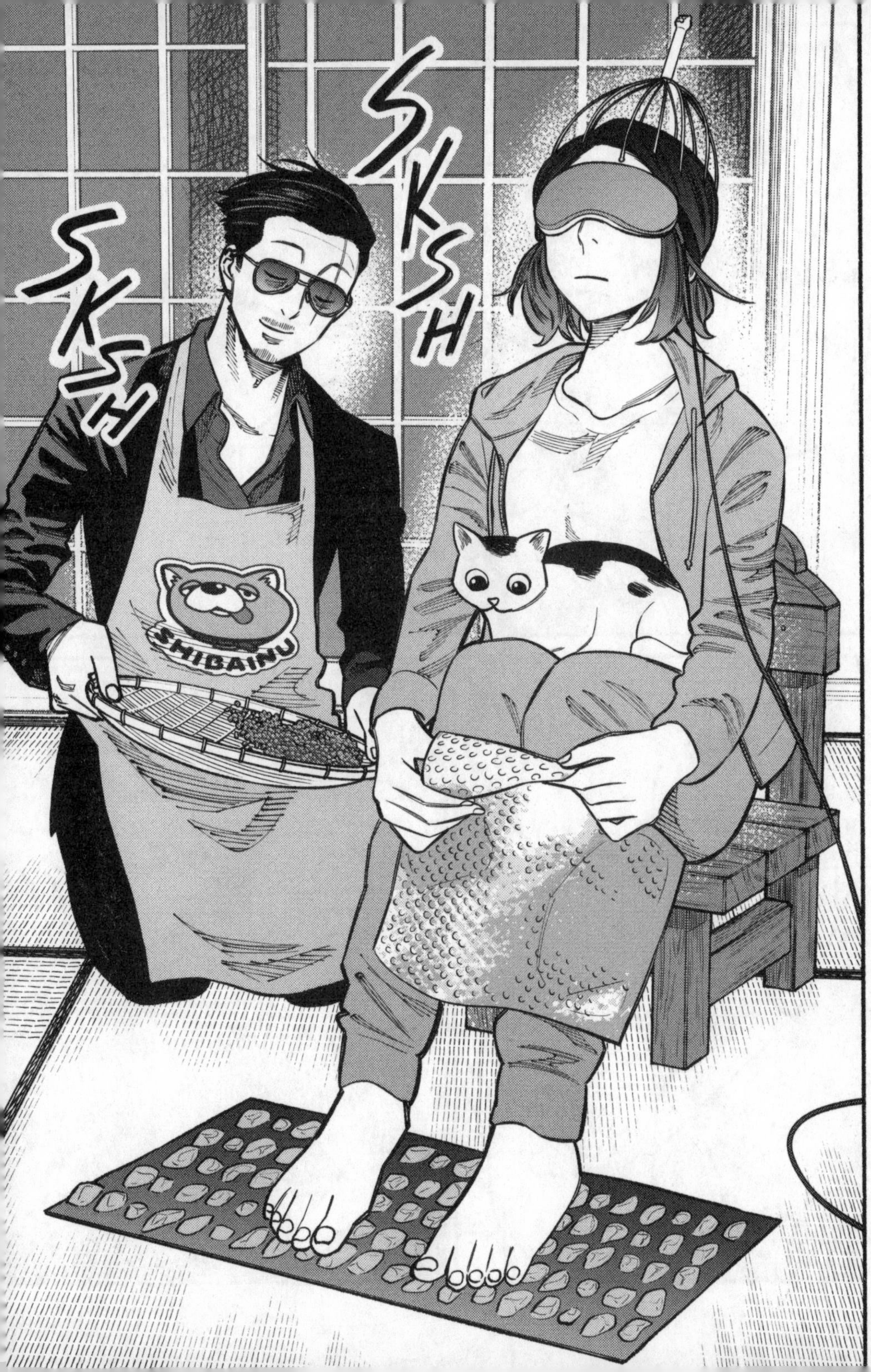
SKSH
SKSH
SHIBAINU

FOR YOUR HEAD, A WIRE SCALP MASSAGER.
ON THE EYES, A HOT EYE COMPRESS.
BUBBLE WRAP FOR YOUR HANDS TO POP...
...AND A MAT TO MASSAGE YOUR FEET.
SKSH SKSH
SOME BEANS TO CREATE THE SOOTHING SOUND OF OCEAN WAVES...
... AND LAST BUT NOT LEAST, A CAT ON YOUR LAP.

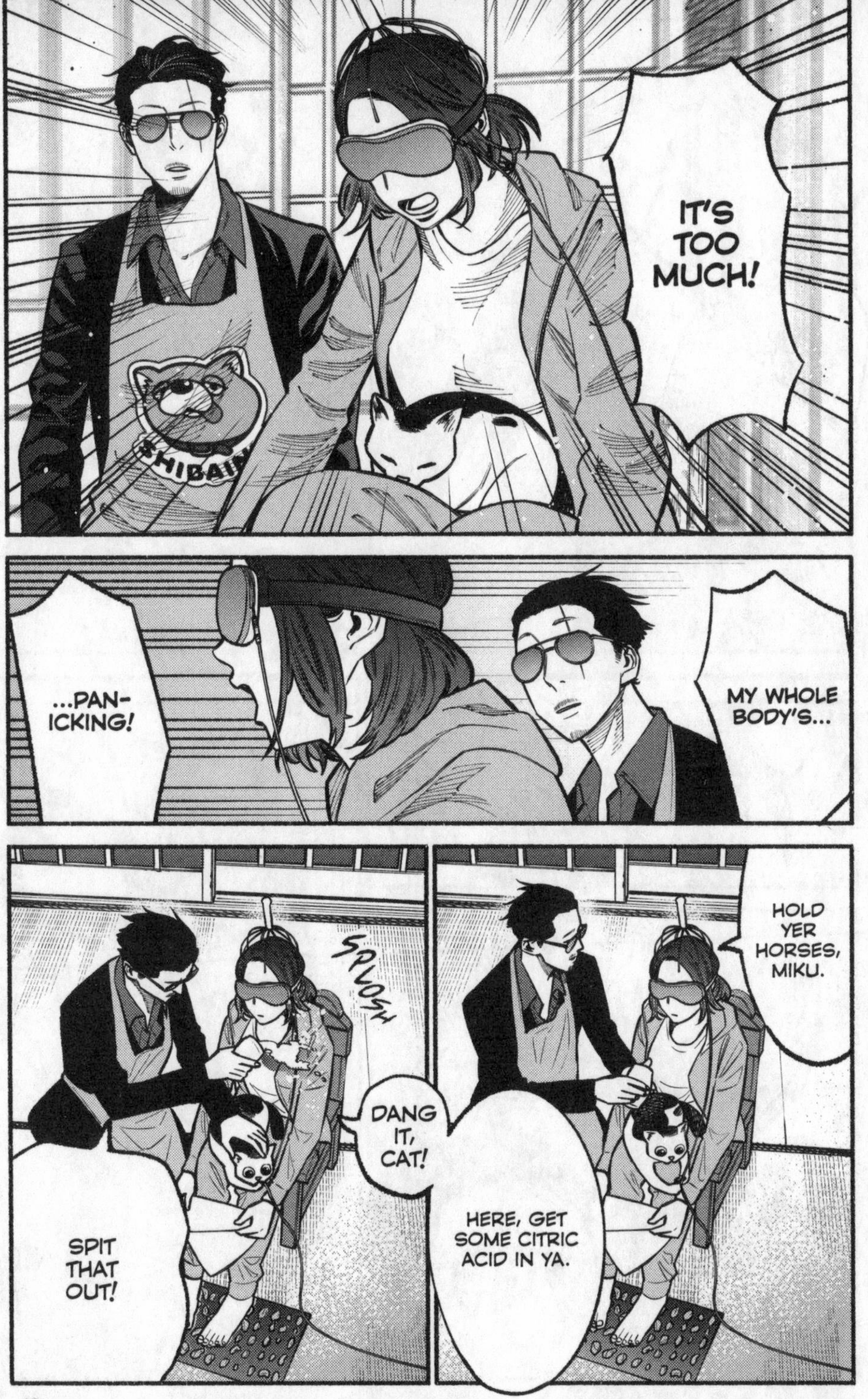
IT'S TOO MUCH!
MY WHOLE BODY'S...
...PAN-ICKING!
HOLD YER HORSES, MIKU.
HERE, GET SOME CITRIC ACID IN YA.
SPLOSH
DANG IT, CAT!
SPIT THAT OUT!

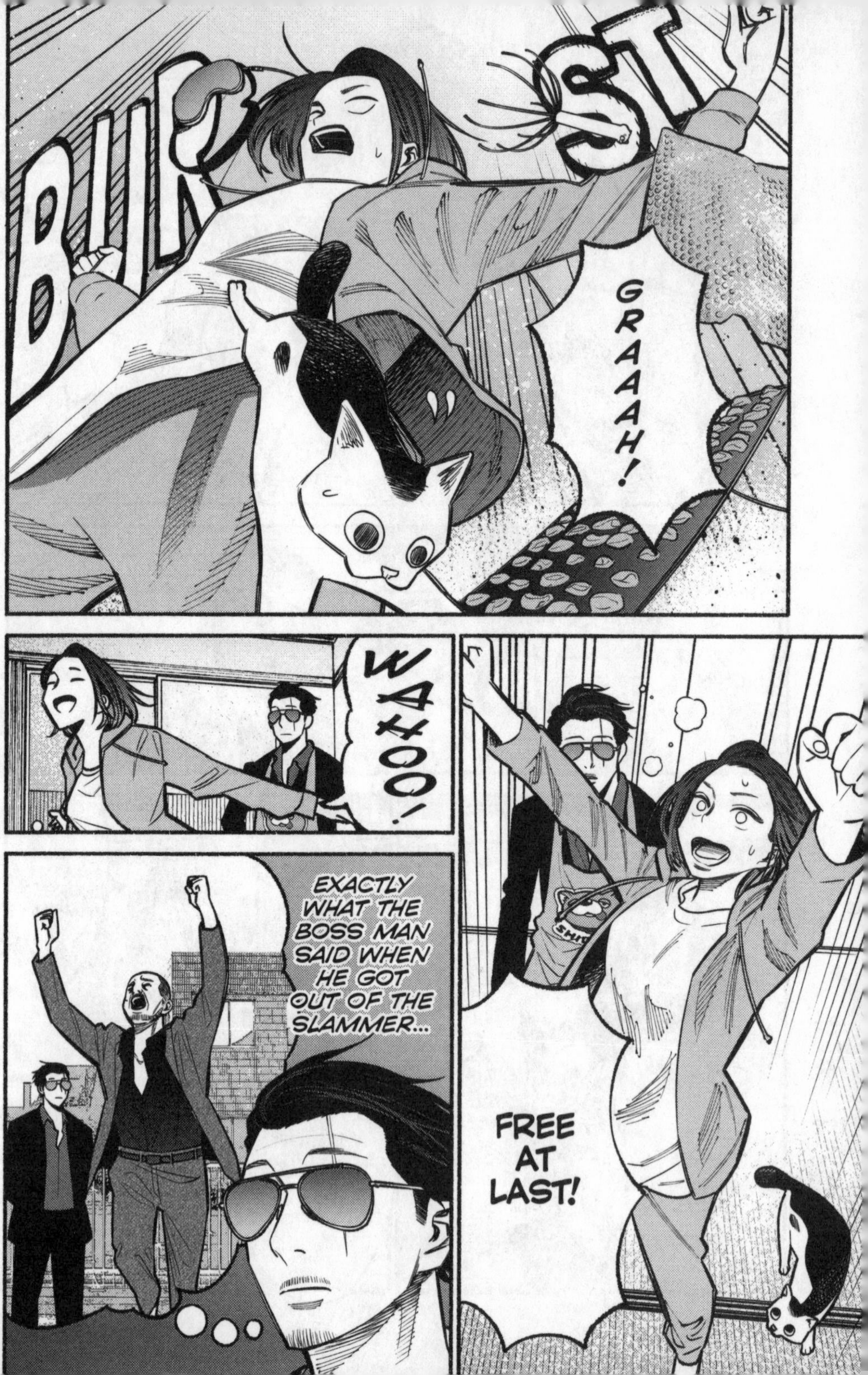
BURST
GRAAAAH!
WAHOO!
FREE AT LAST!
EXACTLY WHAT THE BOSS MAN SAID WHEN HE GOT OUT OF THE SLAMMER...

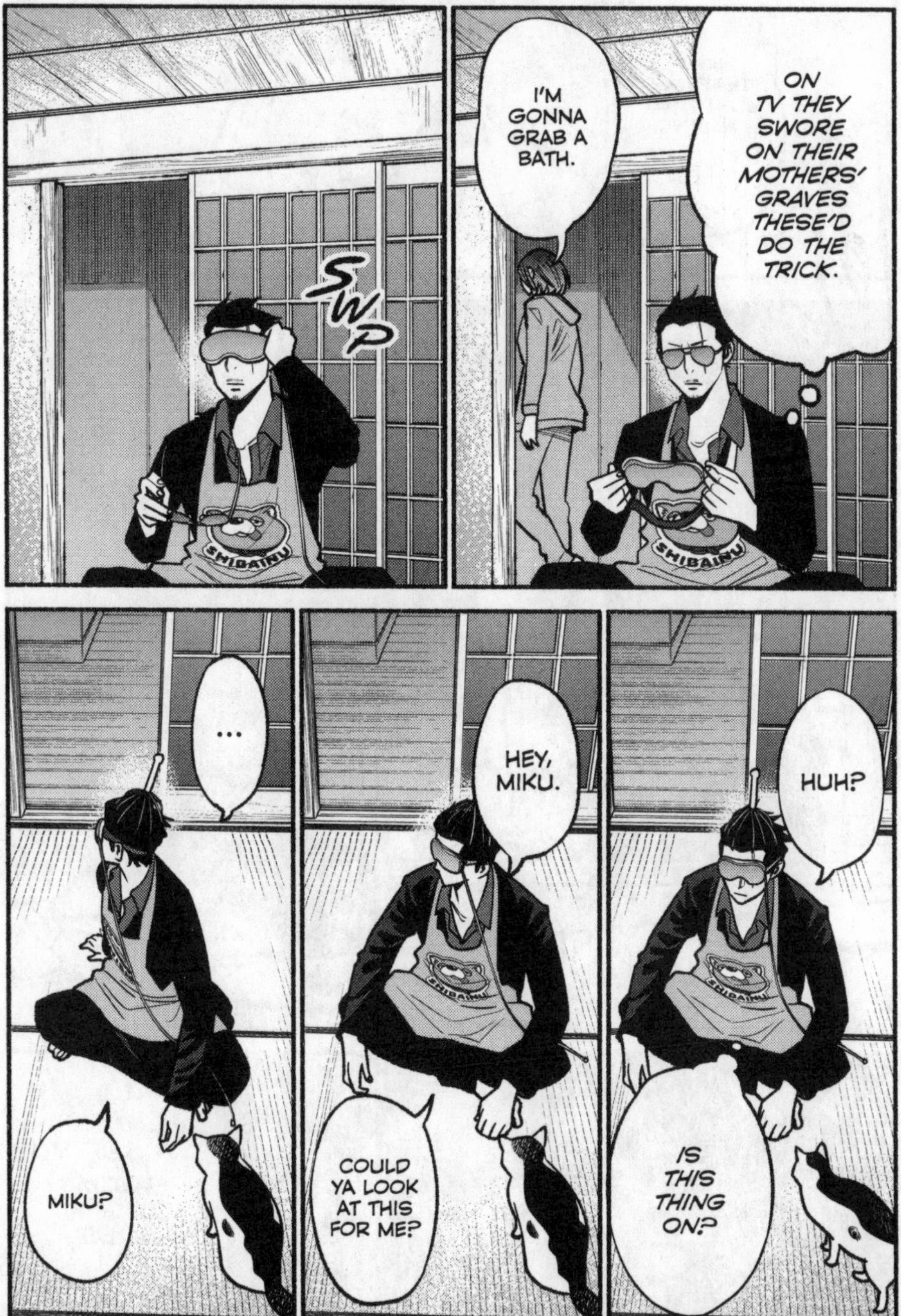
ON TV THEY SWORE ON THEIR MOTHERS' GRAVES THESE'D DO THE TRICK.
I'M GONNA GRAB A BATH.
SWP
HUH?
IS THIS THING ON?
HEY, MIKU.
COULD YA LOOK AT THIS FOR ME?
...
MIKU?
SHIBAINU

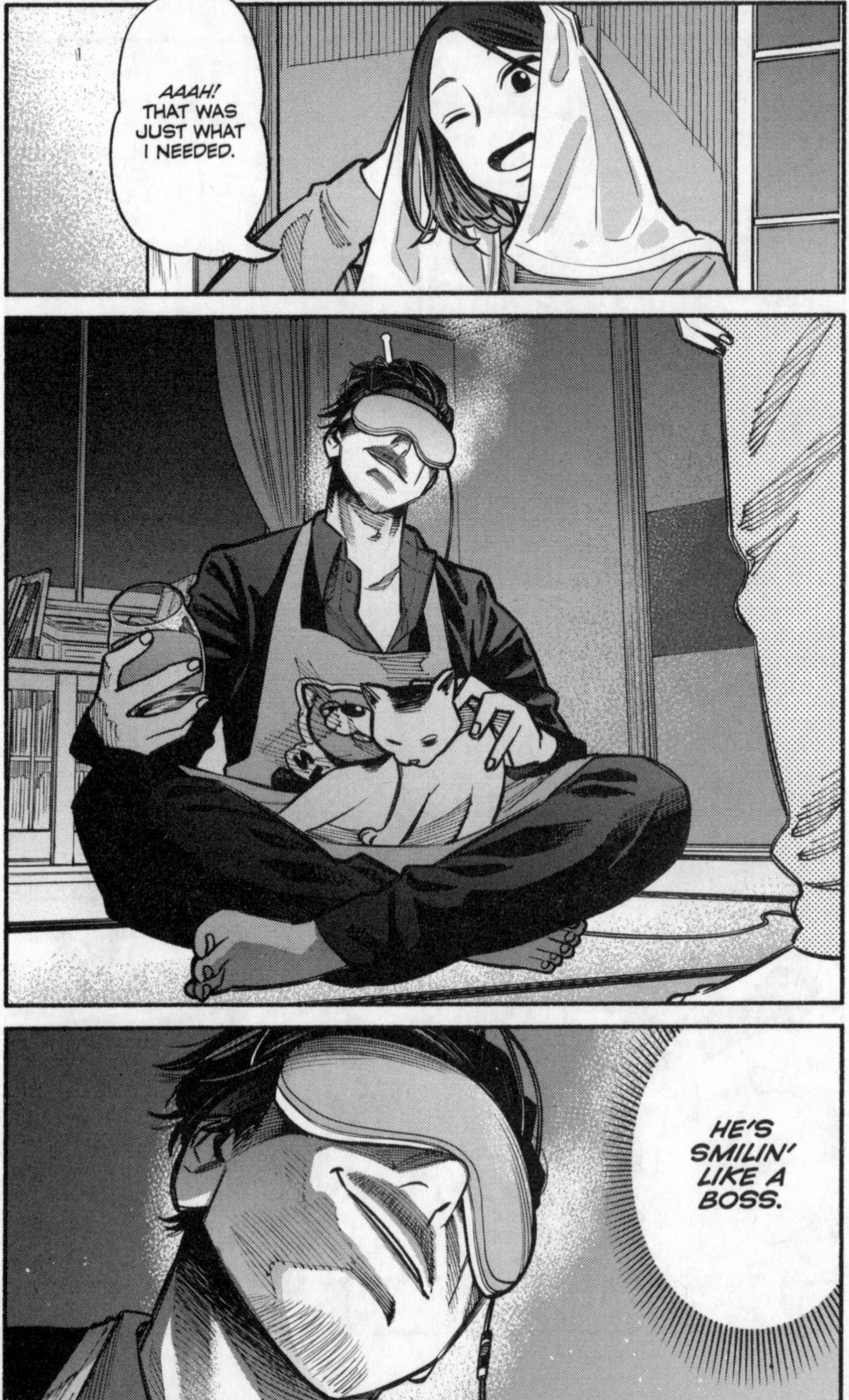
AAAH! THAT WAS JUST WHAT I NEEDED.
HE'S SMILIN' LIKE A BOSS.

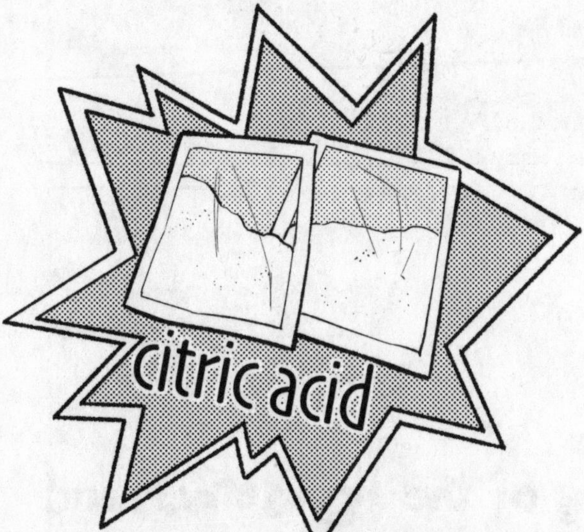
citric acid

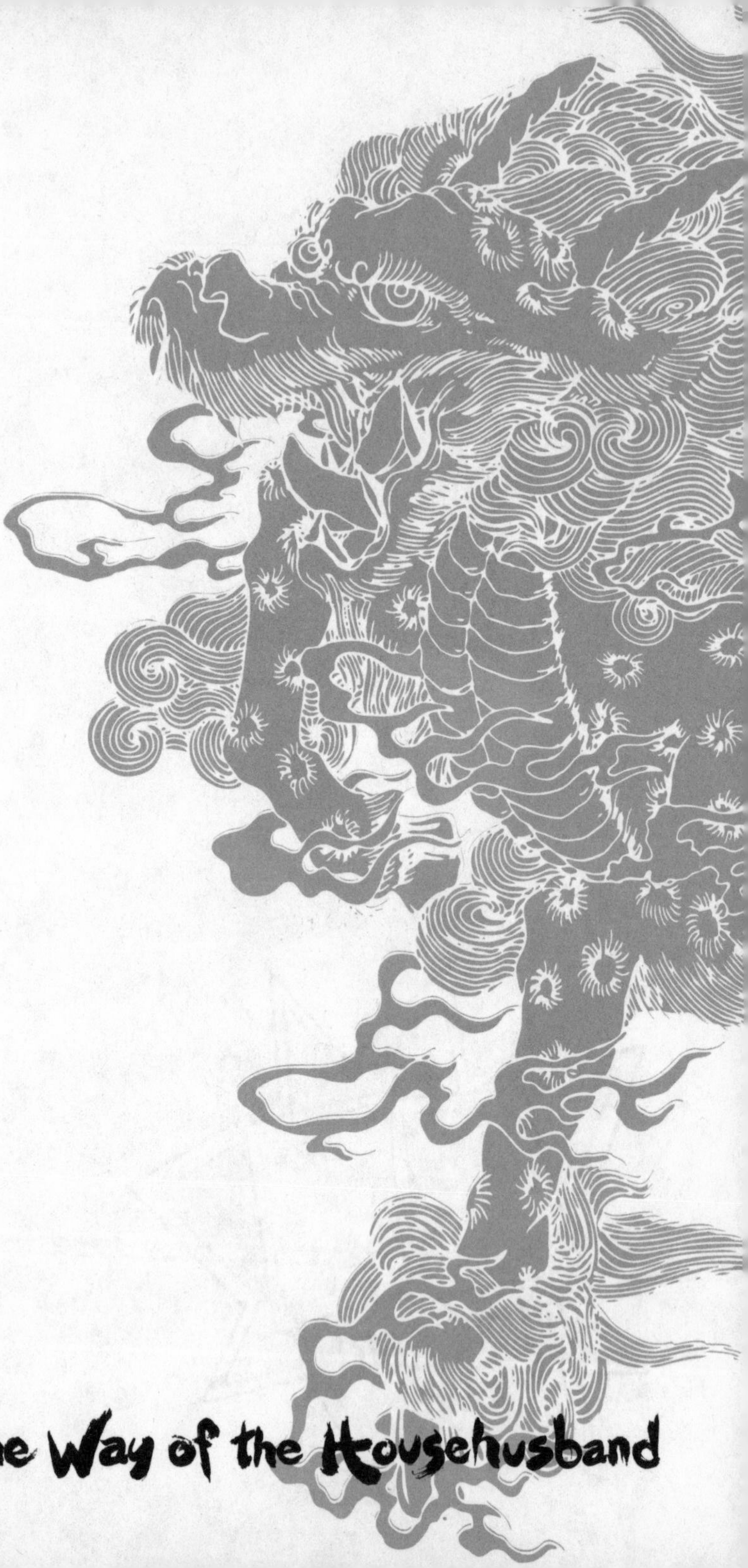

The Way of the Househusband

CHAPTER 22

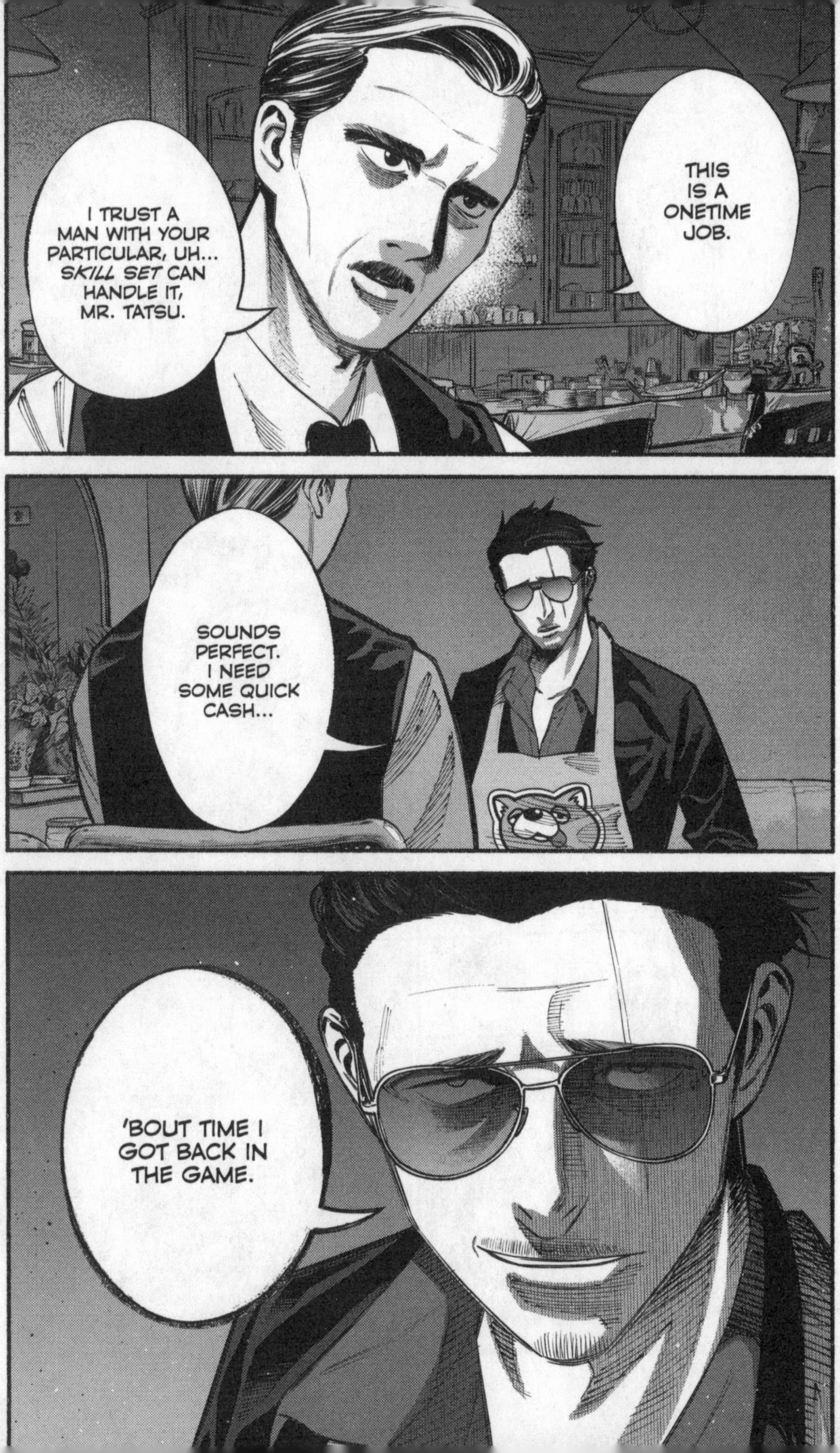
THIS IS A ONETIME JOB.
I TRUST A MAN WITH YOUR PARTICULAR, UH... *SKILL SET* CAN HANDLE IT, MR. TATSU.
SOUNDS PERFECT. I NEED SOME QUICK CASH...
'BOUT TIME I GOT BACK IN THE GAME.

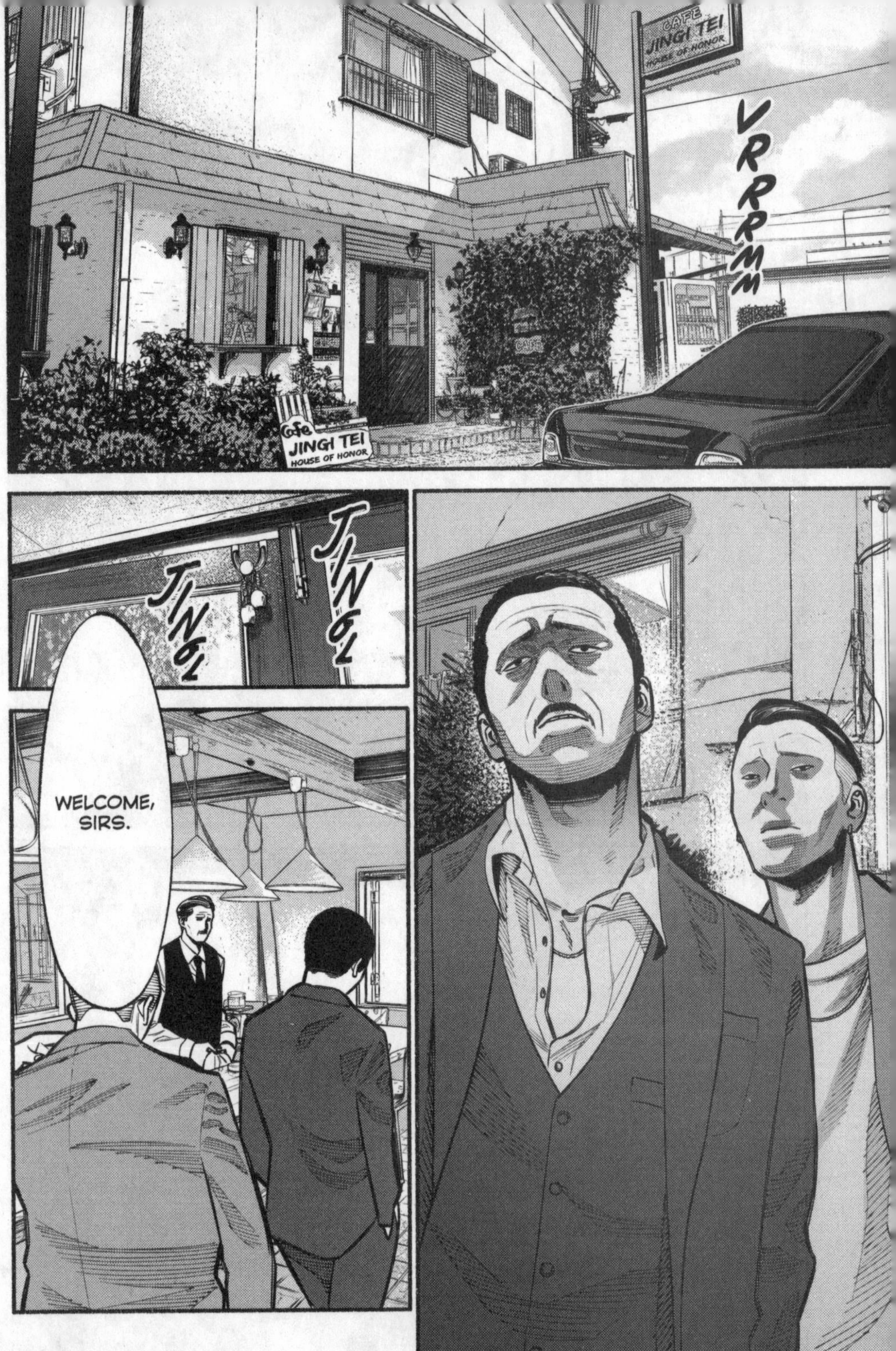
CAFE
JINGI TEI
HOUSE OF HONOR
VRRRMM
Cafe
JINGI TEI
HOUSE OF HONOR
JINGL
JINGL
WELCOME, SIRS.

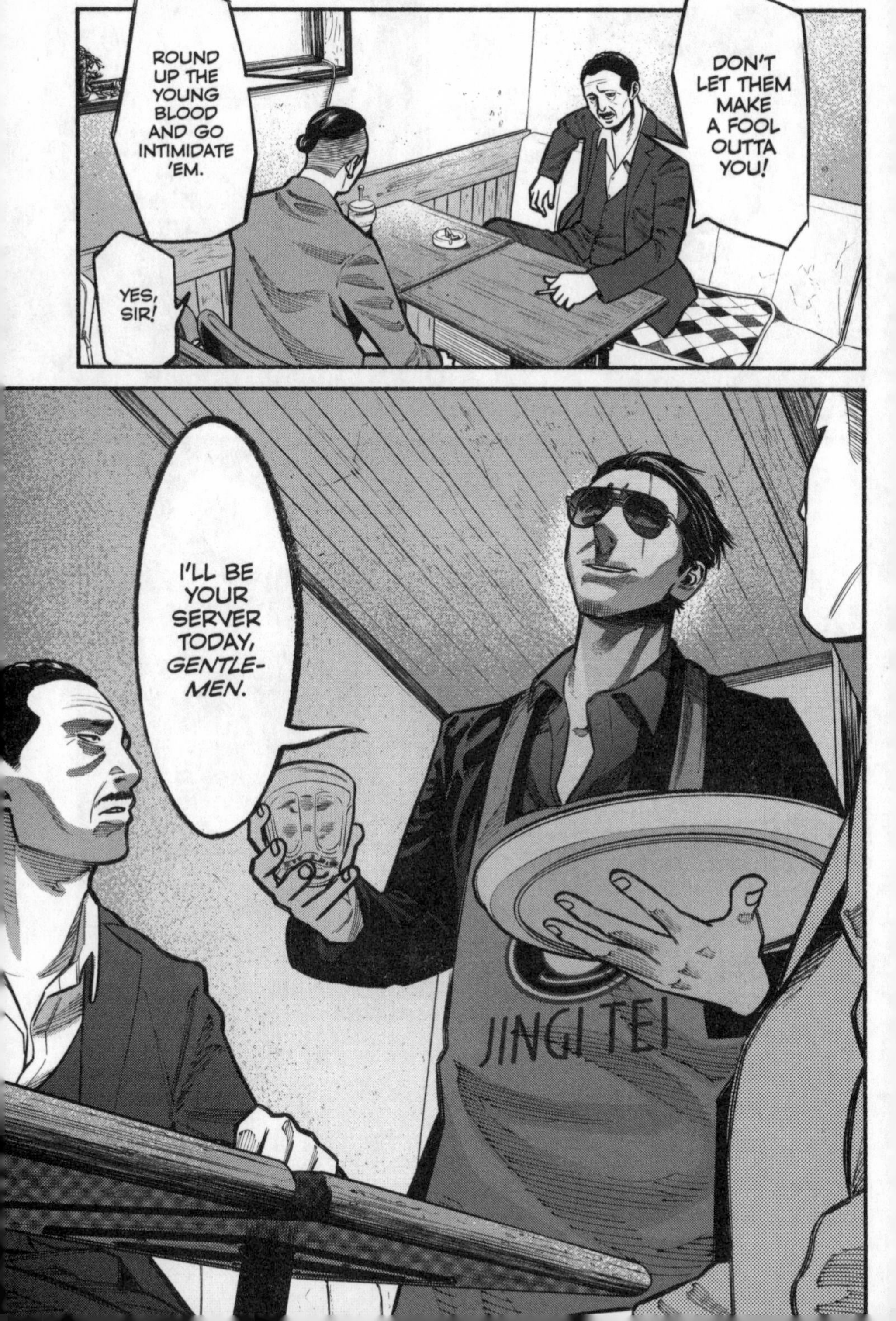
DON'T LET THEM MAKE A FOOL OUTTA YOU!
ROUND UP THE YOUNG BLOOD AND GO INTIMIDATE 'EM.
YES, SIR!
I'LL BE YOUR SERVER TODAY, *GENTLE-MEN*.
JINGI TEI

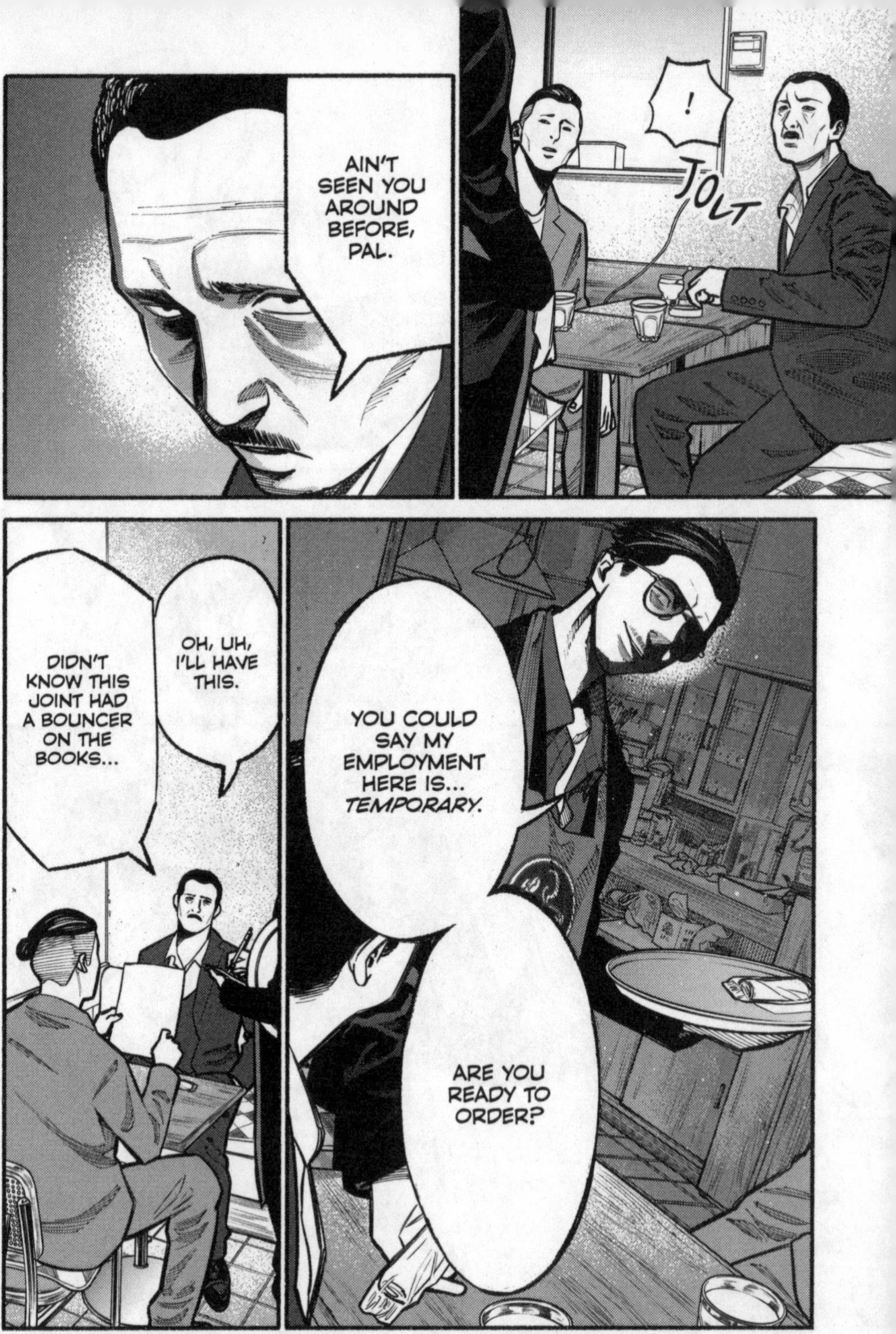
!
JOLT
AIN'T SEEN YOU AROUND BEFORE, PAL.
YOU COULD SAY MY EMPLOYMENT HERE IS... *TEMPORARY.*
ARE YOU READY TO ORDER?
OH, UH, I'LL HAVE THIS.
DIDN'T KNOW THIS JOINT HAD A BOUNCER ON THE BOOKS...

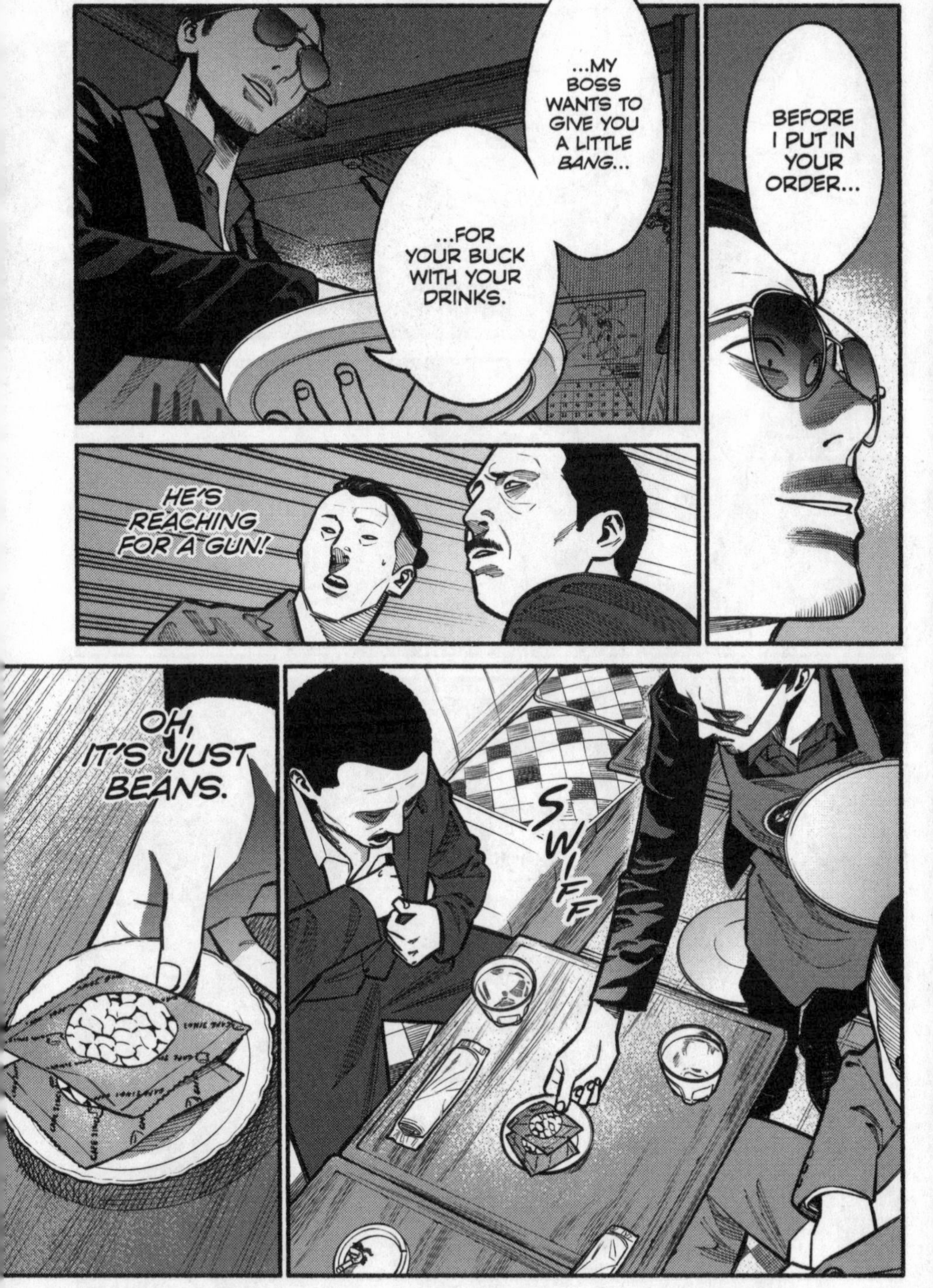
BEFORE I PUT IN YOUR ORDER...
...MY BOSS WANTS TO GIVE YOU A LITTLE *BANG*...
...FOR YOUR BUCK WITH YOUR DRINKS.
HE'S REACHING FOR A GUN!
SWIFF
OH, IT'S JUST BEANS.

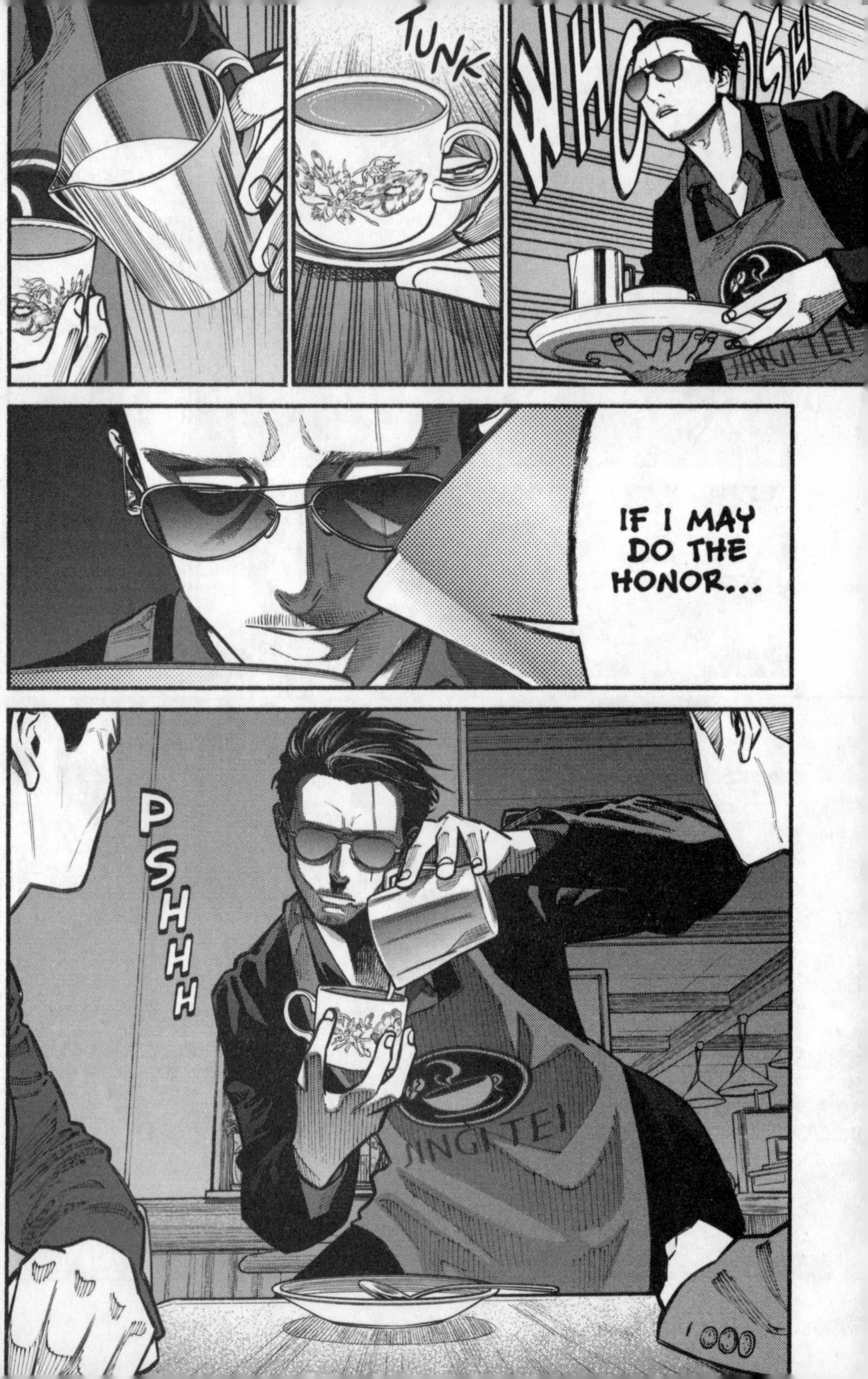
WHOOSH
TUNK
IF I MAY DO THE HONOR...
PSHHH

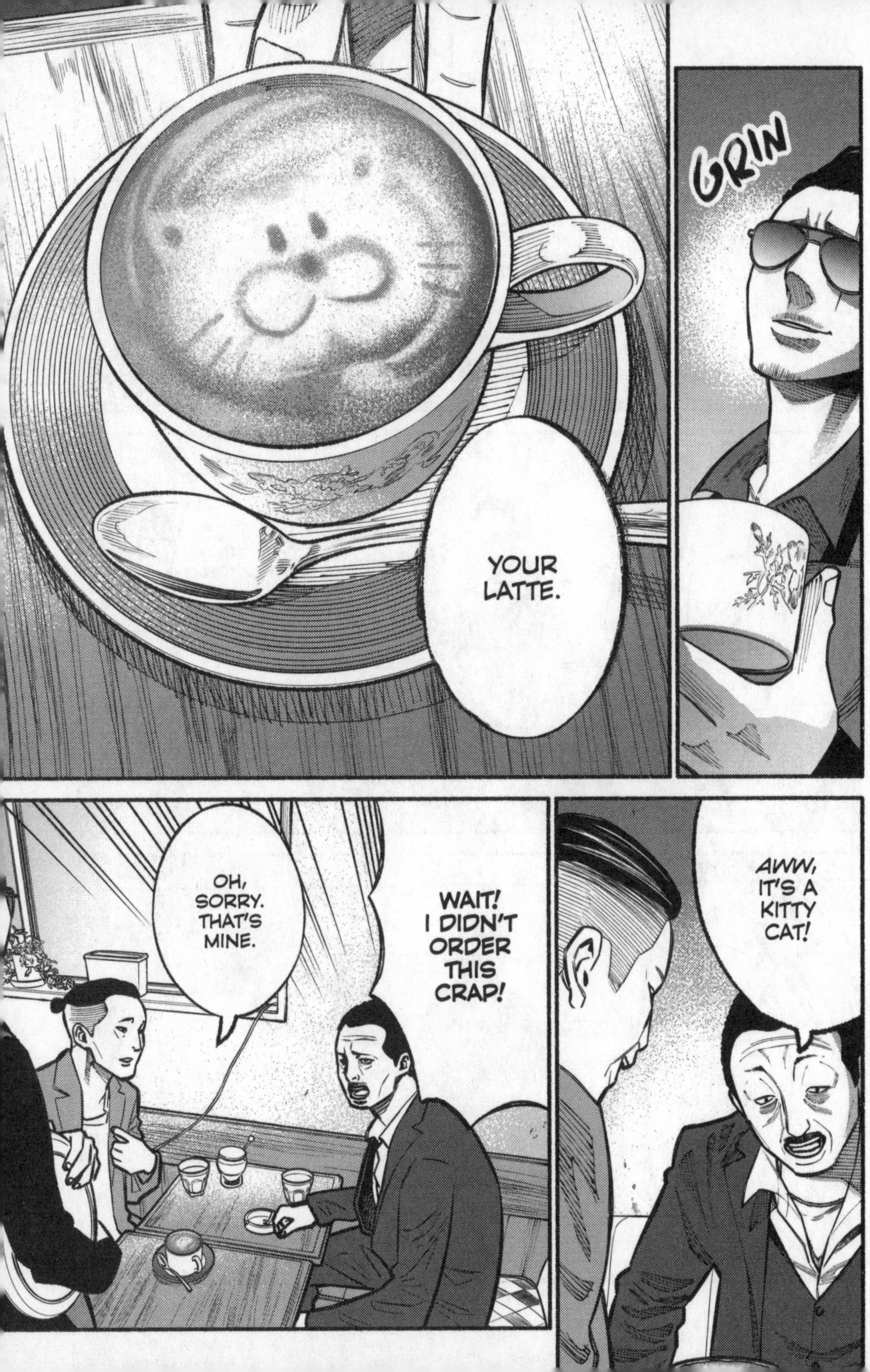
GRIN
YOUR LATTE.
AWW, IT'S A KITTY CAT!
WAIT! I DIDN'T ORDER THIS CRAP!
OH, SORRY. THAT'S MINE.

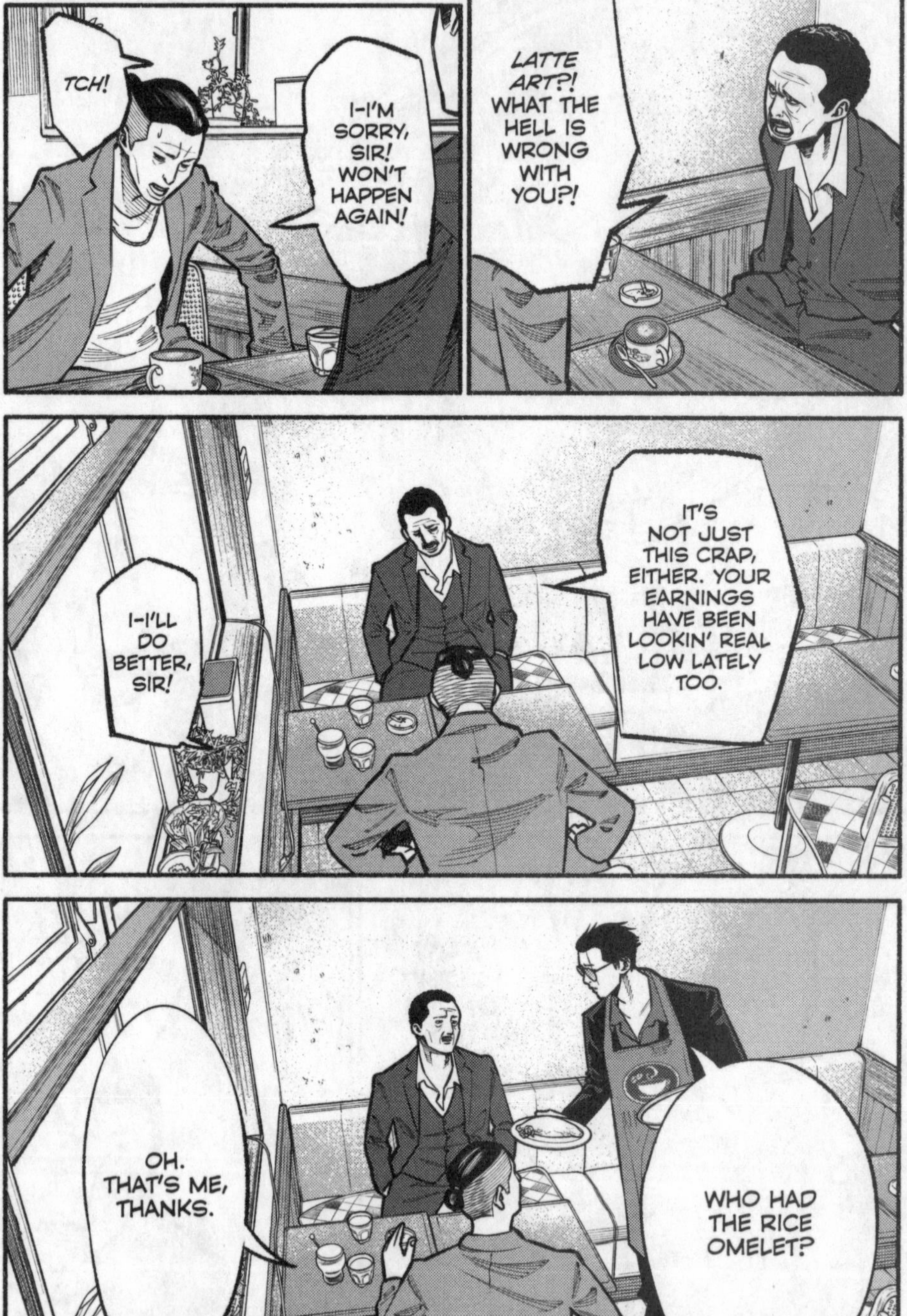

LATTE ART?! WHAT THE HELL IS WRONG WITH YOU?!
I-I'M SORRY, SIR! WON'T HAPPEN AGAIN!
TCH!
IT'S NOT JUST THIS CRAP, EITHER. YOUR EARNINGS HAVE BEEN LOOKIN' REAL LOW LATELY TOO.
I-I'LL DO BETTER, SIR!
WHO HAD THE RICE OMELET?
OH. THAT'S ME, THANKS.

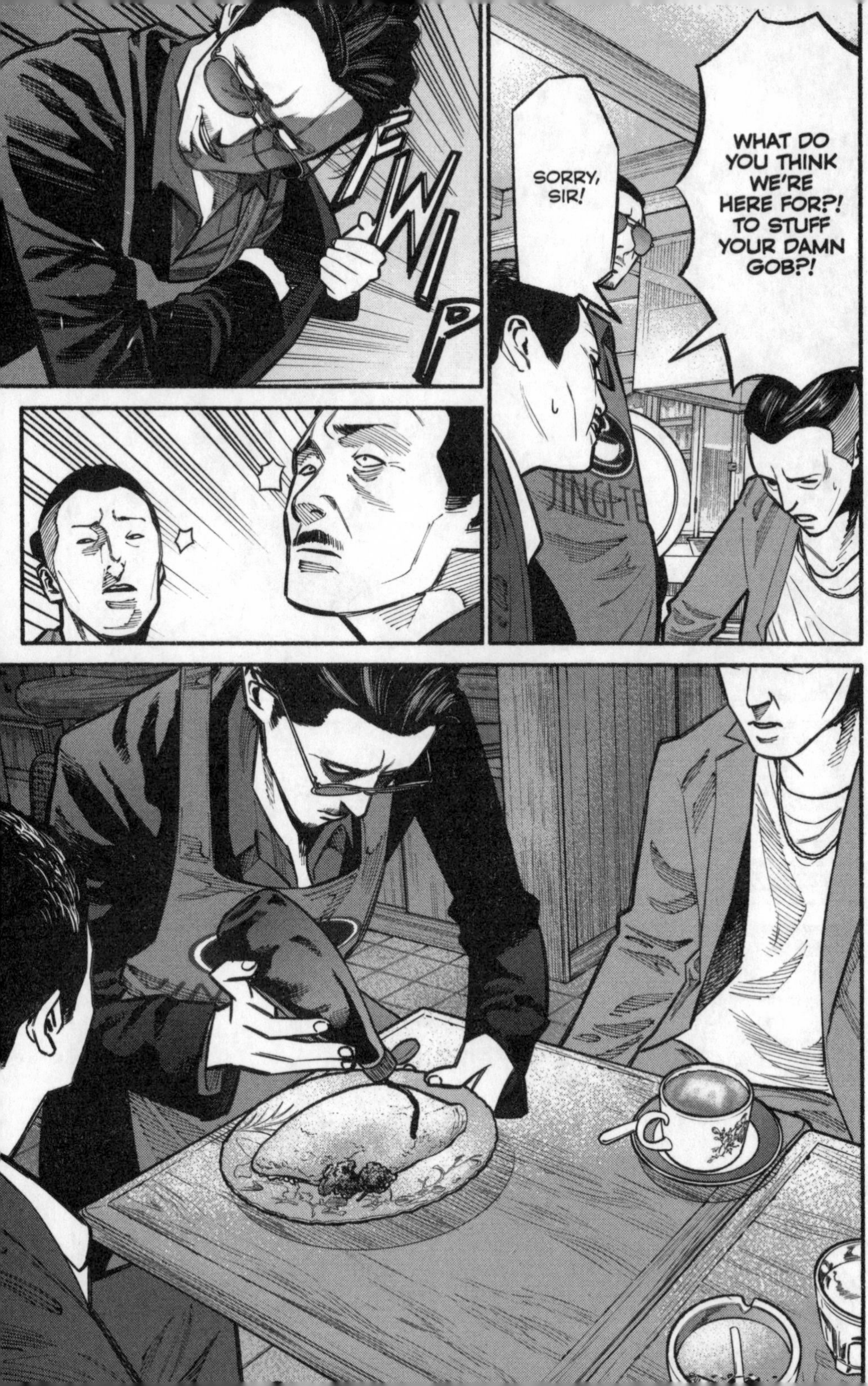
WHAT DO YOU THINK WE'RE HERE FOR?! TO STUFF YOUR DAMN GOB?!
SORRY, SIR!
JINGITEI
FWIP

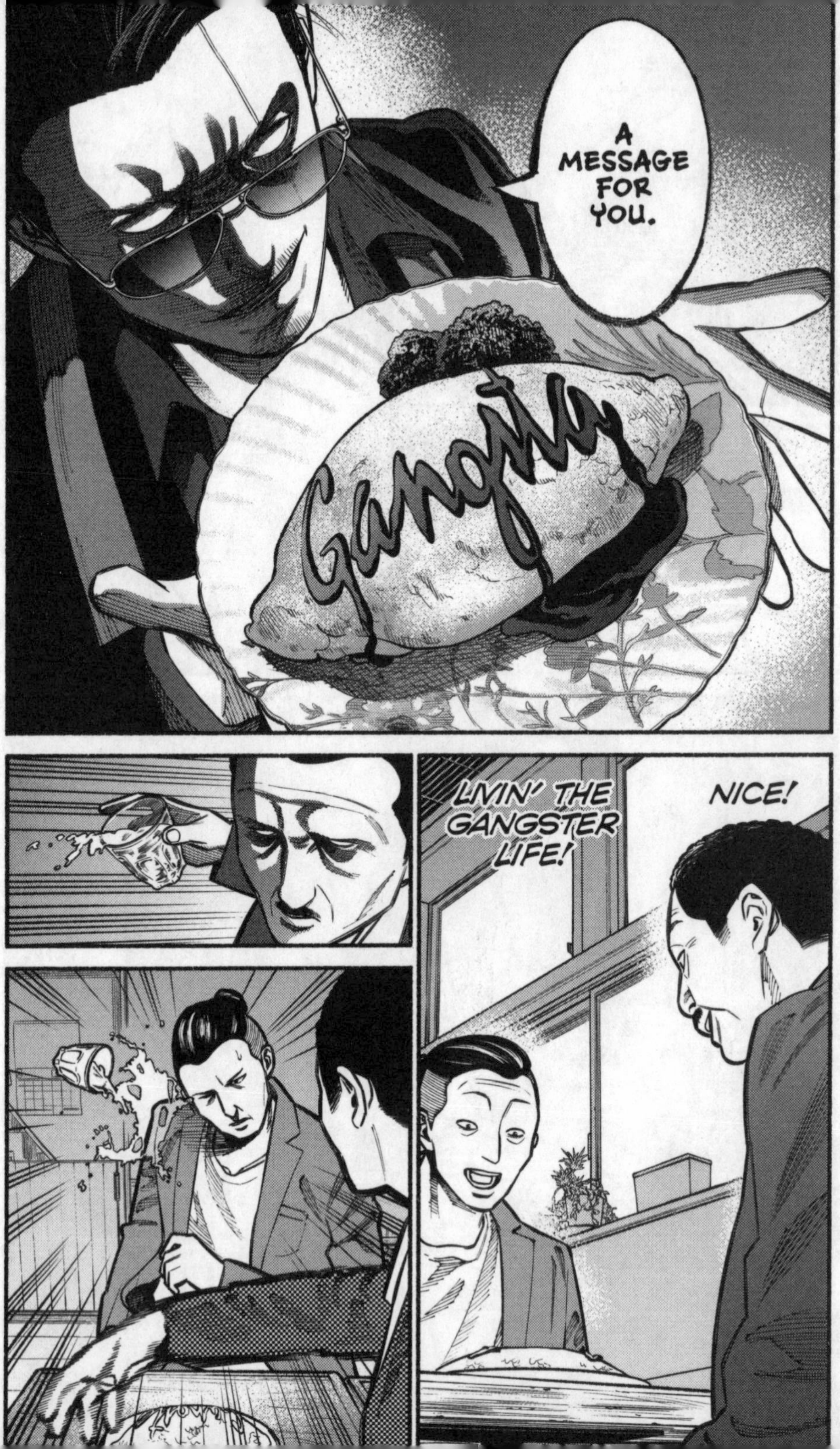
A MESSAGE FOR YOU.
Gangster
NICE!
LIVIN' THE GANGSTER LIFE!

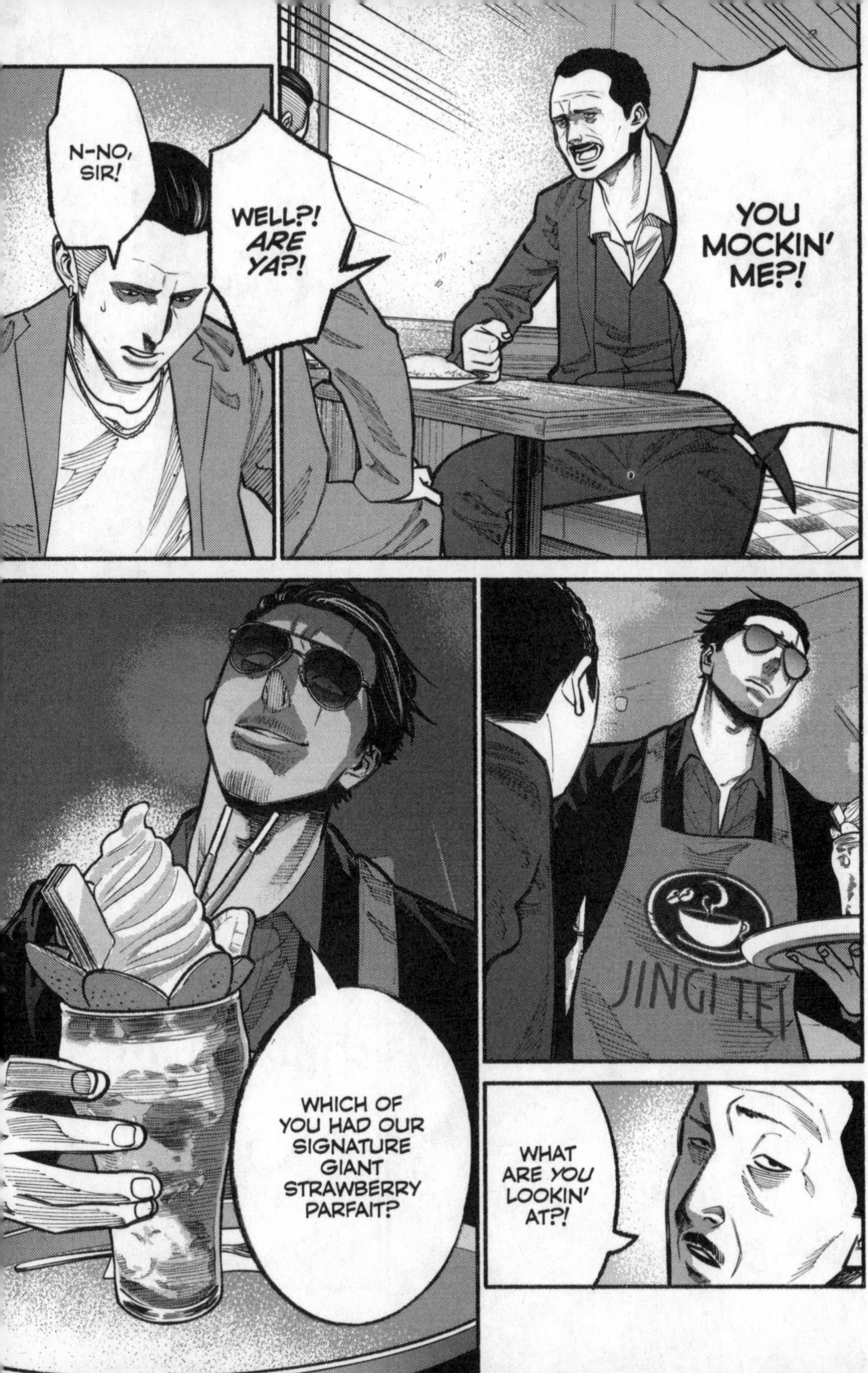
YOU MOCKIN' ME?!
WELL?! ARE YA?!
N-NO, SIR!
JINGI TEI
WHAT ARE YOU LOOKIN' AT?!
WHICH OF YOU HAD OUR SIGNATURE GIANT STRAWBERRY PARFAIT?

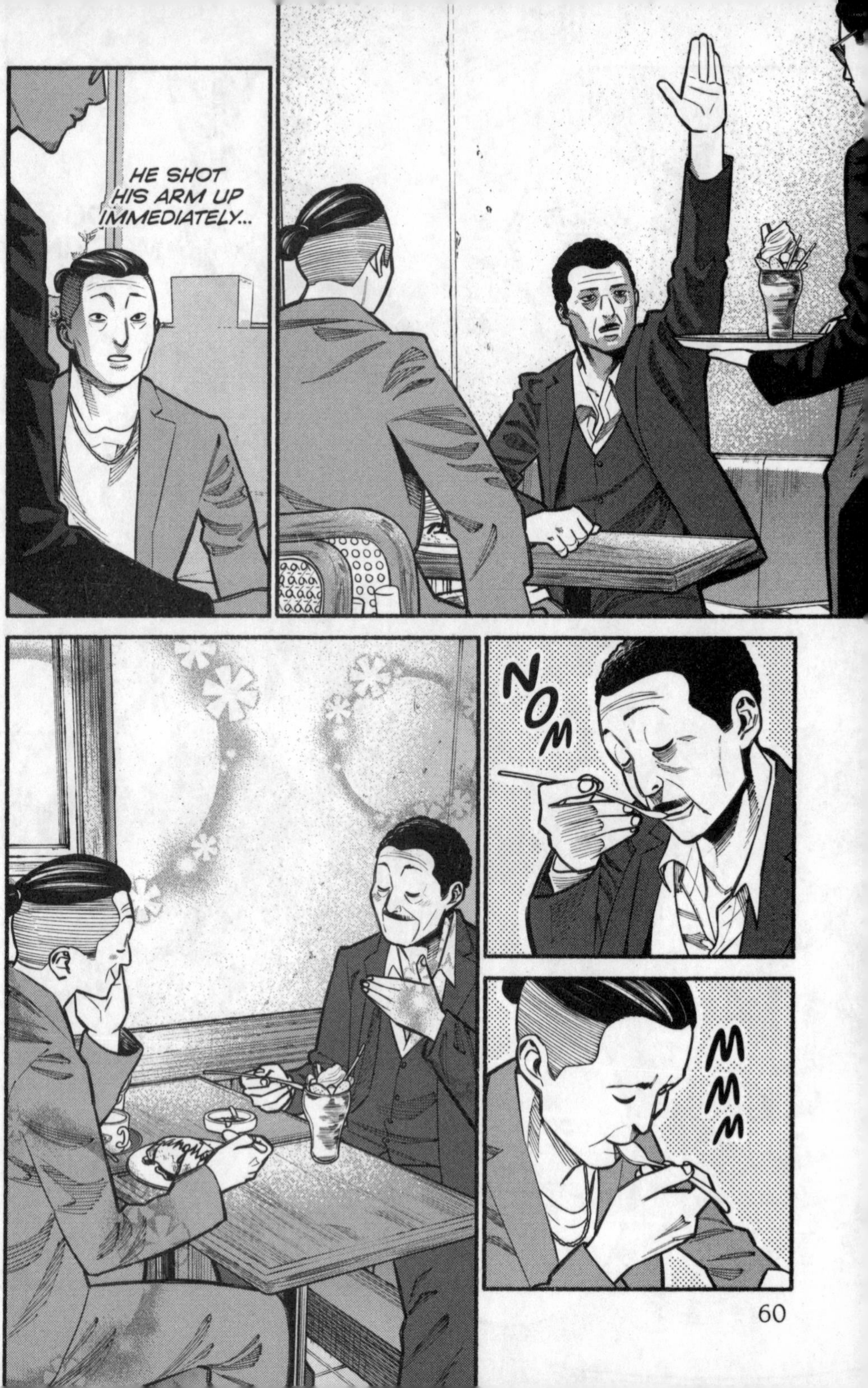
HE SHOT HIS ARM UP IMMEDIATELY...
NOM
MMMM

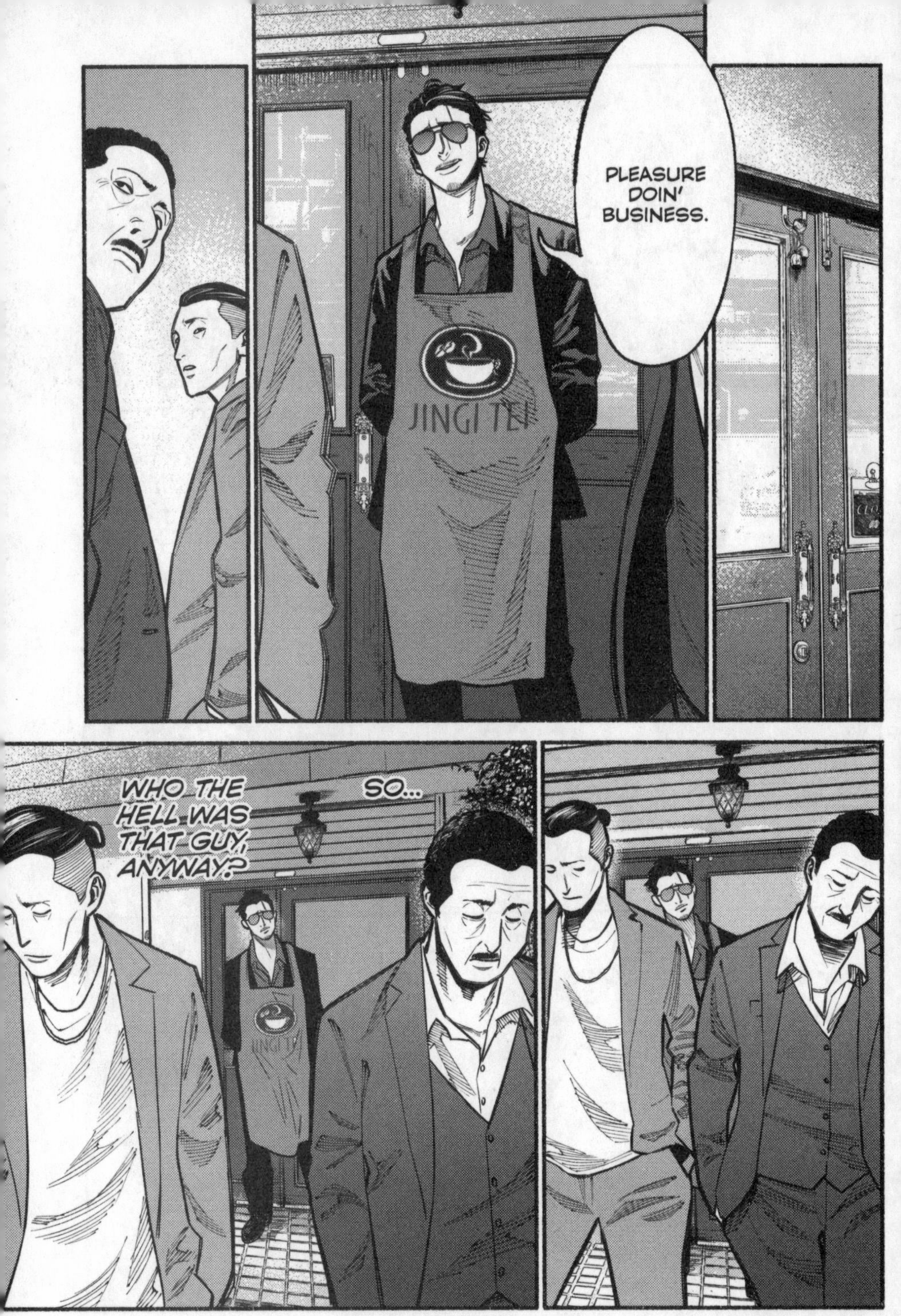
PLEASURE DOIN' BUSINESS.
JINGI TEI
SO...
WHO THE HELL WAS THAT GUY, ANYWAY?

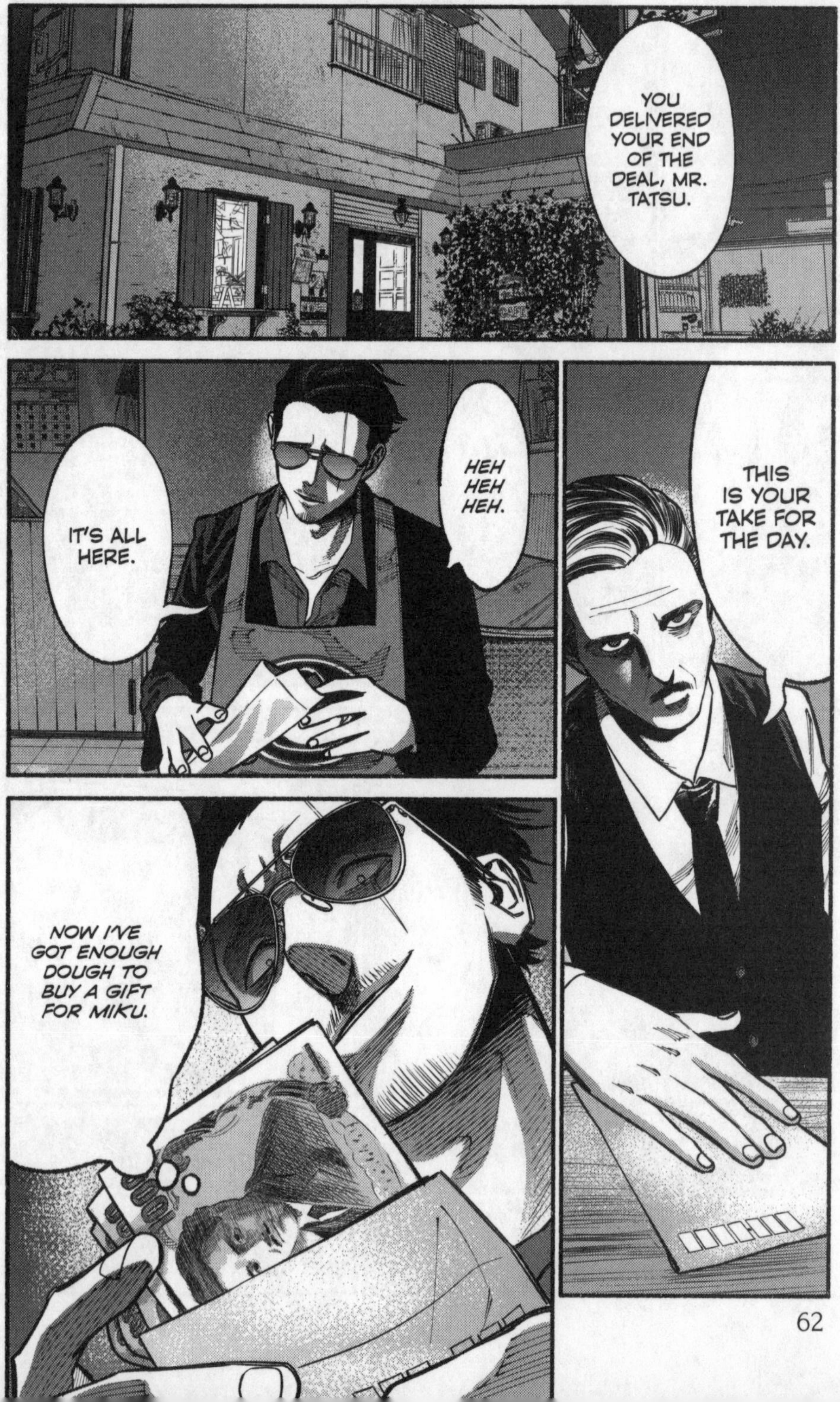
YOU DELIVERED YOUR END OF THE DEAL, MR. TATSU.
THIS IS YOUR TAKE FOR THE DAY.
HEH HEH HEH.
IT'S ALL HERE.
NOW I'VE GOT ENOUGH DOUGH TO BUY A GIFT FOR MIKU.

JINGI TEI

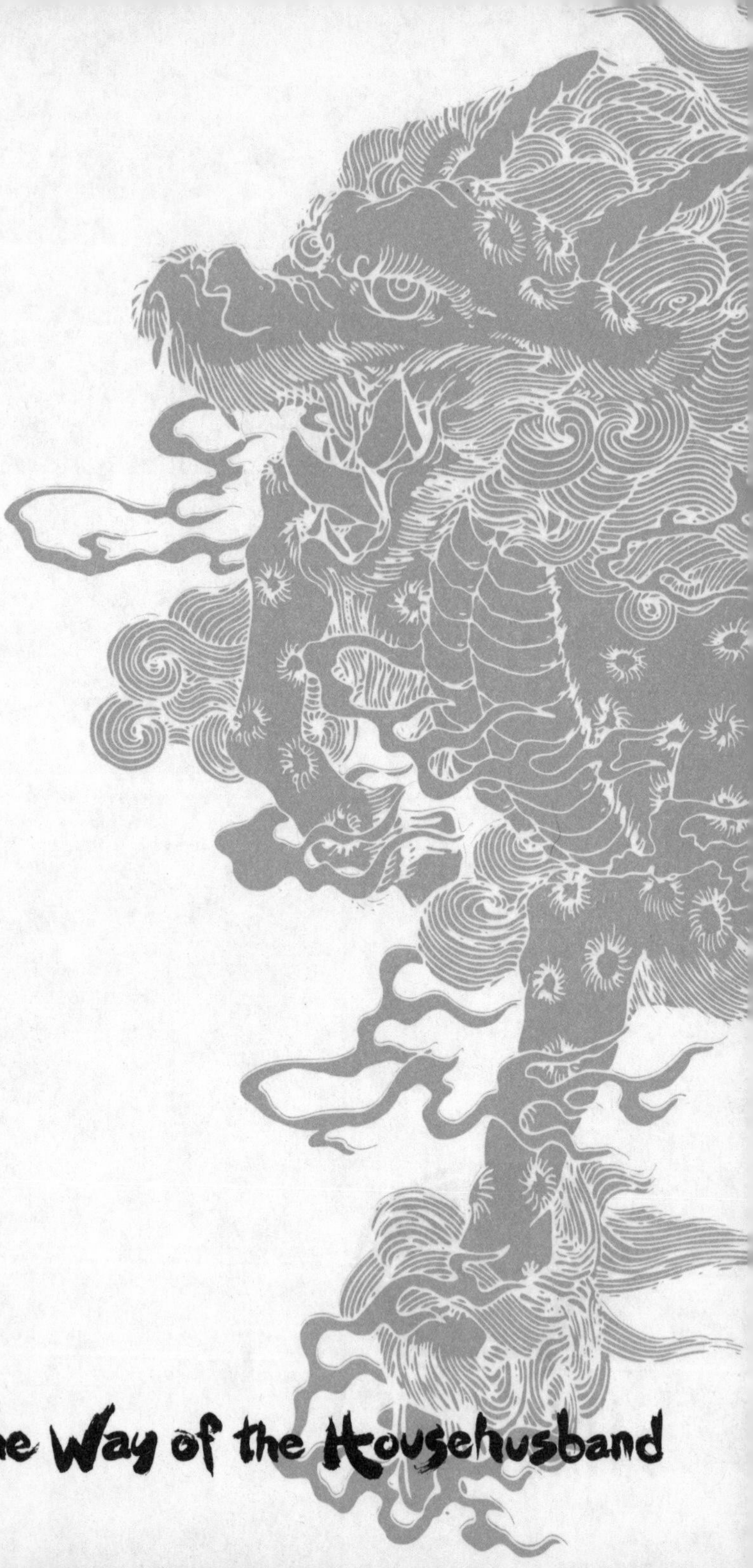

The Way of the Househusband

CHAPTER 23

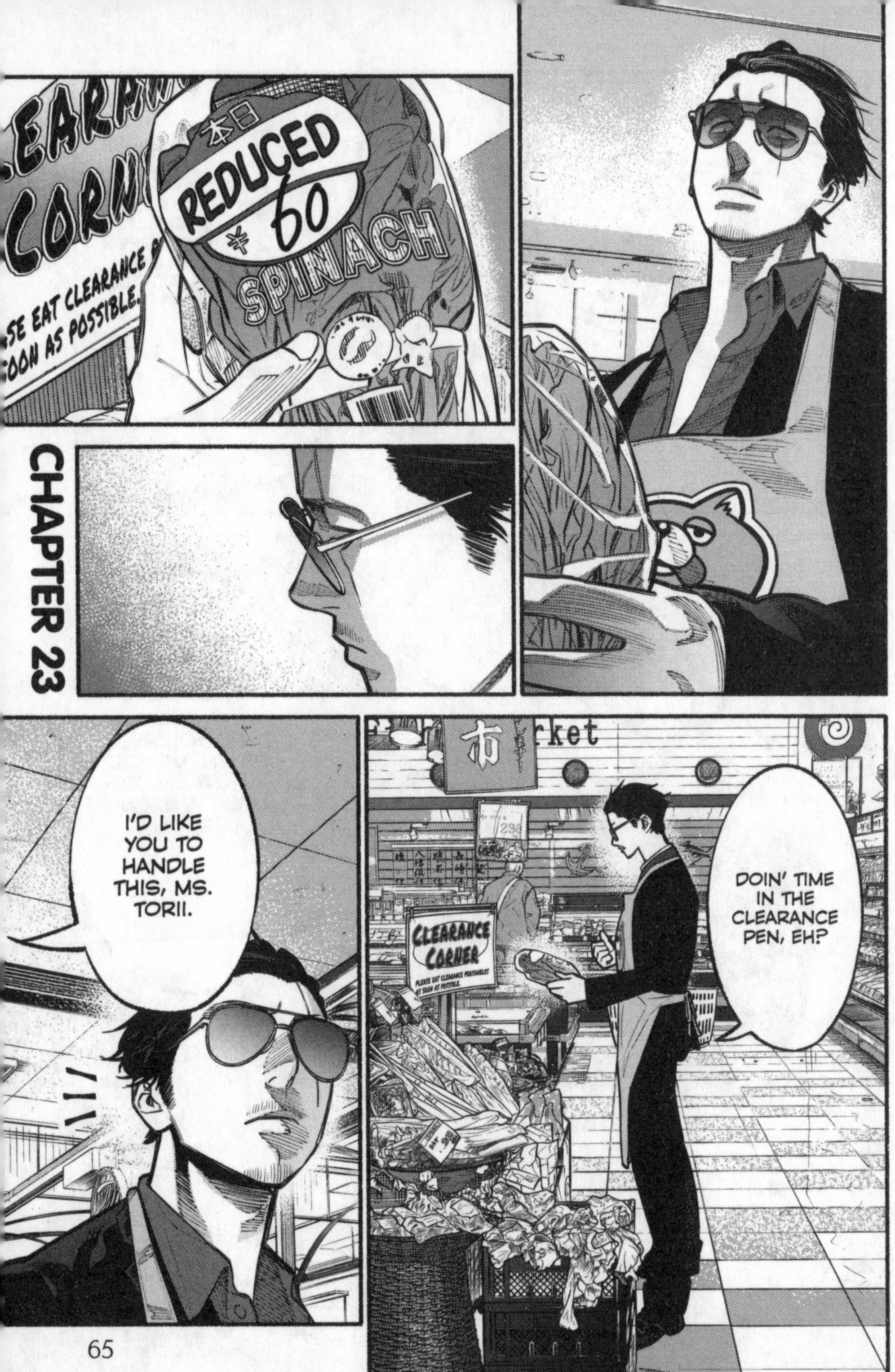
REDUCED
¥60
SPINACH
CLEARANCE CORNER
PLEASE EAT CLEARANCE PERISHABLES AS SOON AS POSSIBLE.
DOIN' TIME IN THE CLEARANCE PEN, EH?
I'D LIKE YOU TO HANDLE THIS, MS. TORII.

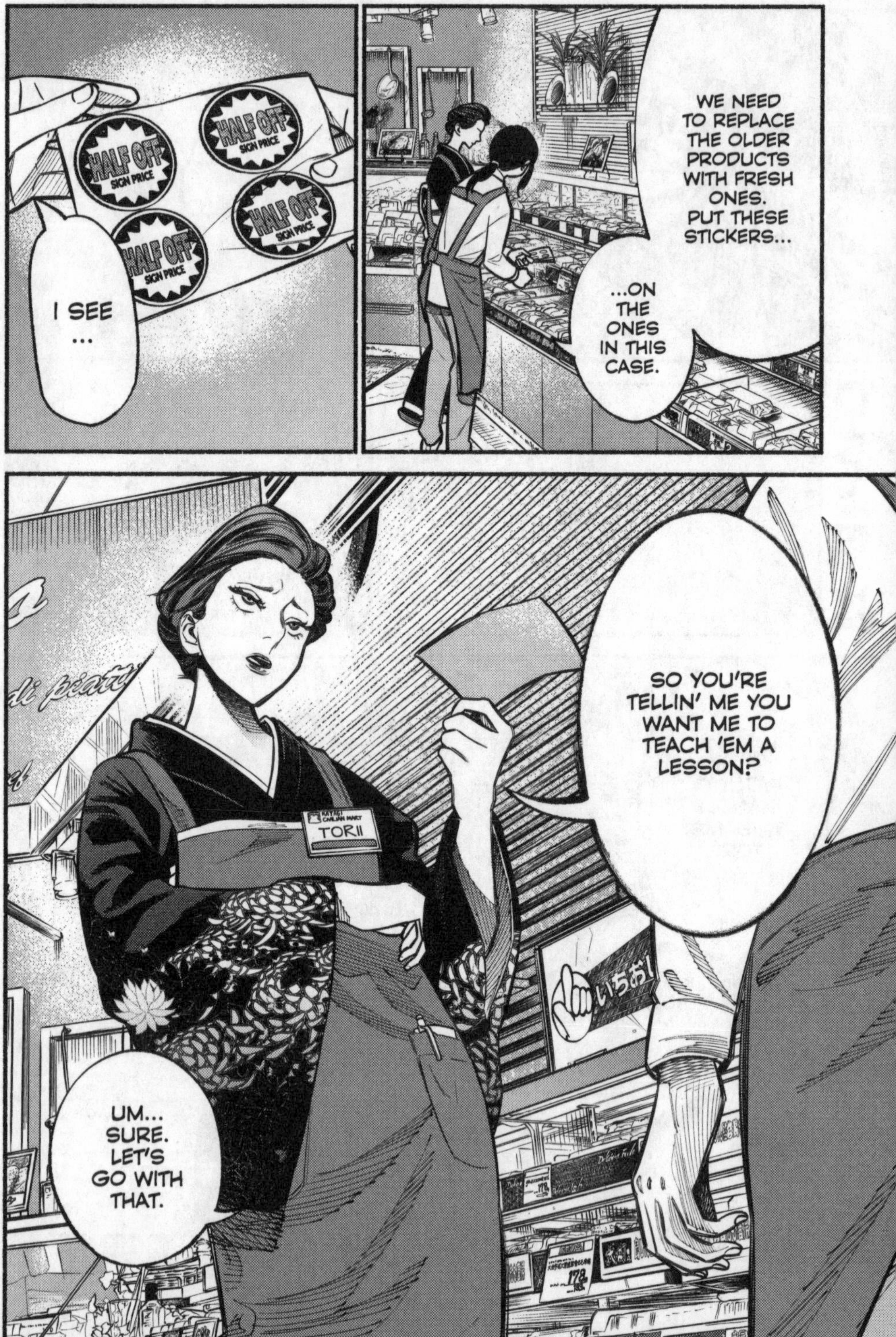
WE NEED TO REPLACE THE OLDER PRODUCTS WITH FRESH ONES. PUT THESE STICKERS...
...ON THE ONES IN THIS CASE.
HALF OFF SIGN PRICE
HALF OFF SIGN PRICE
HALF OFF SIGN PRICE
HALF OFF SIGN PRICE
I SEE ...
SO YOU'RE TELLIN' ME YOU WANT ME TO TEACH 'EM A LESSON?
いちおし
TORII
UM... SURE. LET'S GO WITH THAT.

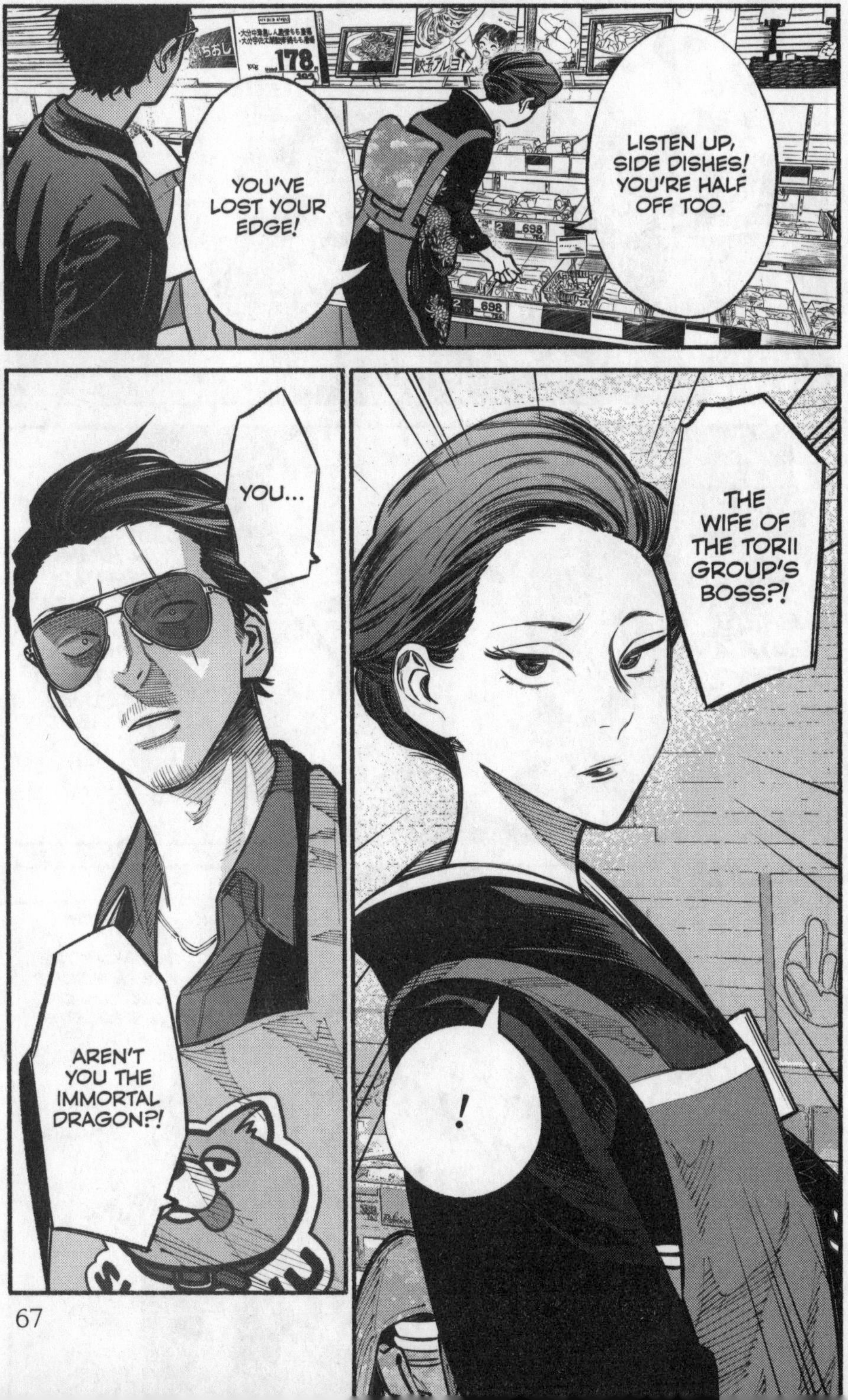
LISTEN UP, SIDE DISHES! YOU'RE HALF OFF TOO.
YOU'VE LOST YOUR EDGE!
THE WIFE OF THE TORII GROUP'S BOSS?!
!
YOU...
AREN'T YOU THE IMMORTAL DRAGON?!

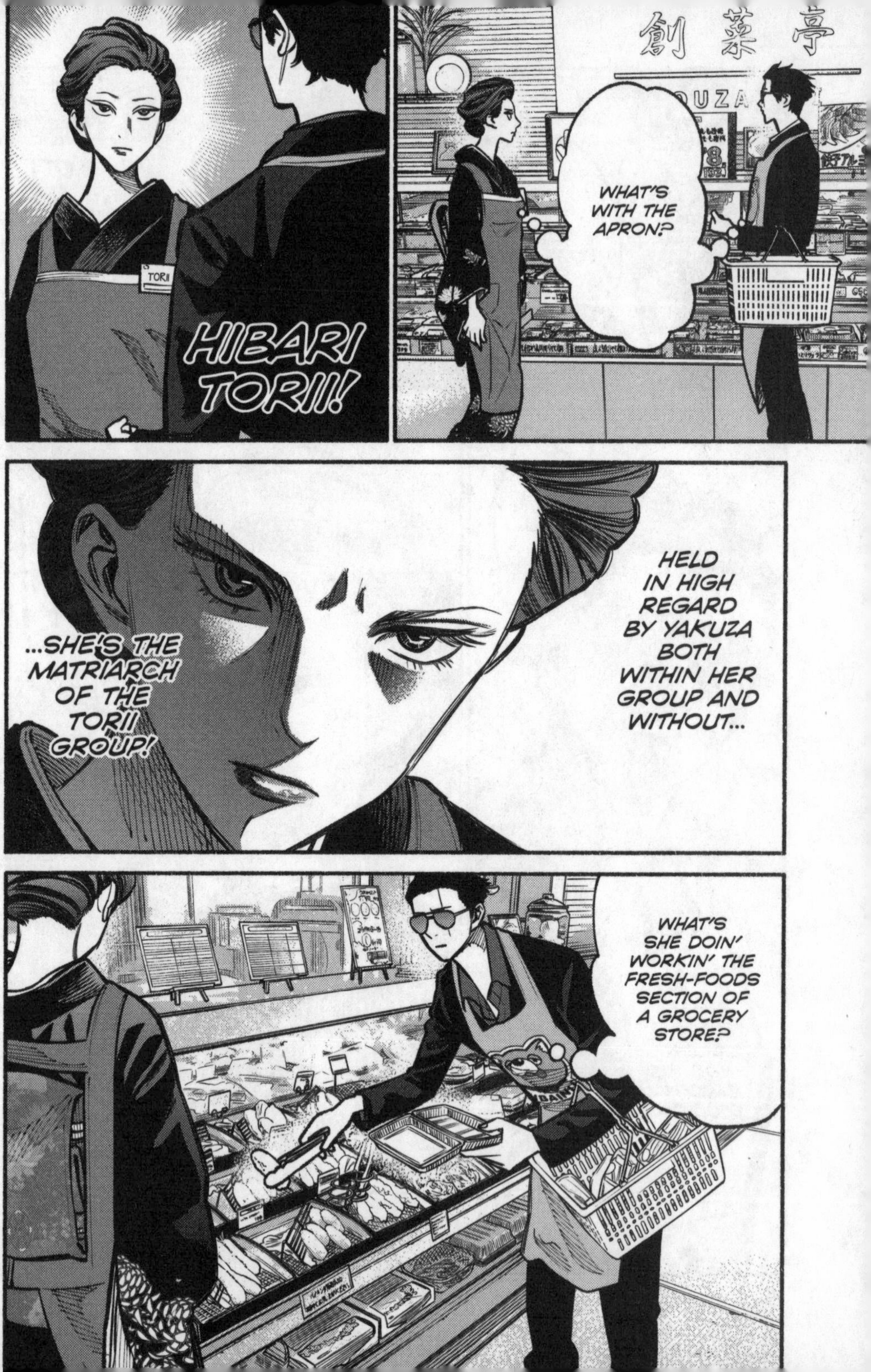
創菜亭
WHAT'S WITH THE APRON?
HIBARI TORII!
TORII
HELD IN HIGH REGARD BY YAKUZA BOTH WITHIN HER GROUP AND WITHOUT...
...SHE'S THE MATRIARCH OF THE TORII GROUP!
WHAT'S SHE DOIN' WORKIN' THE FRESH-FOODS SECTION OF A GROCERY STORE?

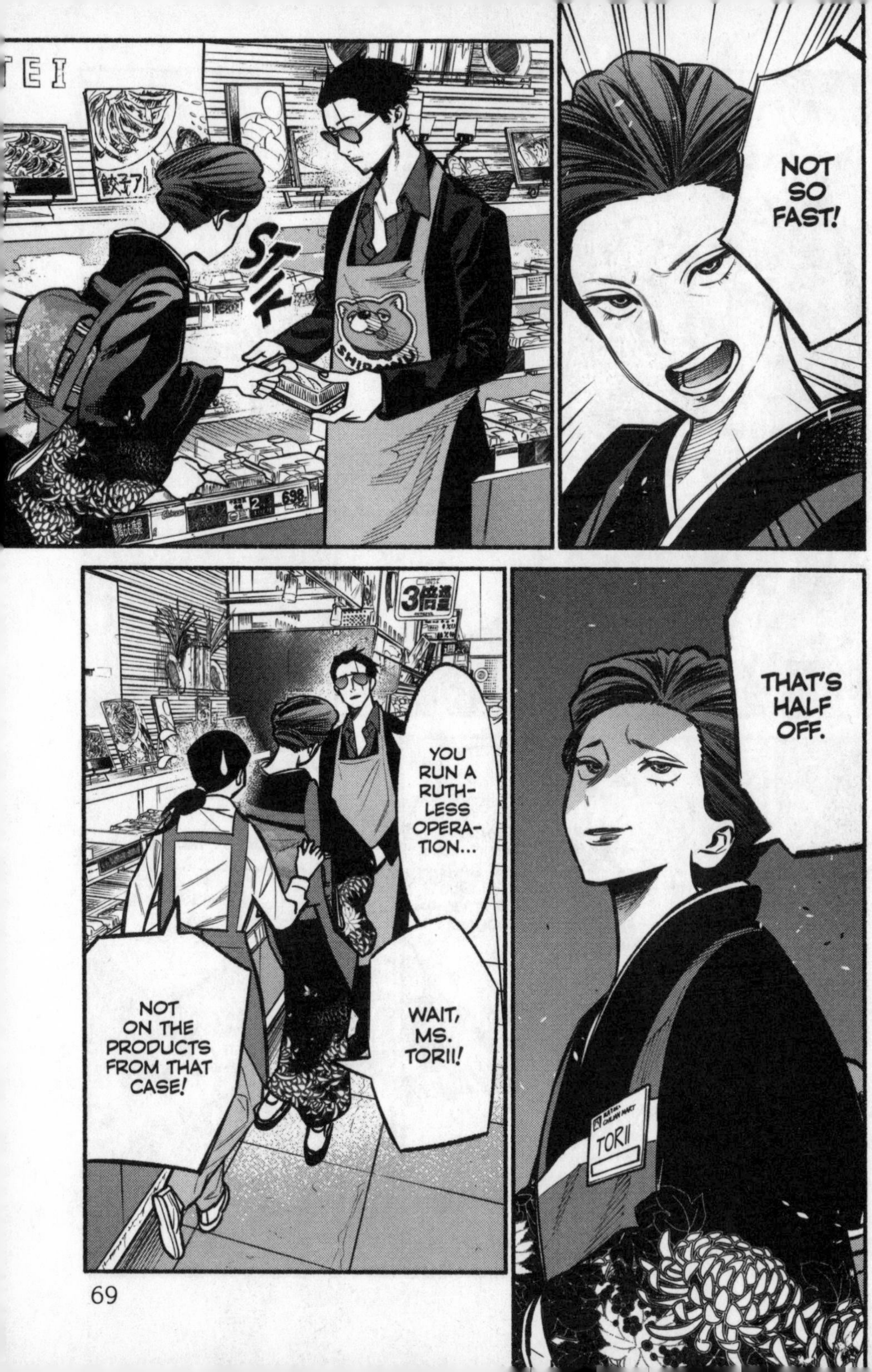
NOT SO FAST!
TEI
STIK
THAT'S HALF OFF.
TORII
YOU RUN A RUTHLESS OPERATION...
WAIT, MS. TORII!
NOT ON THE PRODUCTS FROM THAT CASE!

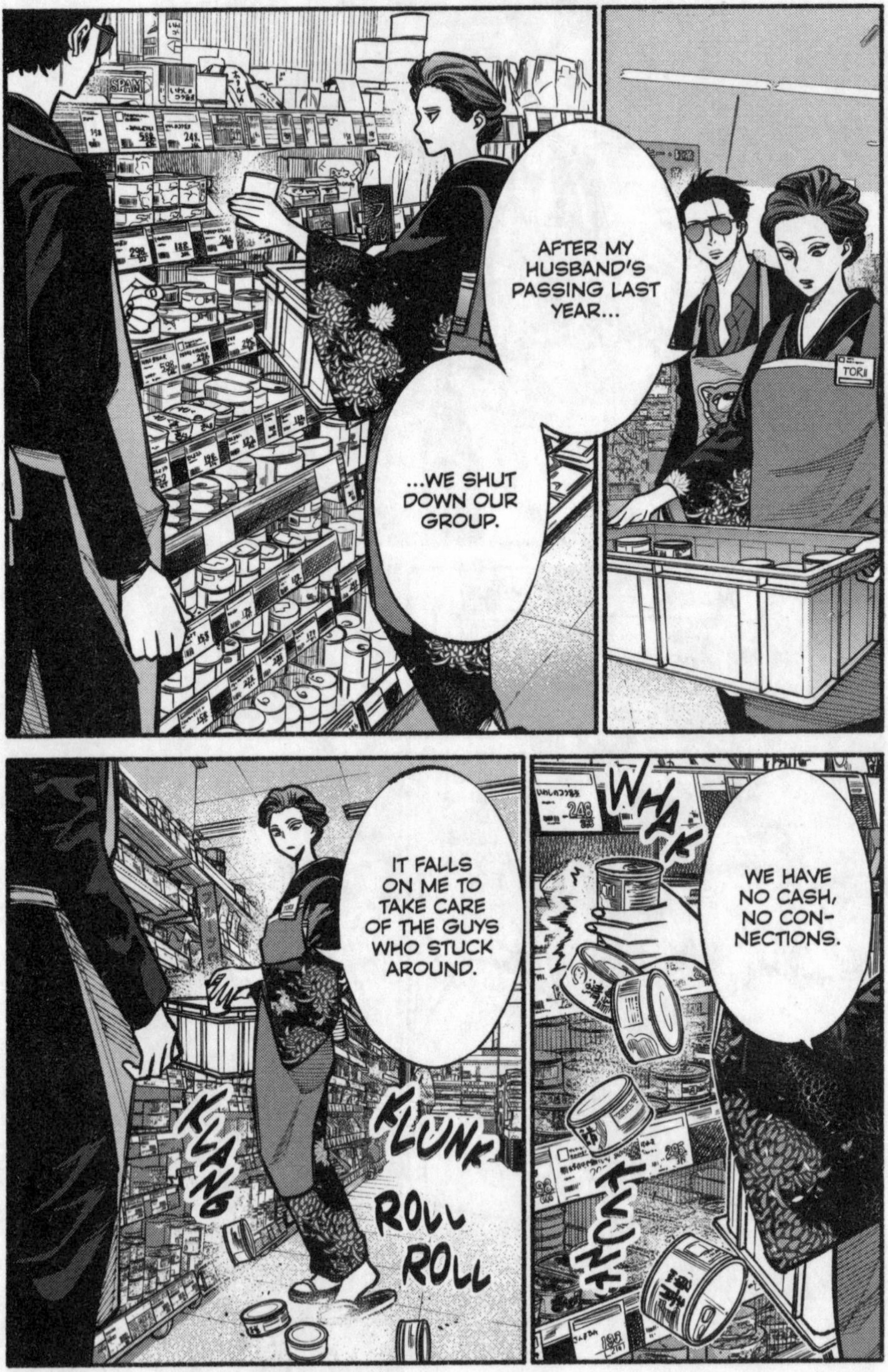
AFTER MY HUSBAND'S PASSING LAST YEAR...
...WE SHUT DOWN OUR GROUP.
WHAK
WE HAVE NO CASH, NO CON- NECTIONS.
KLUNK
IT FALLS ON ME TO TAKE CARE OF THE GUYS WHO STUCK AROUND.
KLUNK
ROLL
ROLL
KLANG

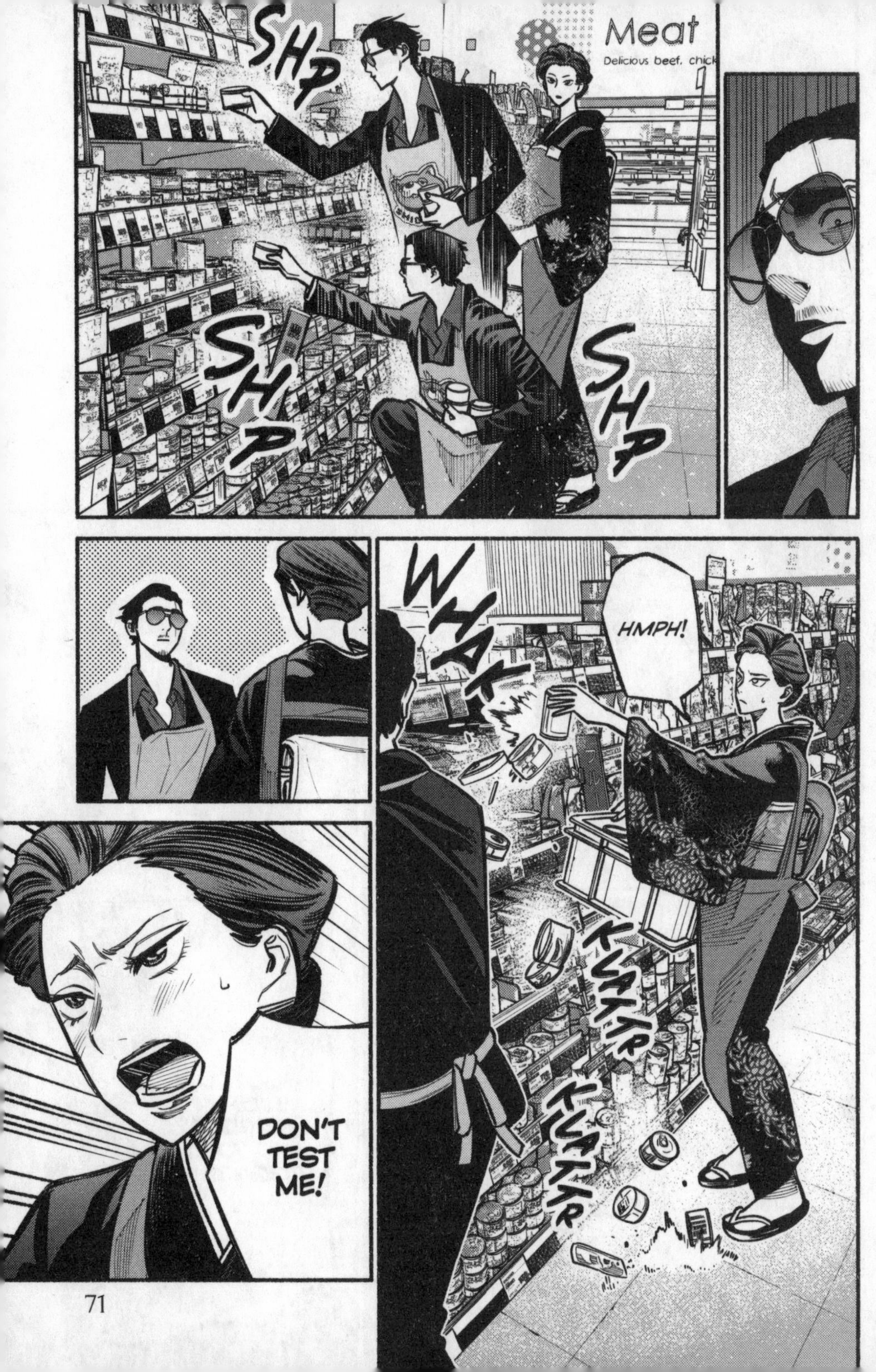
SHP
Meat
Delicious beef, chick
SHP
SHP
WHAK
HMPH!
KLAKR
KLAKR
DON'T TEST ME!

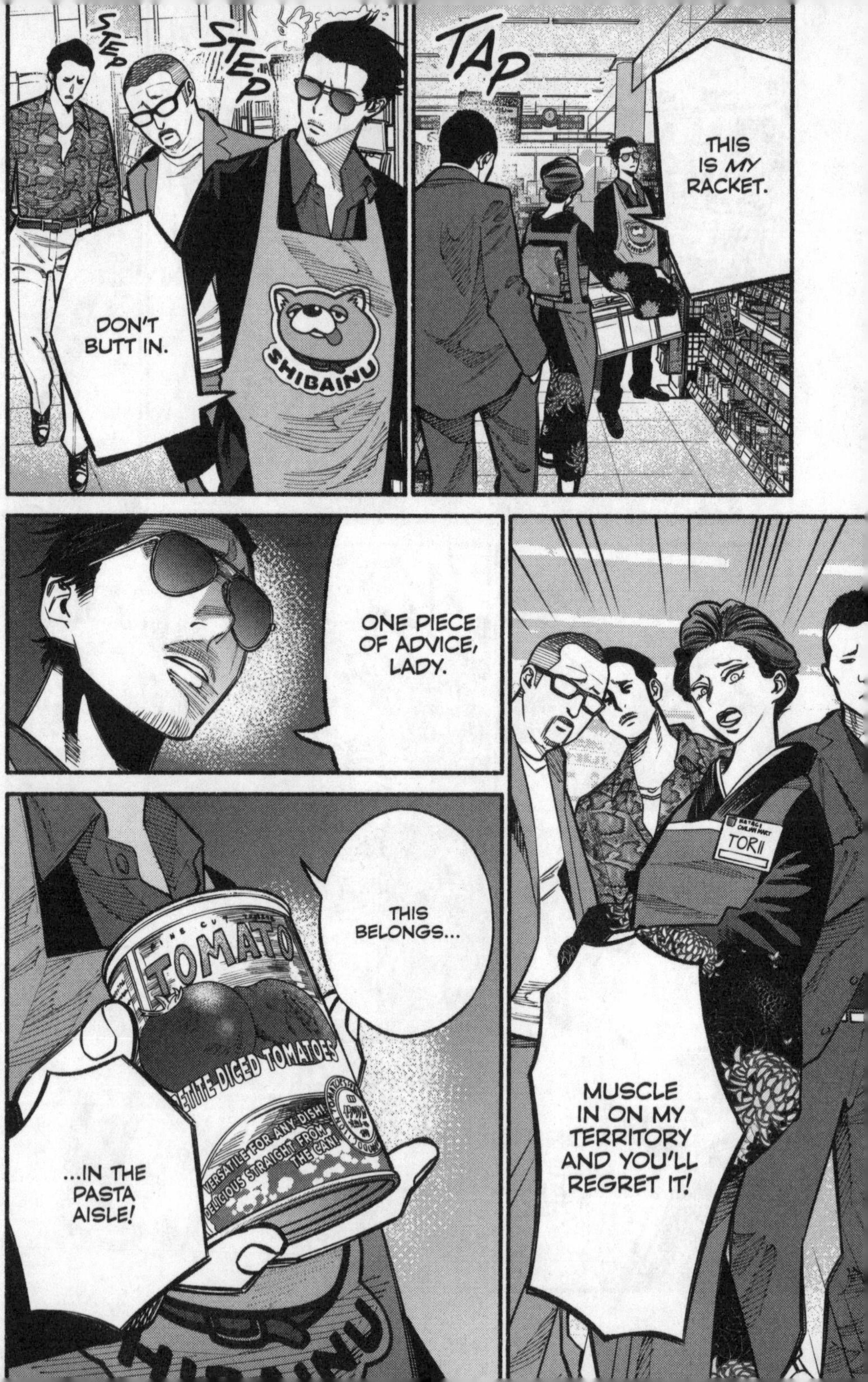
TAP
THIS IS MY RACKET.
STEP
STEP
DON'T BUTT IN.
SHIBAINU
TORII
MUSCLE IN ON MY TERRITORY AND YOU'LL REGRET IT!
ONE PIECE OF ADVICE, LADY.
THIS BELONGS...
TOMATO
ETITE-DICED TOMATOES
VERSATILE FOR ANY DISH! DELICIOUS STRAIGHT FROM THE CAN!
...IN THE PASTA AISLE!

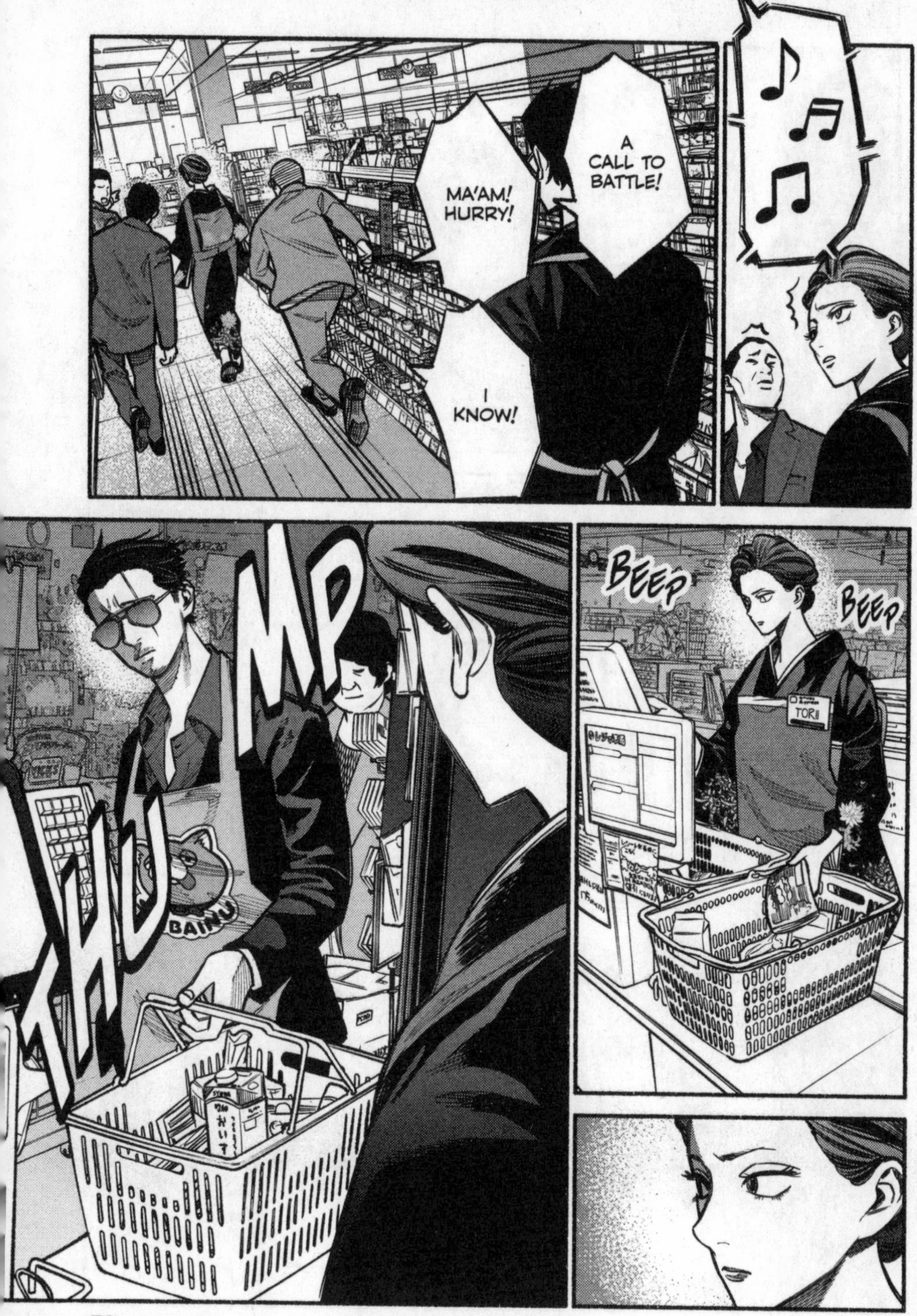
A CALL TO BATTLE!
MA'AM! HURRY!
I KNOW!
BEEP
BEEP
TORII
THUMP
BAINU

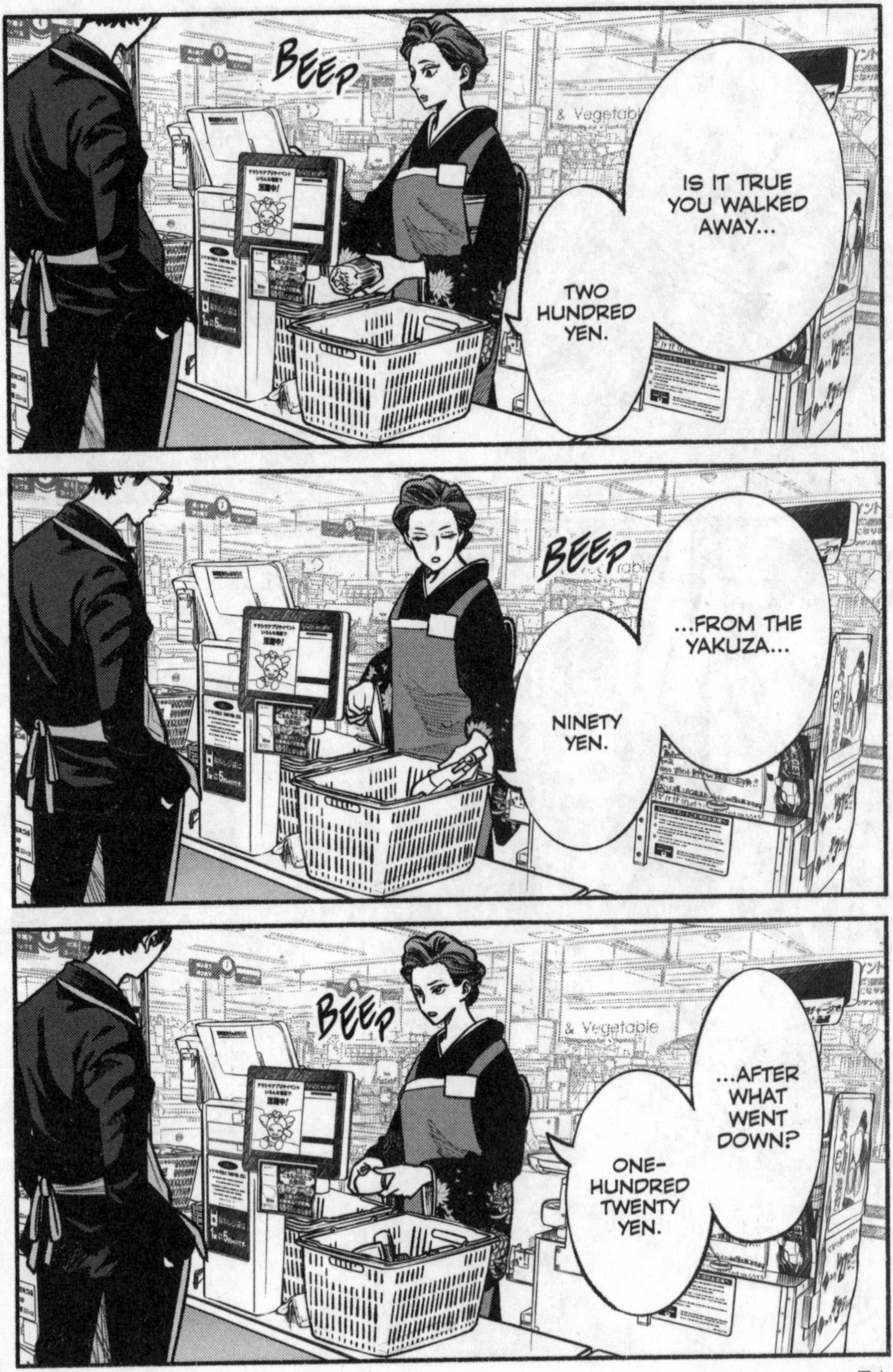
IS IT TRUE YOU WALKED AWAY...
BEEP
TWO HUNDRED YEN.
...FROM THE YAKUZA...
BEEP
NINETY YEN.
...AFTER WHAT WENT DOWN?
BEEP
ONE-HUNDRED TWENTY YEN.

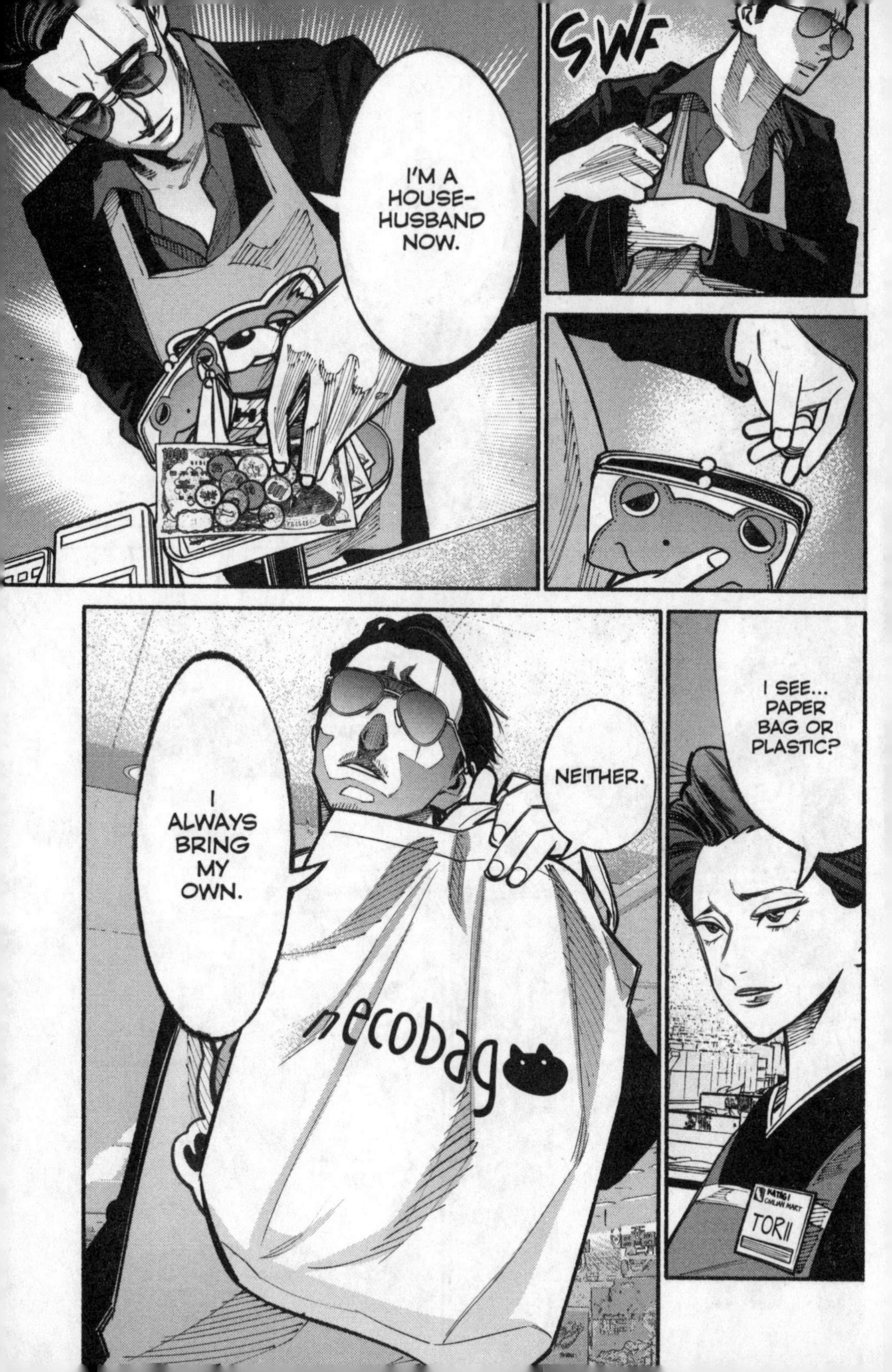
SWF
I'M A HOUSE-HUSBAND NOW.
I SEE... PAPER BAG OR PLASTIC?
TORII
NEITHER.
I ALWAYS BRING MY OWN.
necobag

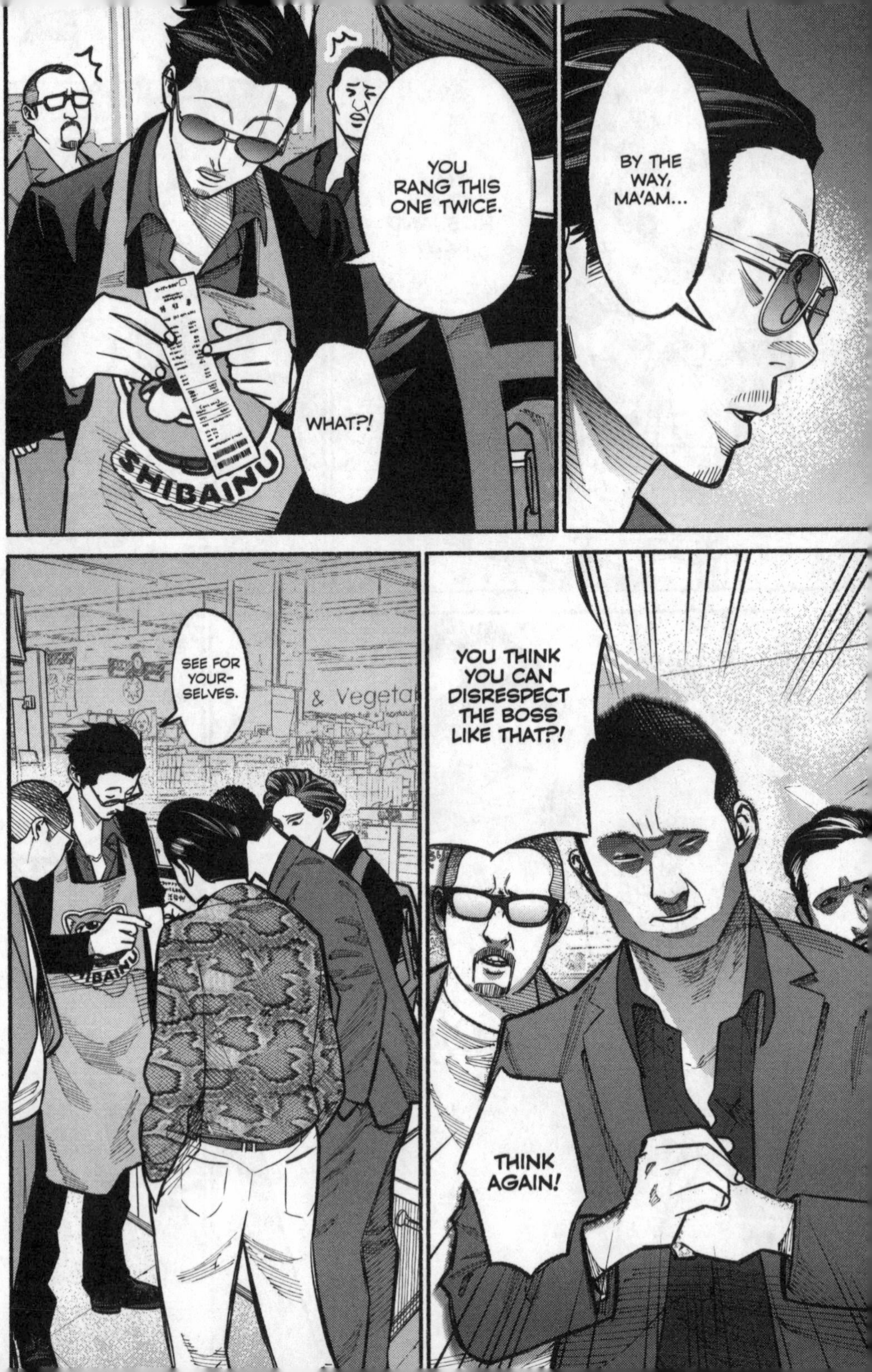
BY THE WAY, MA'AM...
YOU RANG THIS ONE TWICE.
WHAT?!
SHIBAINU
YOU THINK YOU CAN DISRESPECT THE BOSS LIKE THAT?!
THINK AGAIN!
SEE FOR YOURSELVES.

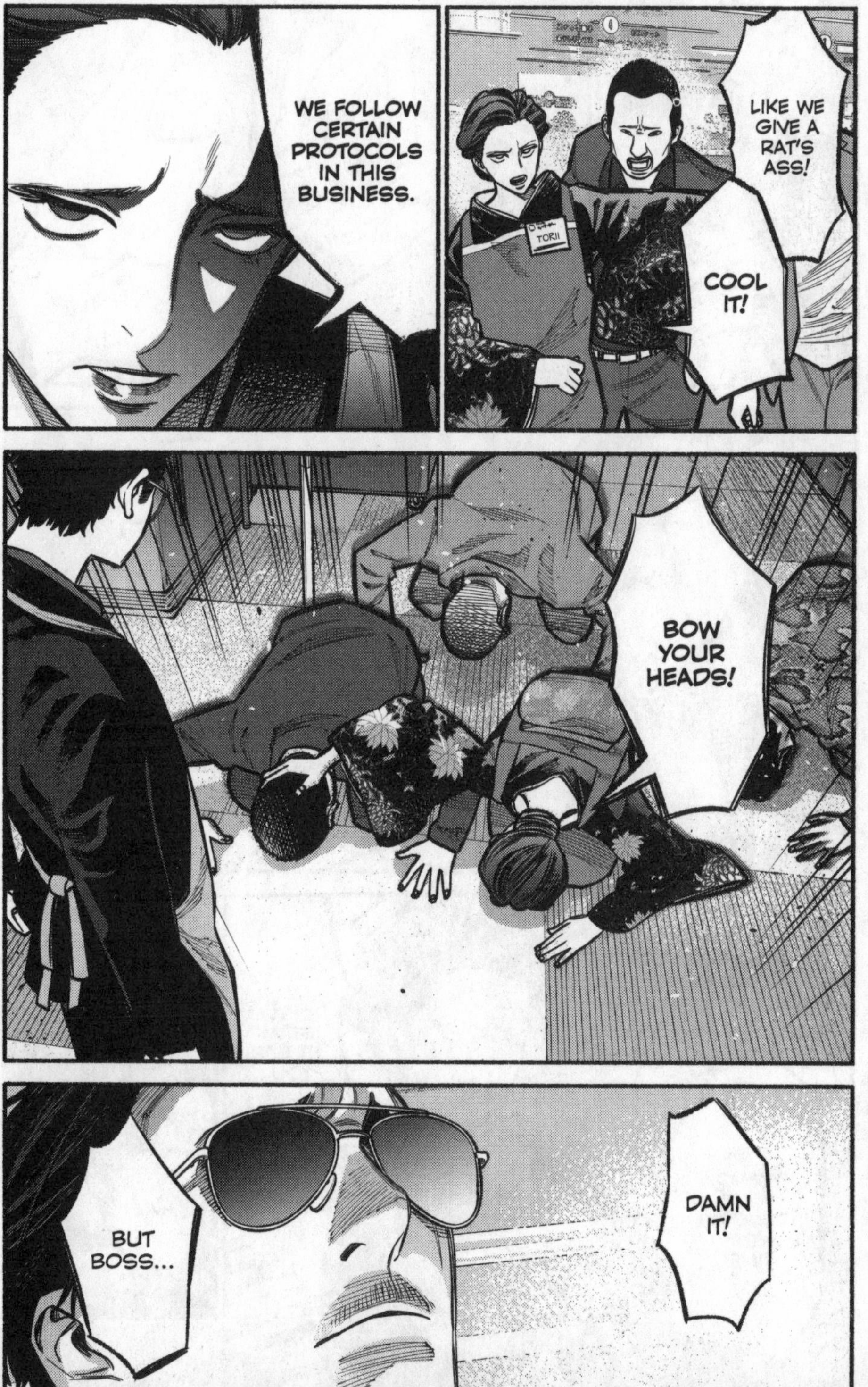

LIKE WE GIVE A RAT'S ASS!
TORII
COOL IT!
WE FOLLOW CERTAIN PROTOCOLS IN THIS BUSINESS.
BOW YOUR HEADS!
DAMN IT!
BUT BOSS...

ALL RIGHT. WE'RE SQUARE NOW...

KLINK

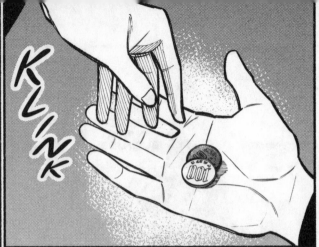

ONE MORE THING. I FORGOT MY POINT CARD TODAY.

I'LL STAMP IT FOR YOU...

...SO BRING YOUR RECEIPT NEXT TIME!

TORII

HA!

78

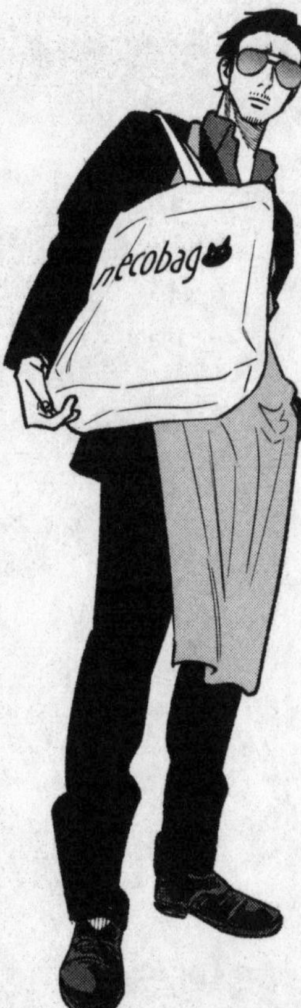
necobag

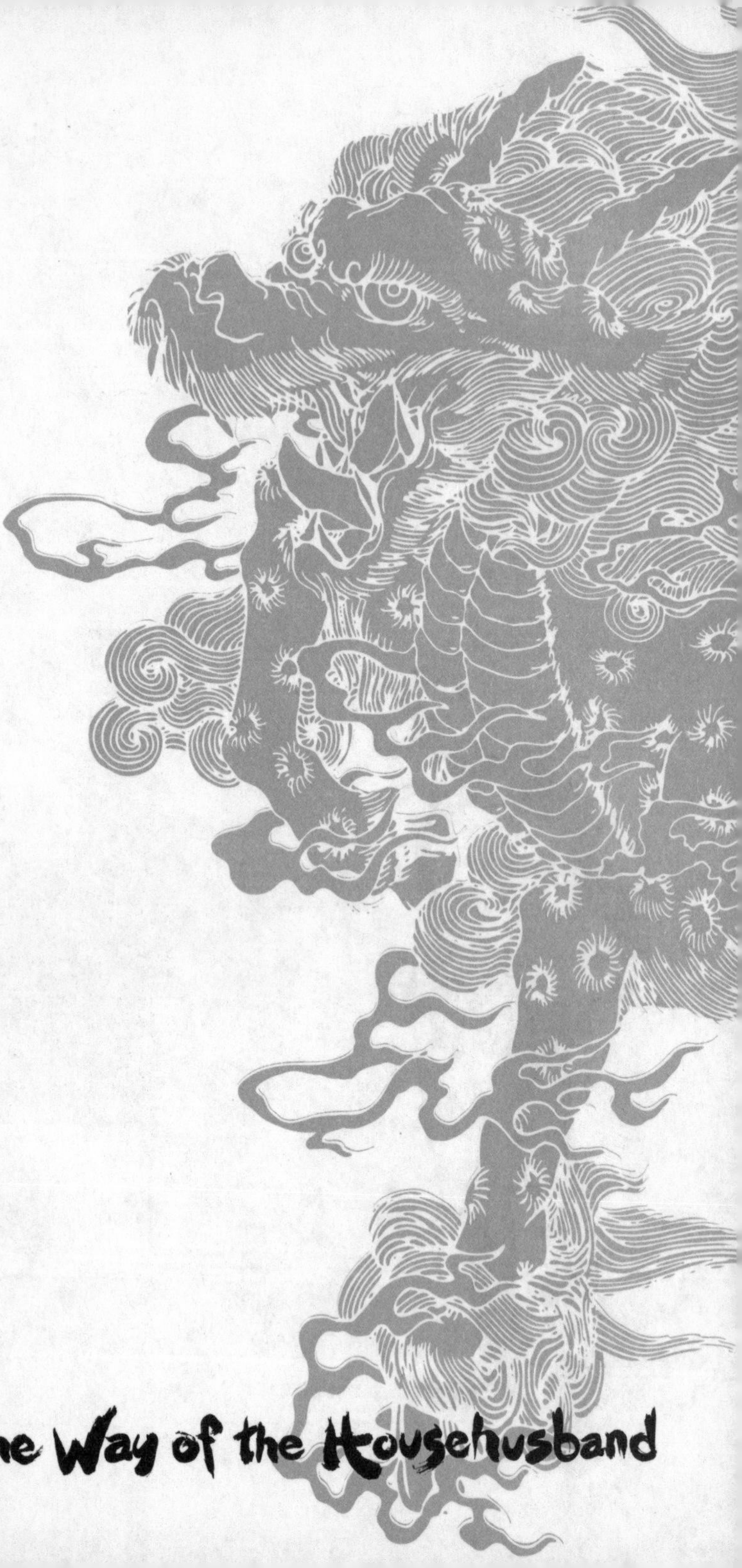

The Way of the Househusband

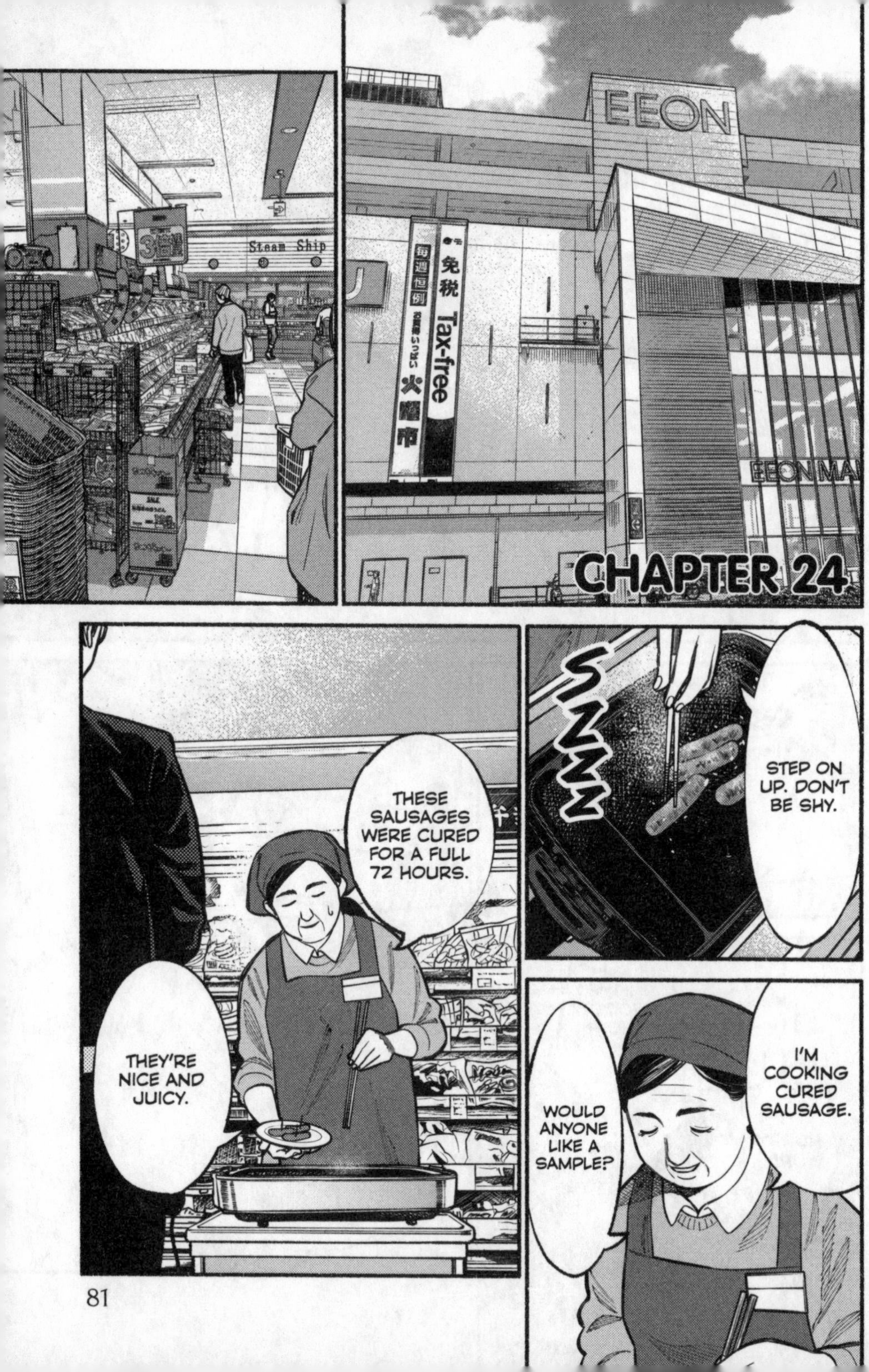
EEON
免税
Tax-free
毎週恒例
火曜市
CHAPTER 24
Steam Ship
STEP ON UP. DON'T BE SHY.
I'M COOKING CURED SAUSAGE.
WOULD ANYONE LIKE A SAMPLE?
THESE SAUSAGES WERE CURED FOR A FULL 72 HOURS.
THEY'RE NICE AND JUICY.

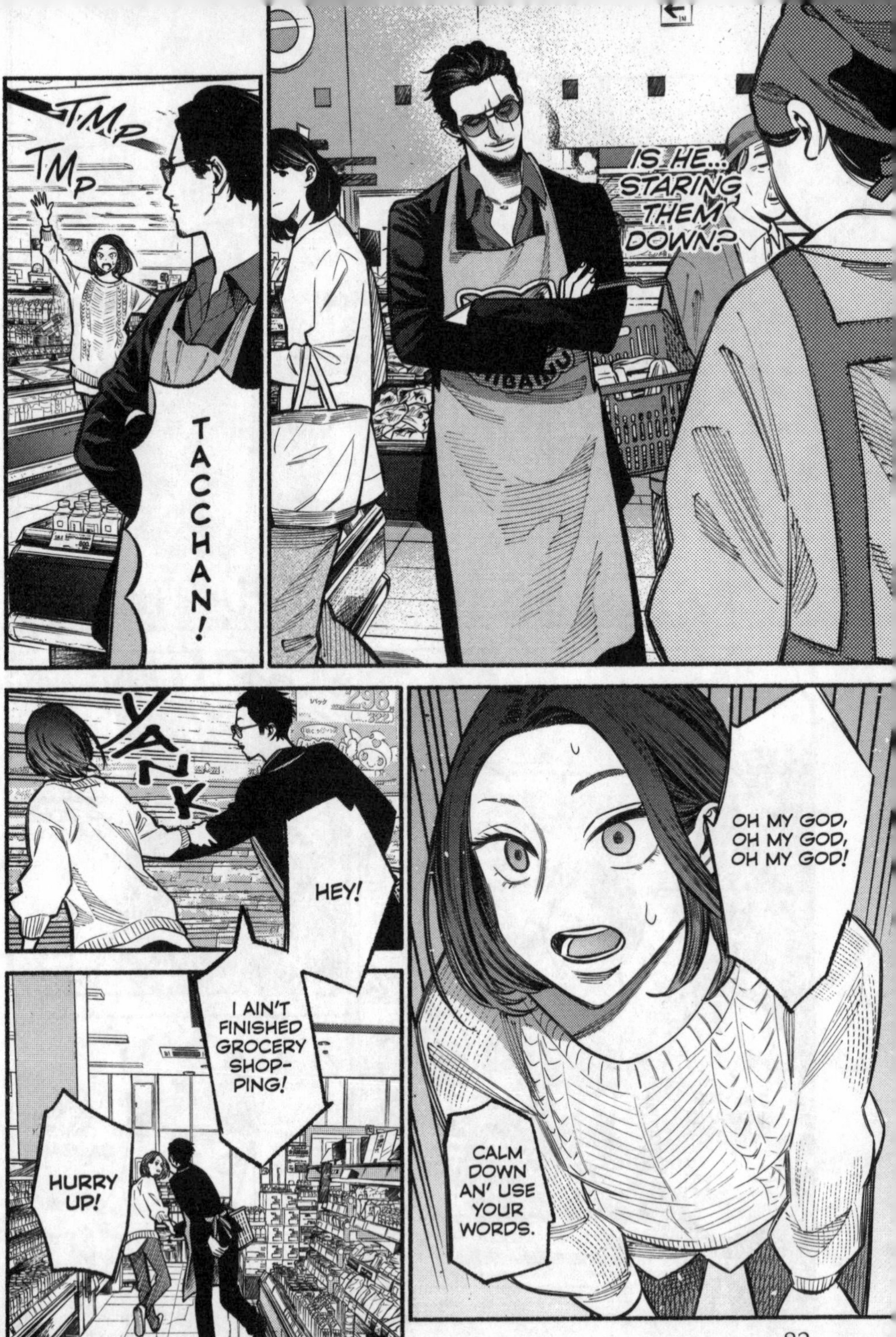
IS HE... STARING THEM DOWN?
TMP
TMP
TACCHAN!
OH MY GOD, OH MY GOD, OH MY GOD!
CALM DOWN AN' USE YOUR WORDS.
YANK
HEY!
I AIN'T FINISHED GROCERY SHOP-PING!
HURRY UP!

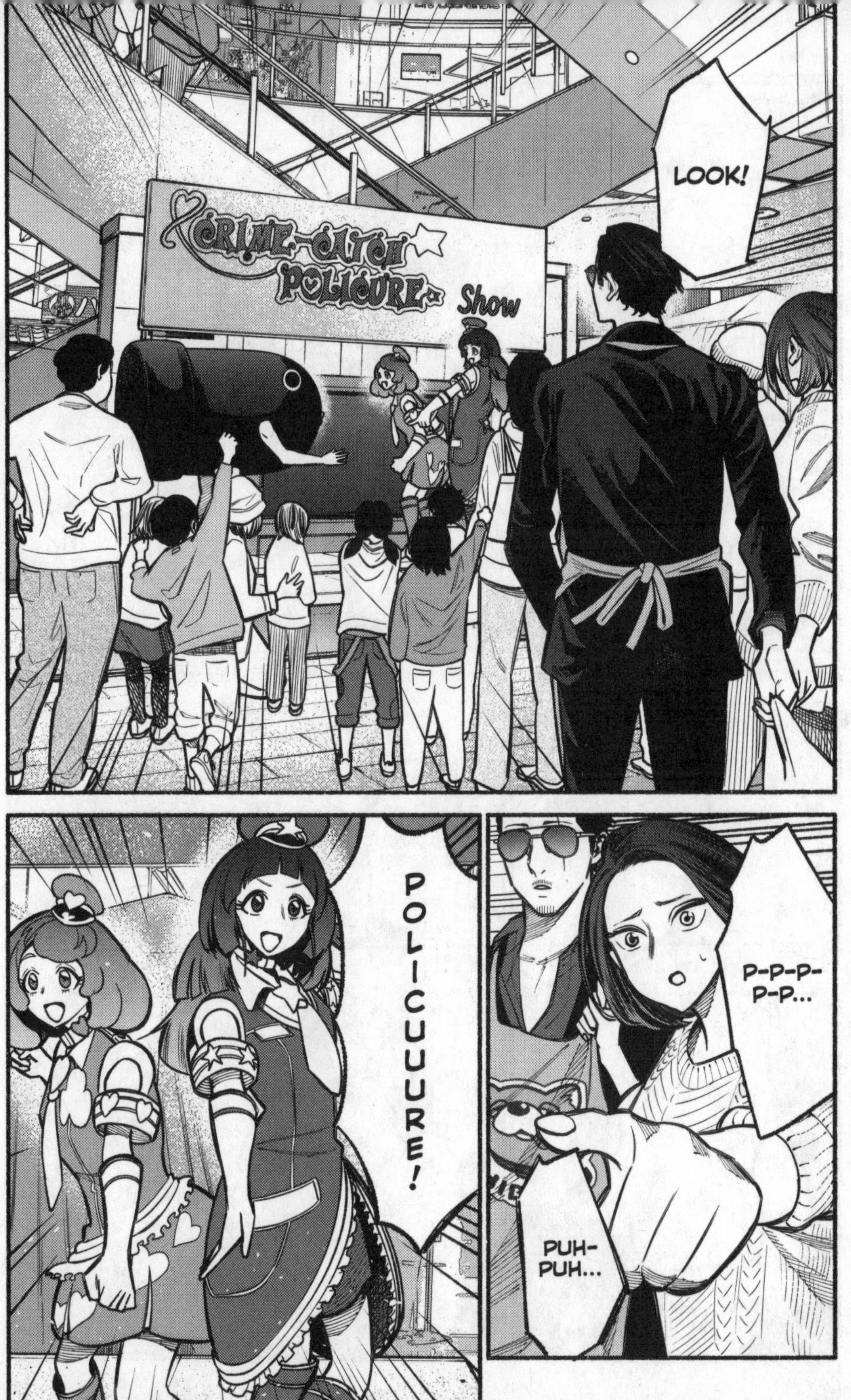
CRIME-CATCH POLICURE Show
LOOK!
P-P-P-P-P...
PUH-PUH...
POLICUUURE!

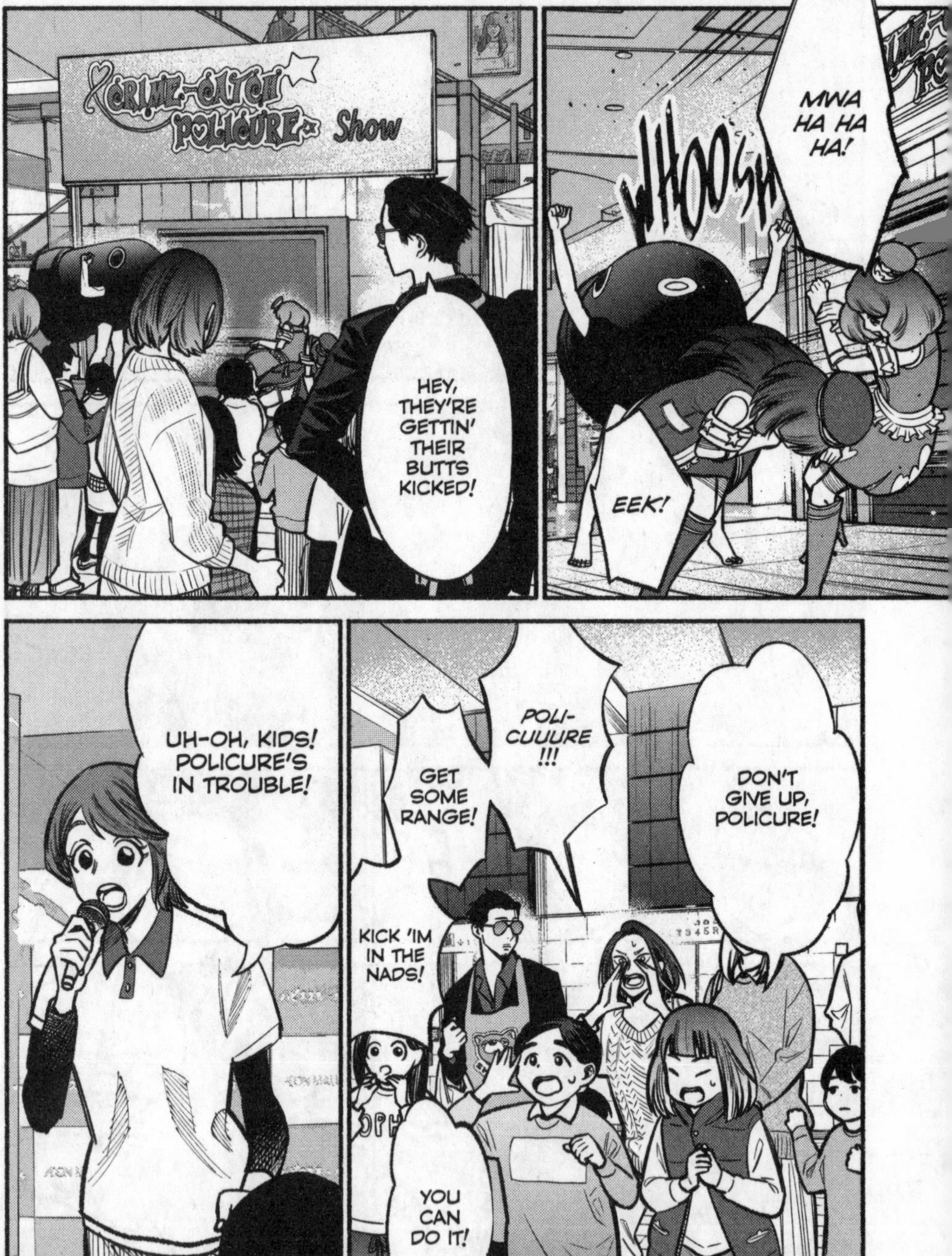
MWA HA HA HA!
WHOOSH
EEK!
CRIME-CATCH POLICURE Show
HEY, THEY'RE GETTIN' THEIR BUTTS KICKED!
POLI-CUUURE!!!
DON'T GIVE UP, POLICURE!
GET SOME RANGE!
KICK 'IM IN THE NADS!
YOU CAN DO IT!
UH-OH, KIDS! POLICURE'S IN TROUBLE!

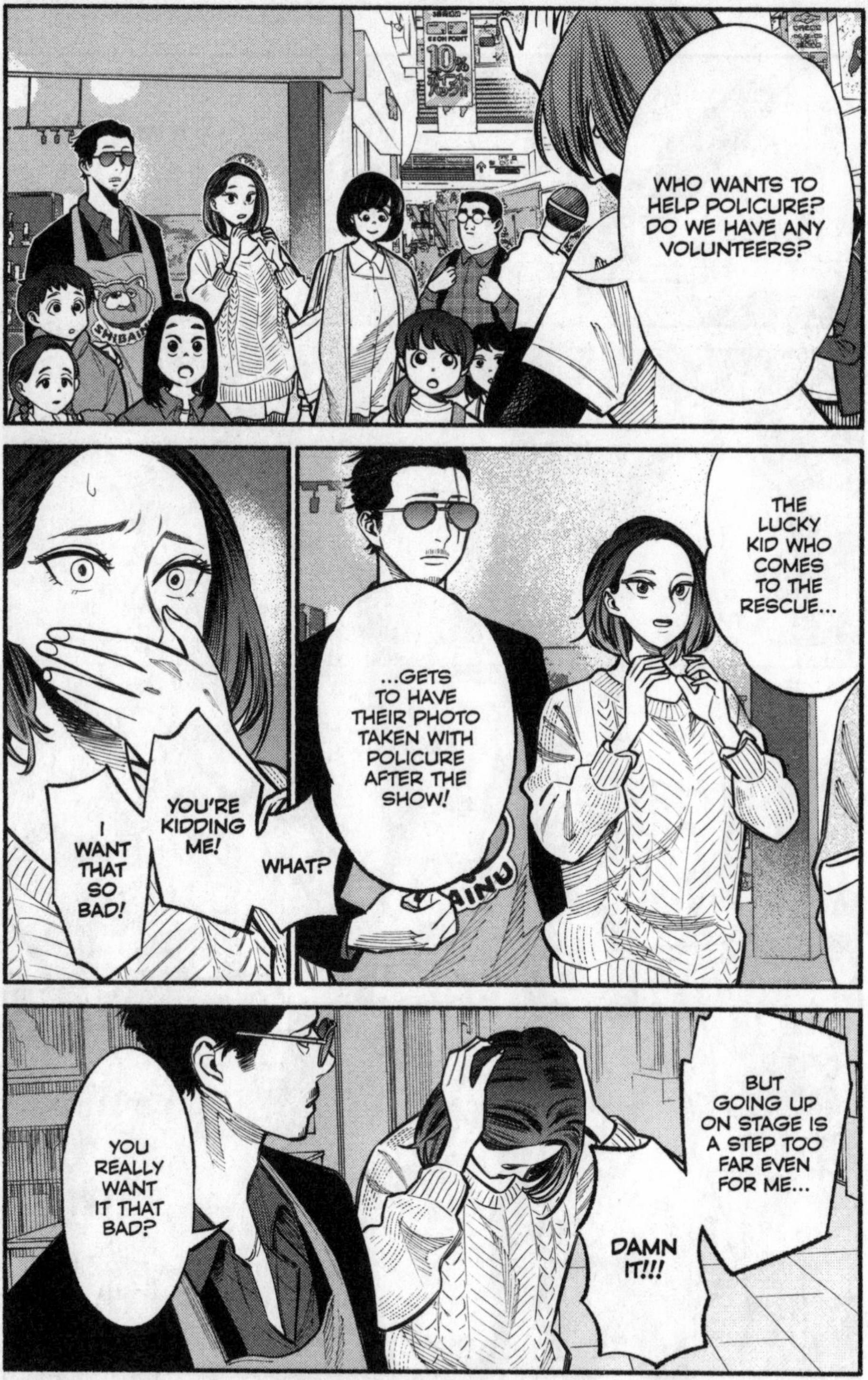
WHO WANTS TO HELP POLICURE? DO WE HAVE ANY VOLUNTEERS?
THE LUCKY KID WHO COMES TO THE RESCUE...
...GETS TO HAVE THEIR PHOTO TAKEN WITH POLICURE AFTER THE SHOW!
WHAT?
YOU'RE KIDDING ME!
I WANT THAT SO BAD!
BUT GOING UP ON STAGE IS A STEP TOO FAR EVEN FOR ME...
DAMN IT!!!
YOU REALLY WANT IT THAT BAD?

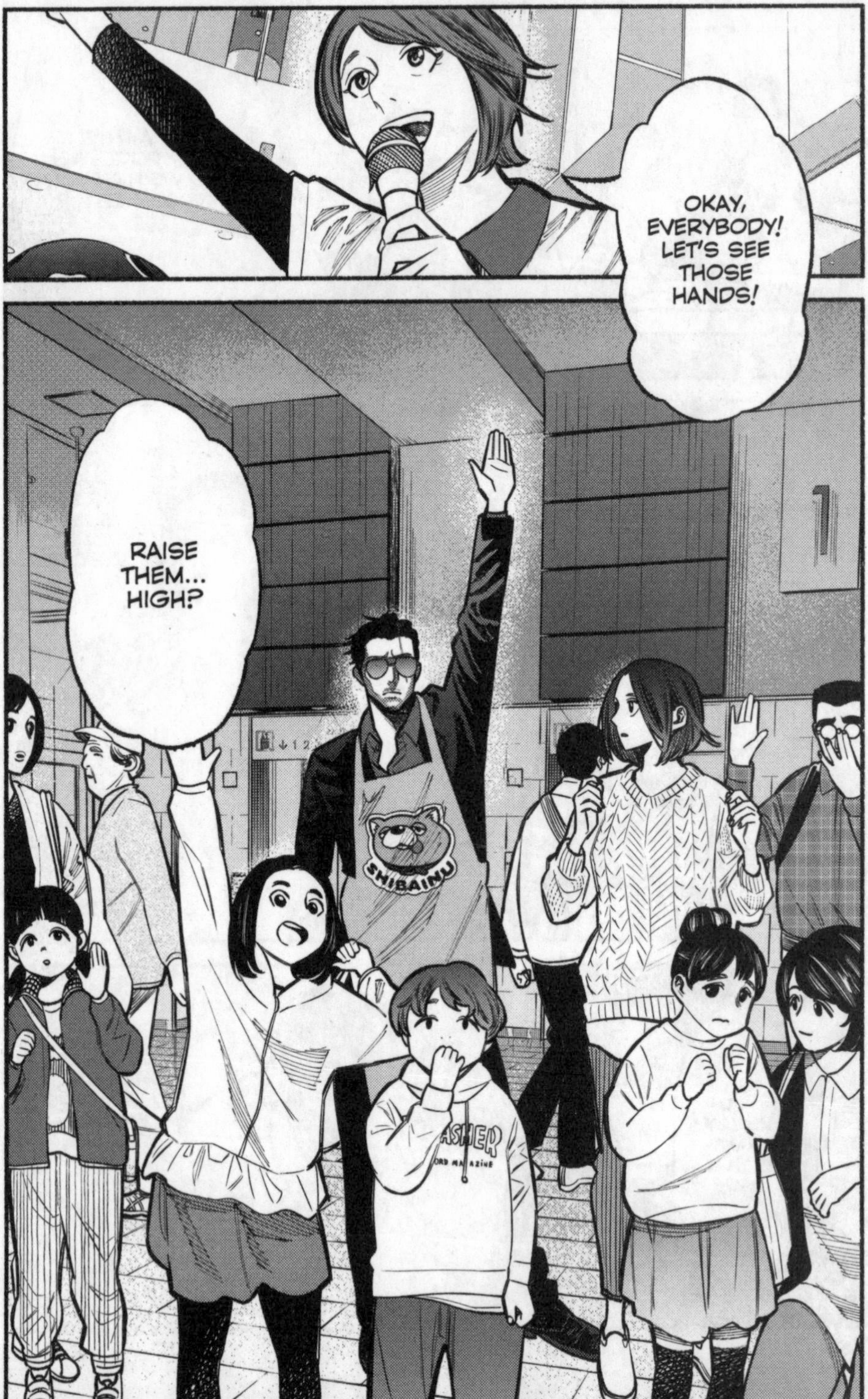
OKAY, EVERYBODY! LET'S SEE THOSE HANDS!
RAISE THEM... HIGH?
SHIBAINU

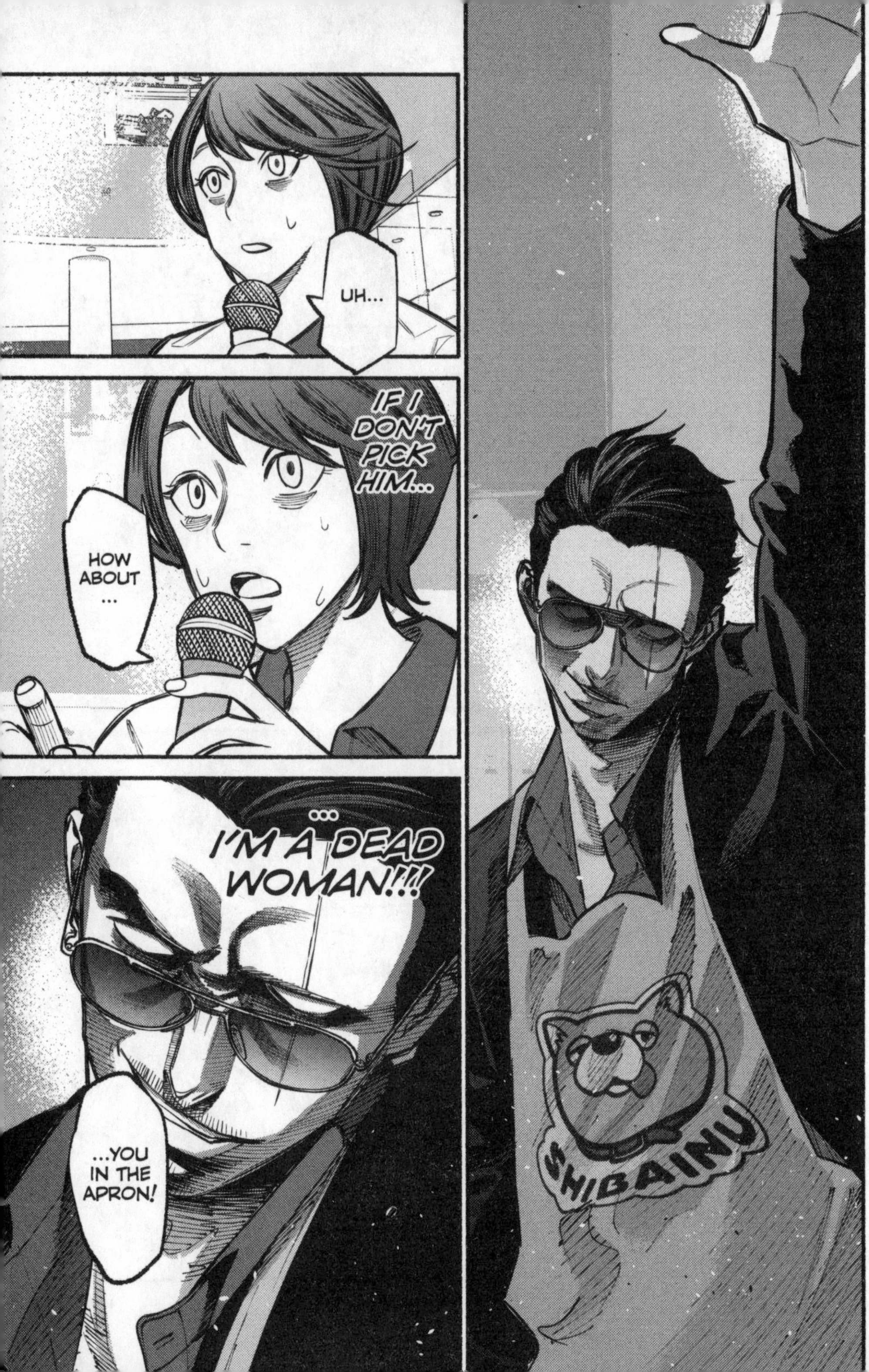
SHIBAINU
UH...
IF I DON'T PICK HIM...
HOW ABOUT ...
... I'M A DEAD WOMAN!!!
...YOU IN THE APRON!

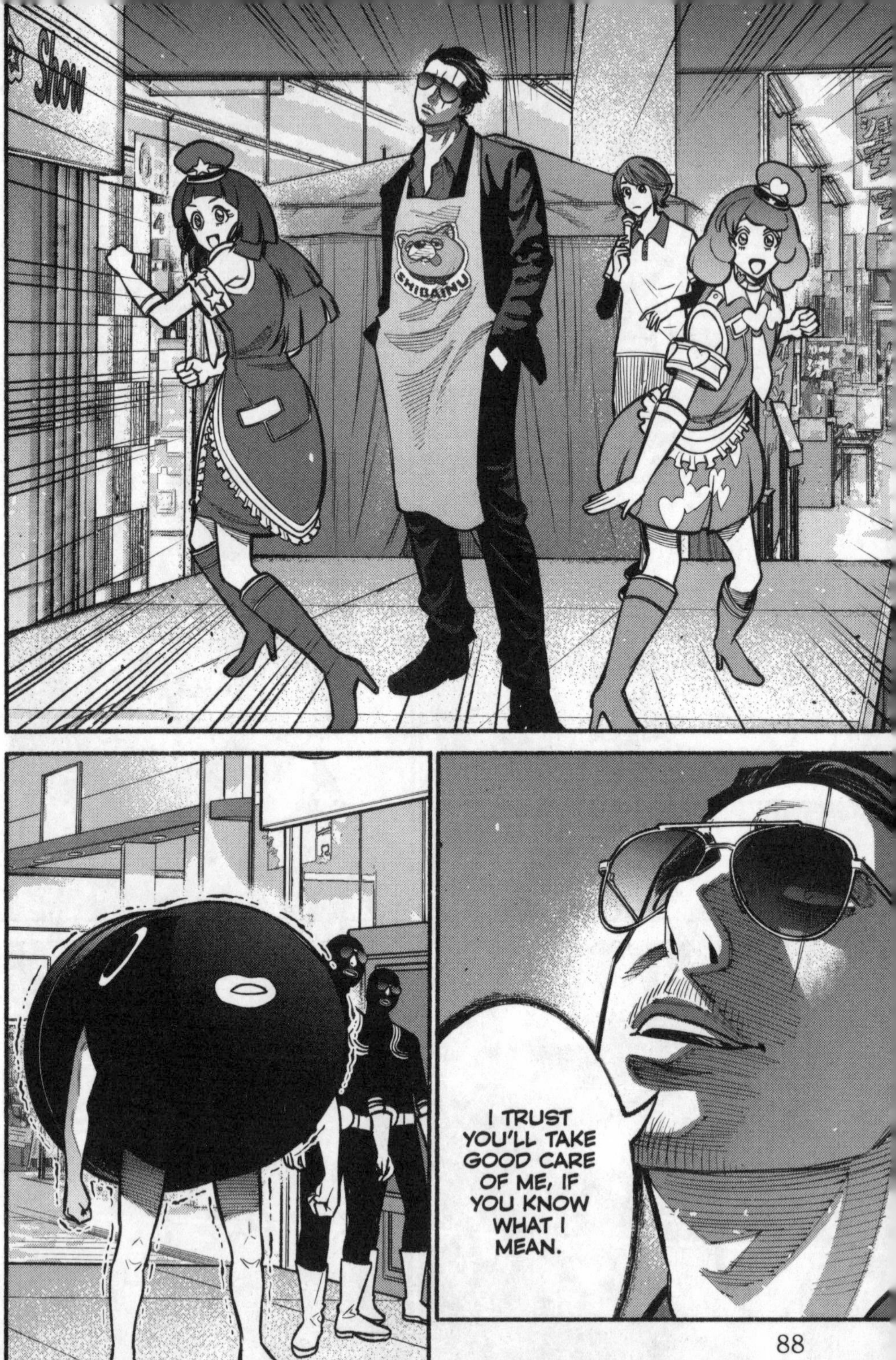
Show
SHIBAINU
I TRUST YOU'LL TAKE GOOD CARE OF ME, IF YOU KNOW WHAT I MEAN.

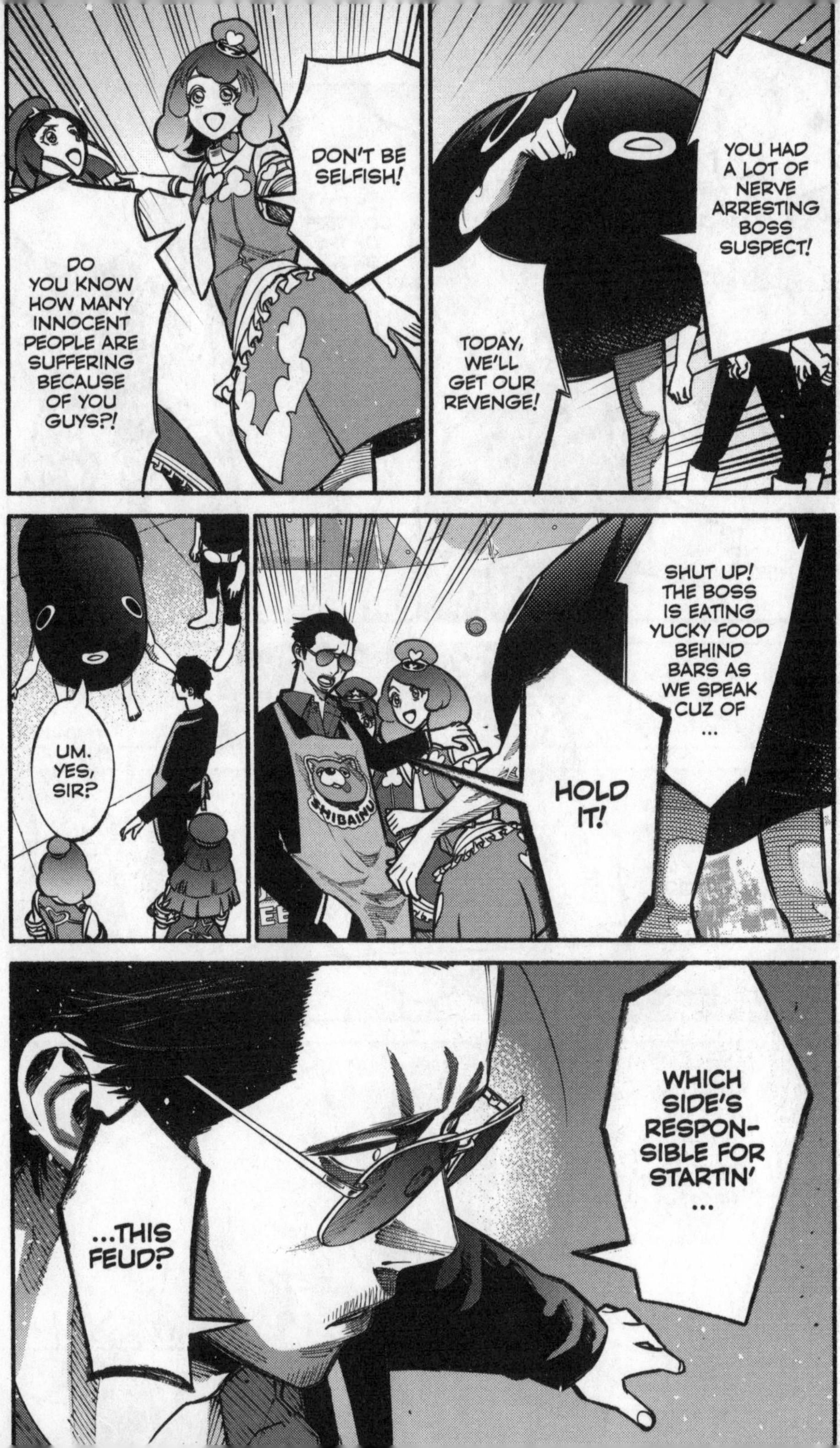
YOU HAD A LOT OF NERVE ARRESTING BOSS SUSPECT!
TODAY, WE'LL GET OUR REVENGE!
DON'T BE SELFISH!
DO YOU KNOW HOW MANY INNOCENT PEOPLE ARE SUFFERING BECAUSE OF YOU GUYS?!
SHUT UP! THE BOSS IS EATING YUCKY FOOD BEHIND BARS AS WE SPEAK CUZ OF ...
HOLD IT!
SHIBAINU
UM. YES, SIR?
WHICH SIDE'S RESPONSIBLE FOR STARTIN' ...
...THIS FEUD?

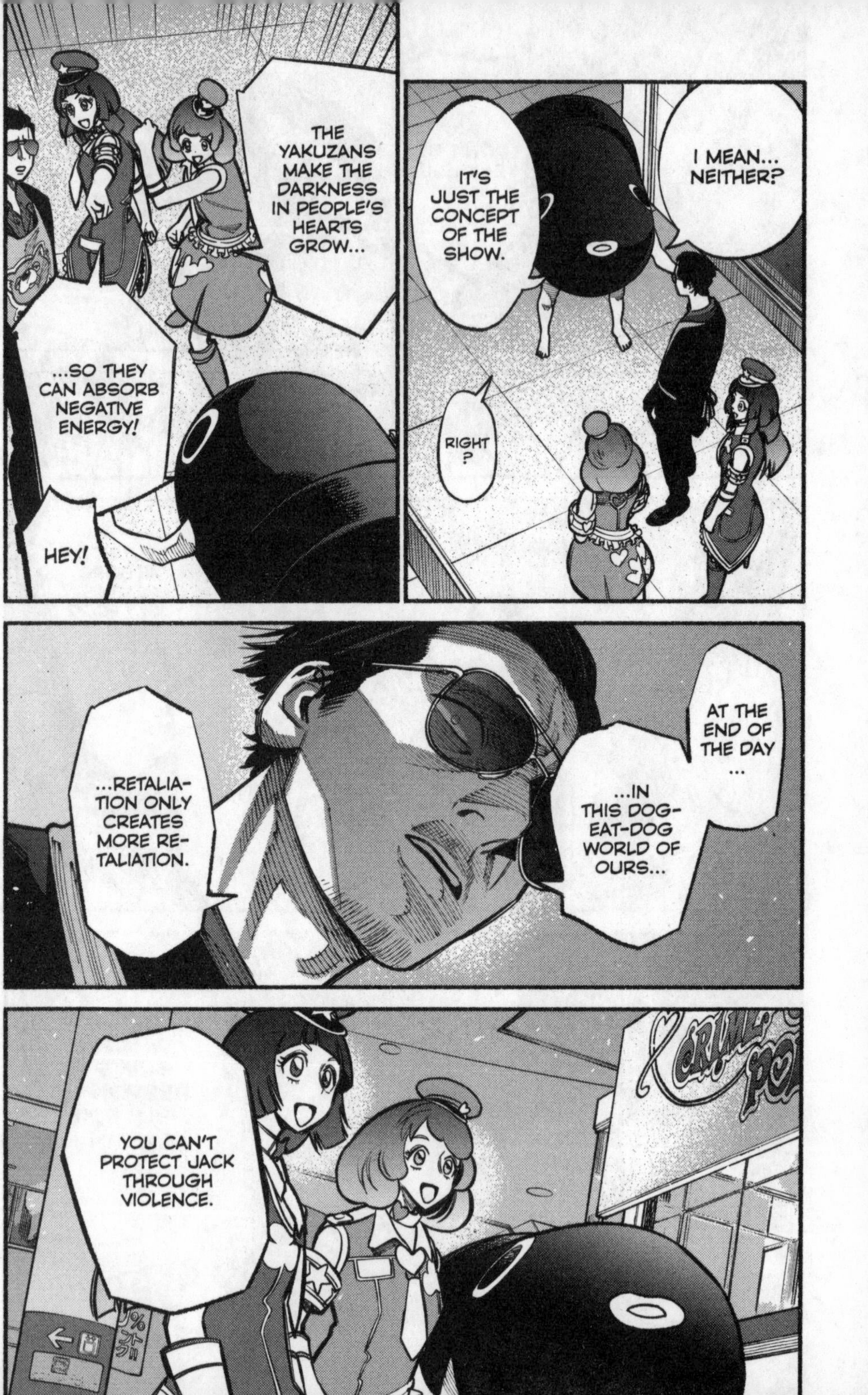

I MEAN... NEITHER?
IT'S JUST THE CONCEPT OF THE SHOW.
RIGHT?
THE YAKUZANS MAKE THE DARKNESS IN PEOPLE'S HEARTS GROW...
...SO THEY CAN ABSORB NEGATIVE ENERGY!
HEY!
AT THE END OF THE DAY...
...IN THIS DOG-EAT-DOG WORLD OF OURS...
...RETALIA-TION ONLY CREATES MORE RE-TALIATION.
YOU CAN'T PROTECT JACK THROUGH VIOLENCE.

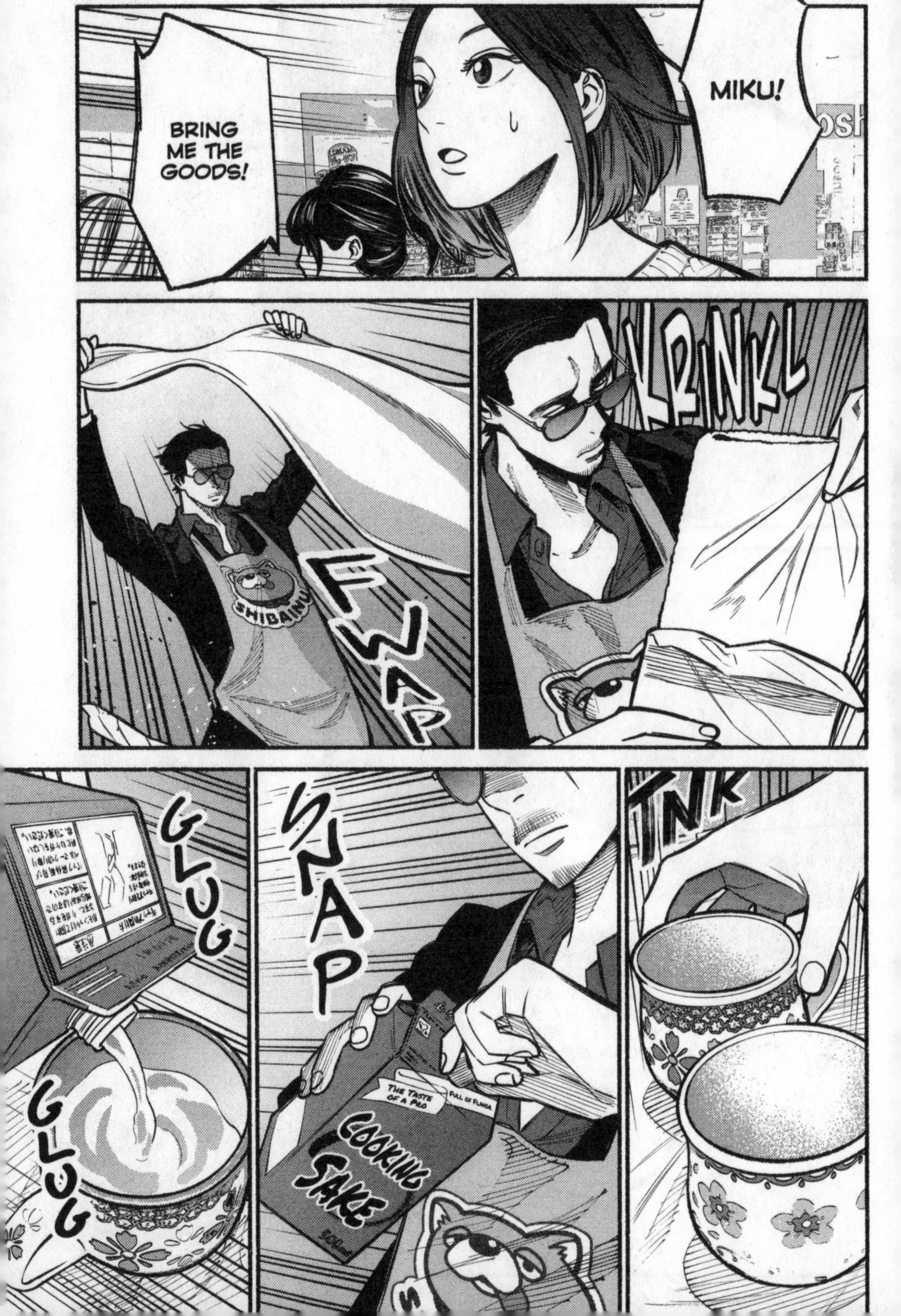
MIKU!
BRING ME THE GOODS!
KRINKL
SHIBAINU
FWAP
TNK
SNAP
THE TASTE OF A PRO
FULL OF FLAVOR
COOKING SAKE
GLUG
GLUG

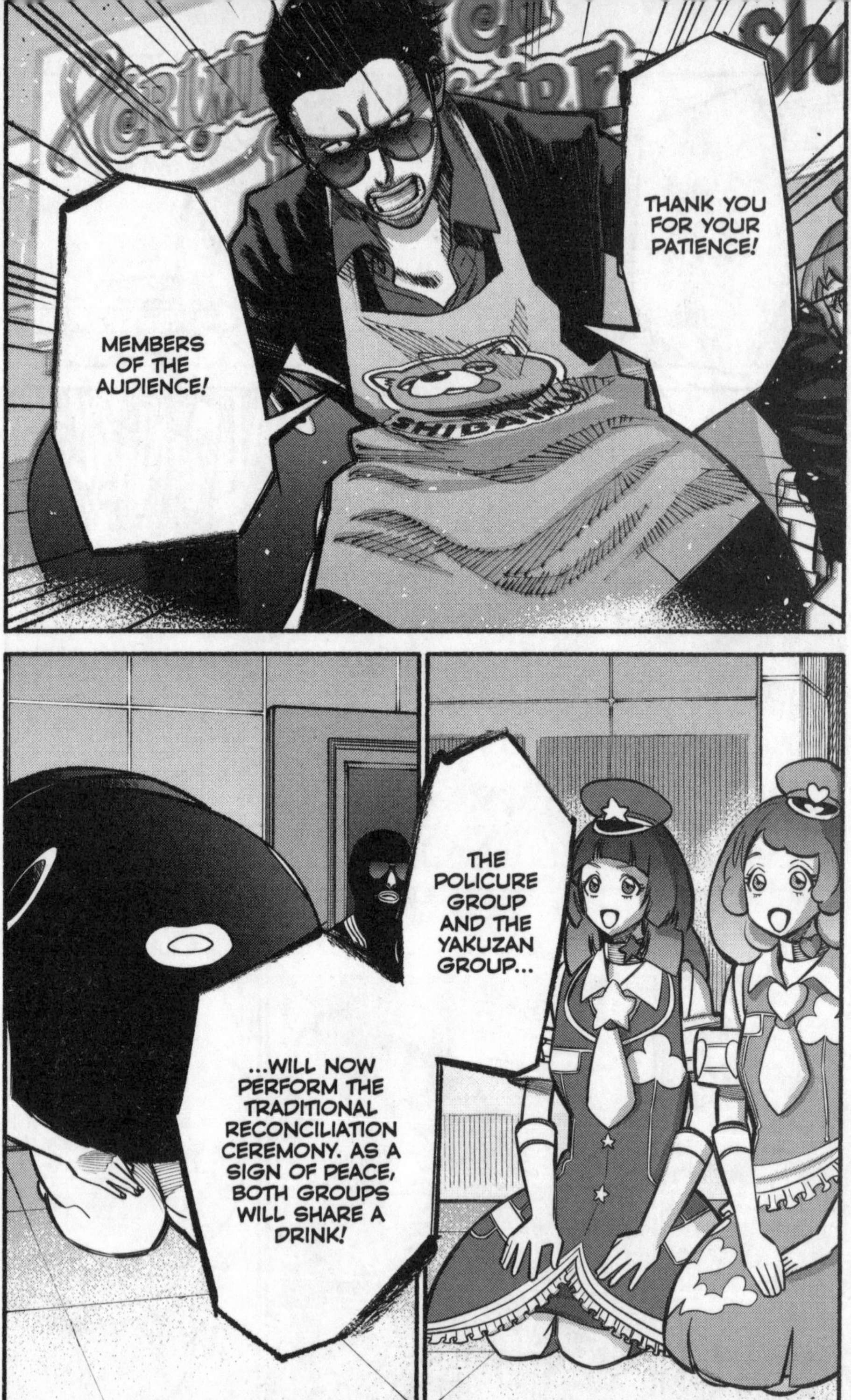
THANK YOU FOR YOUR PATIENCE!
MEMBERS OF THE AUDIENCE!
THE POLICURE GROUP AND THE YAKUZAN GROUP...
...WILL NOW PERFORM THE TRADITIONAL RECONCILIATION CEREMONY. AS A SIGN OF PEACE, BOTH GROUPS WILL SHARE A DRINK!

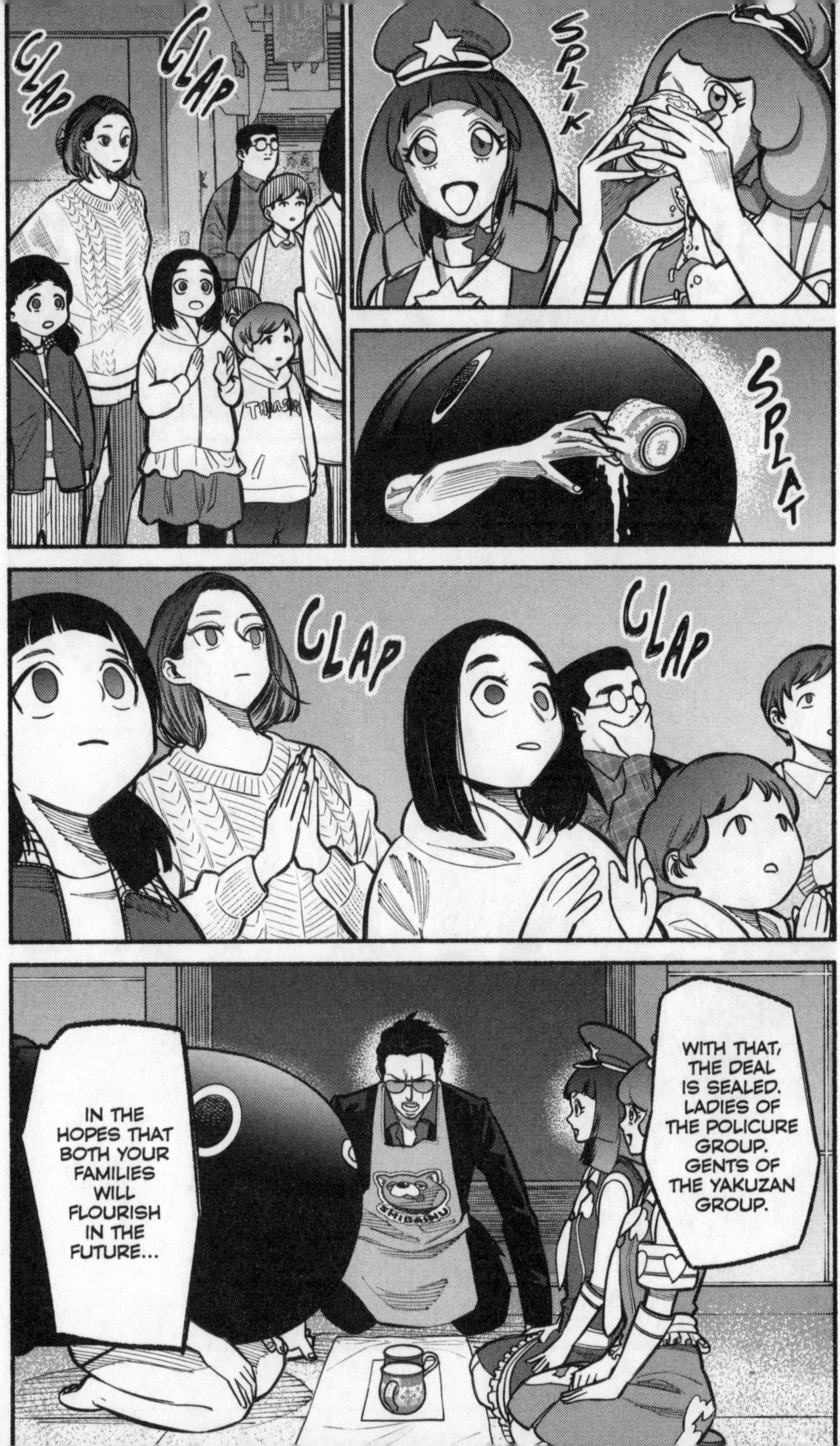
SPLIK
SPLAT
CLAP
CLAP
CLAP
CLAP
WITH THAT, THE DEAL IS SEALED. LADIES OF THE POLICURE GROUP. GENTS OF THE YAKUZAN GROUP.
SHIBAINU
IN THE HOPES THAT BOTH YOUR FAMILIES WILL FLOURISH IN THE FUTURE...

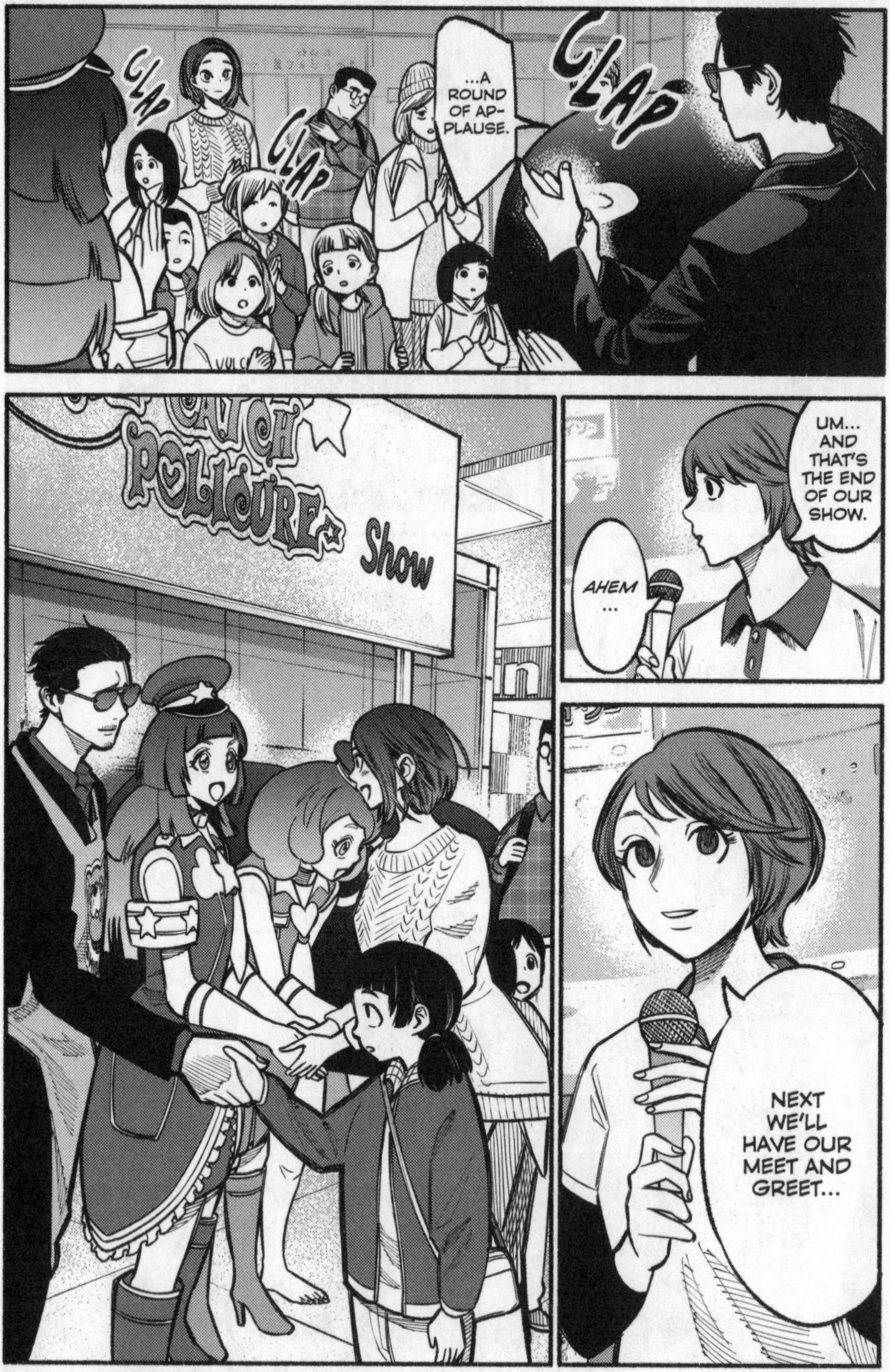
CLAP
...A ROUND OF AP-PLAUSE.
CLAP
CLAP
UM... AND THAT'S THE END OF OUR SHOW.
AHEM...
NEXT WE'LL HAVE OUR MEET AND GREET...
CATCH POLICURE
Show

HE SCARED THE HELL OUT OF ME.

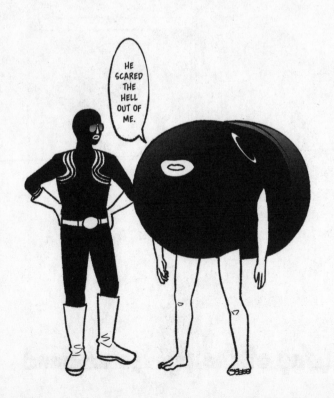

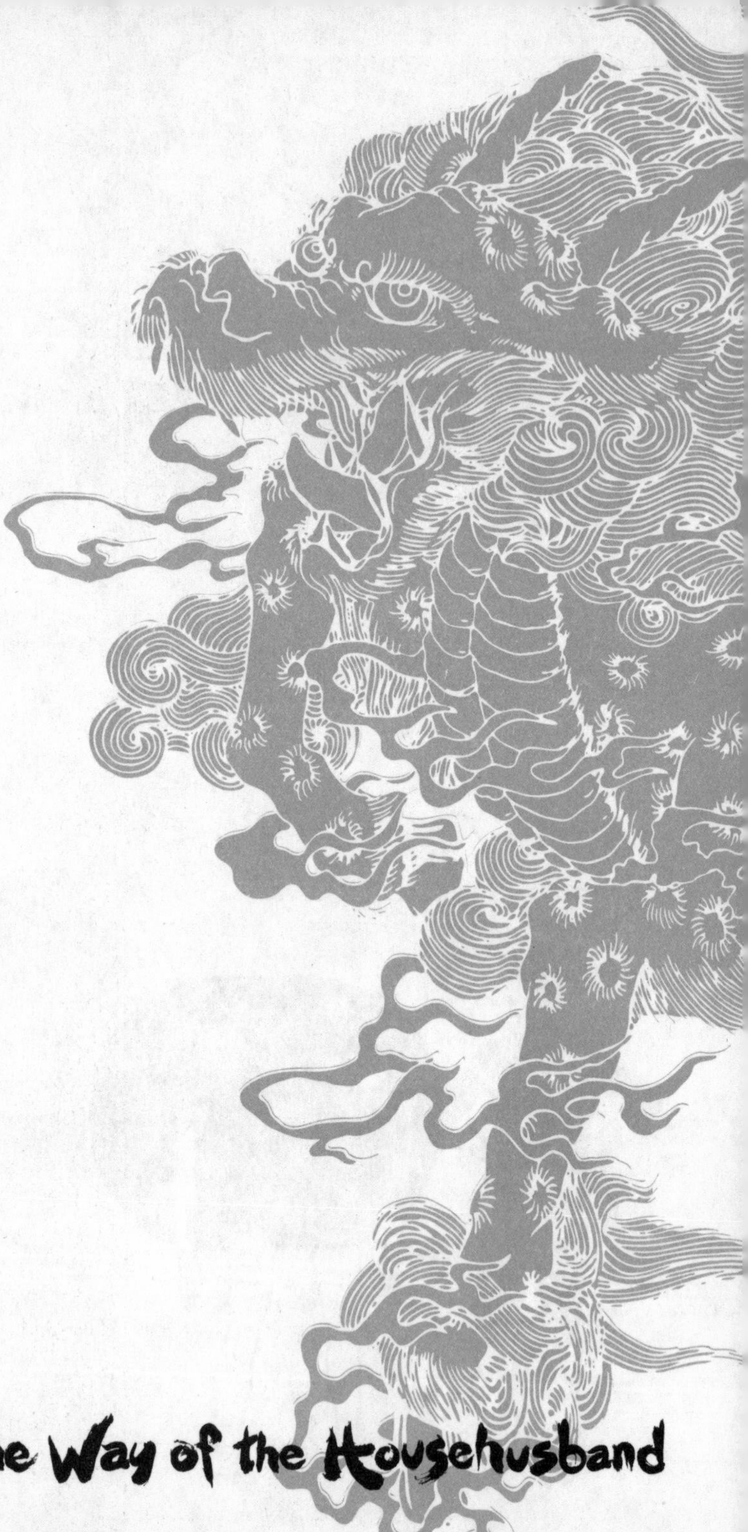

The Way of the Househusband

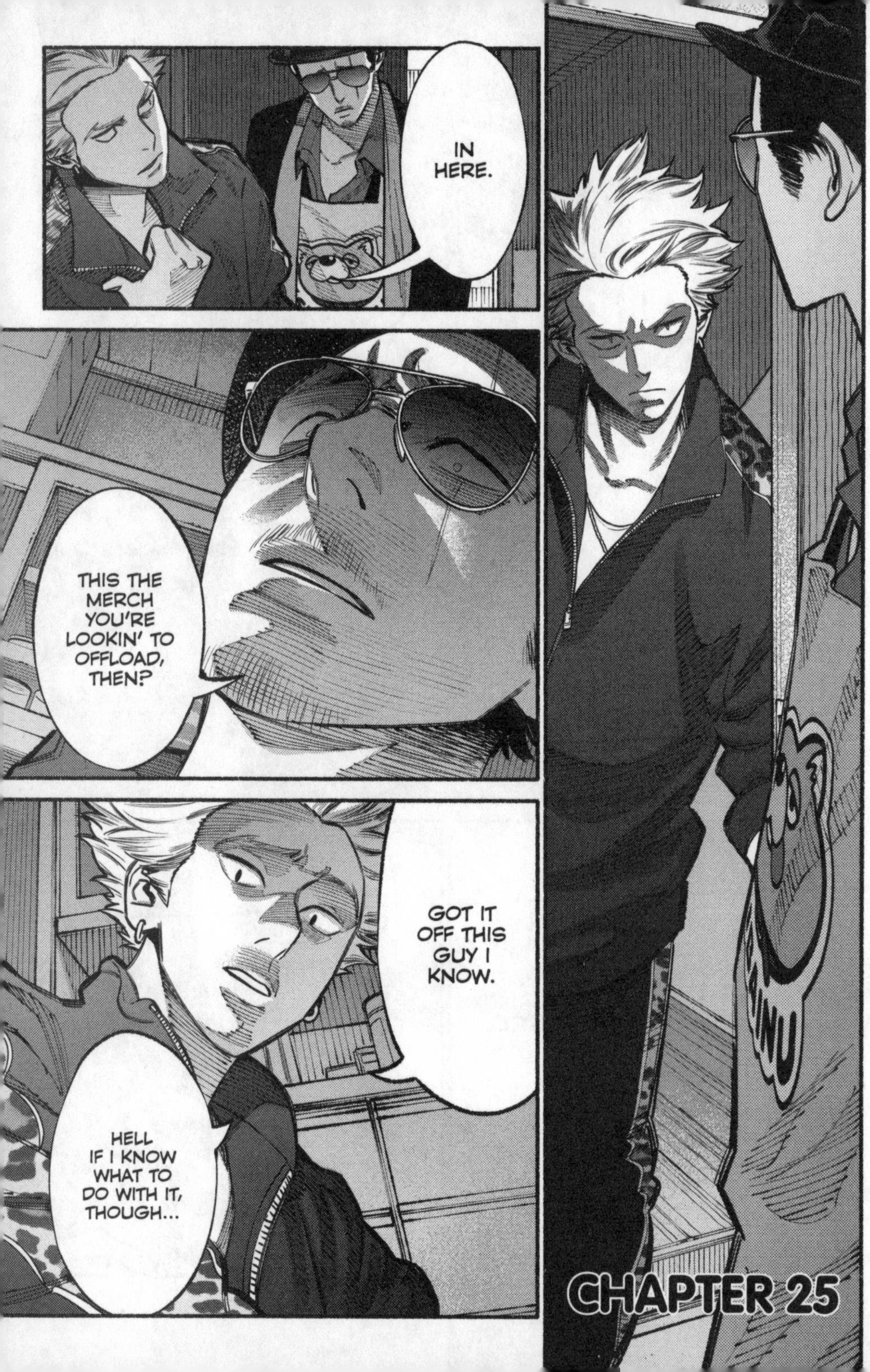
CHAPTER 25
IN HERE.
THIS THE MERCH YOU'RE LOOKIN' TO OFFLOAD, THEN?
GOT IT OFF THIS GUY I KNOW.
HELL IF I KNOW WHAT TO DO WITH IT, THOUGH...

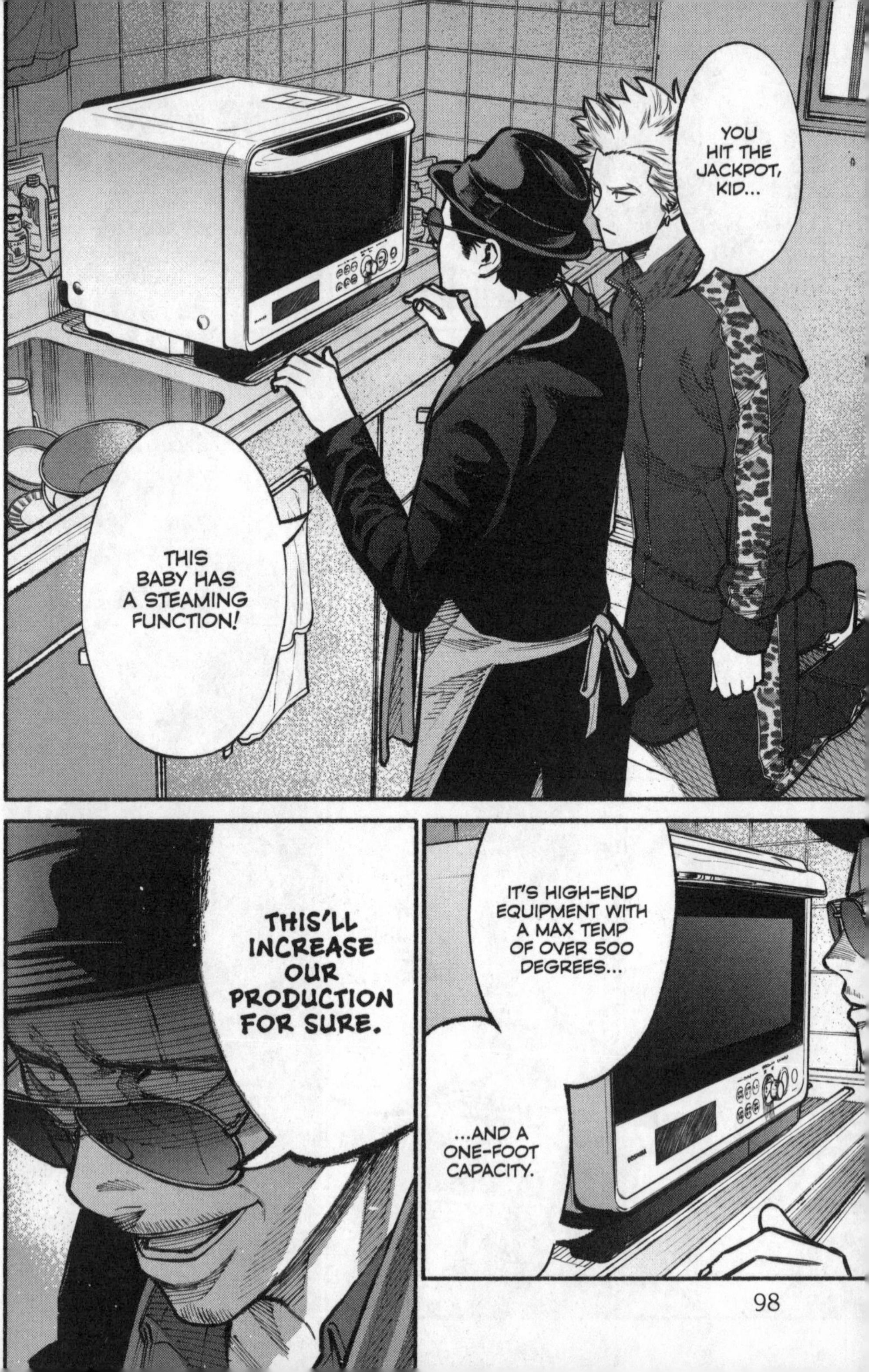
YOU HIT THE JACKPOT, KID...
THIS BABY HAS A STEAMING FUNCTION!
IT'S HIGH-END EQUIPMENT WITH A MAX TEMP OF OVER 500 DEGREES...
...AND A ONE-FOOT CAPACITY.
THIS'LL INCREASE OUR PRODUCTION FOR SURE.

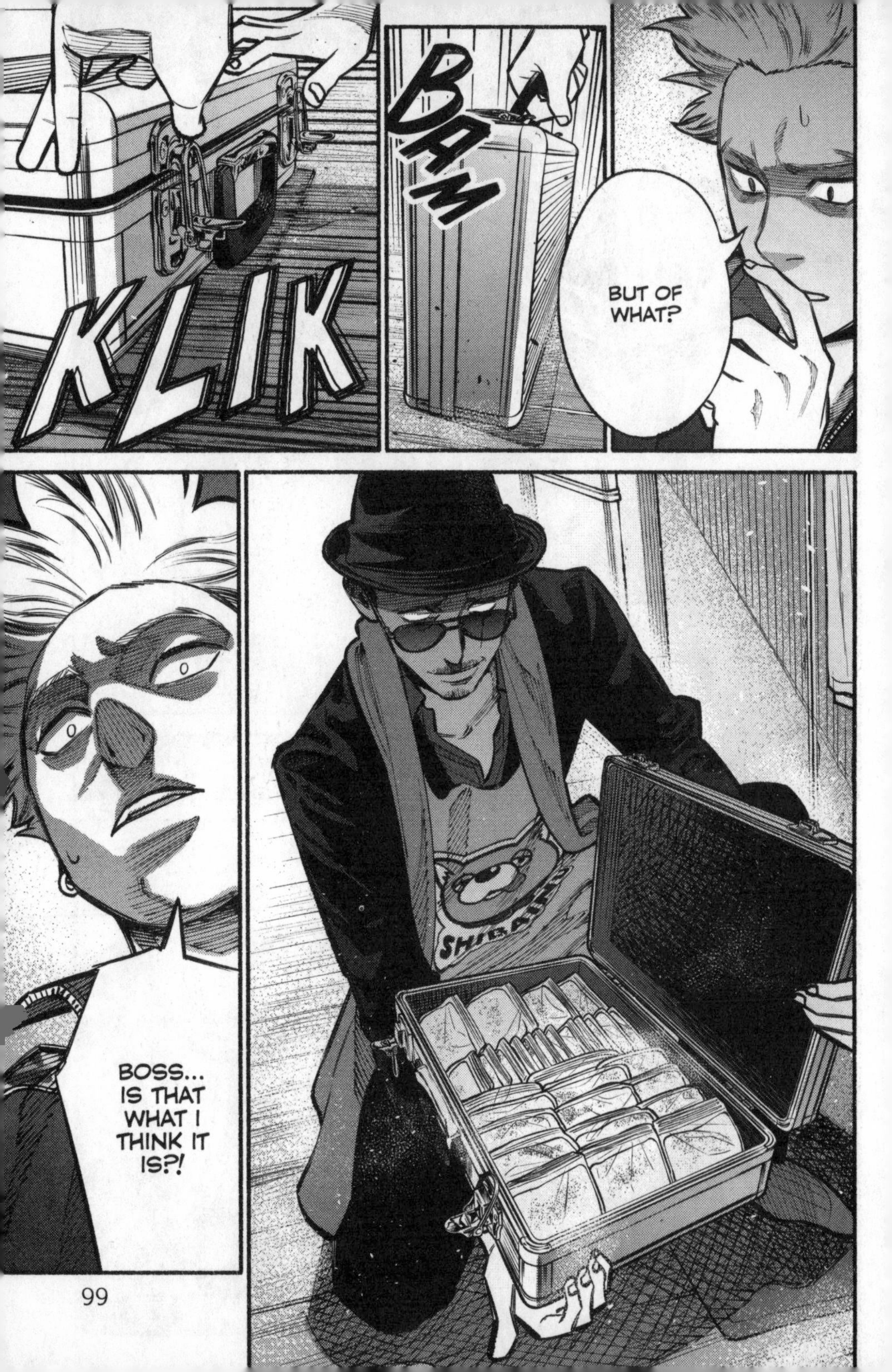
BUT OF WHAT?
BAM
KLIK
BOSS... IS THAT WHAT I THINK IT IS?!

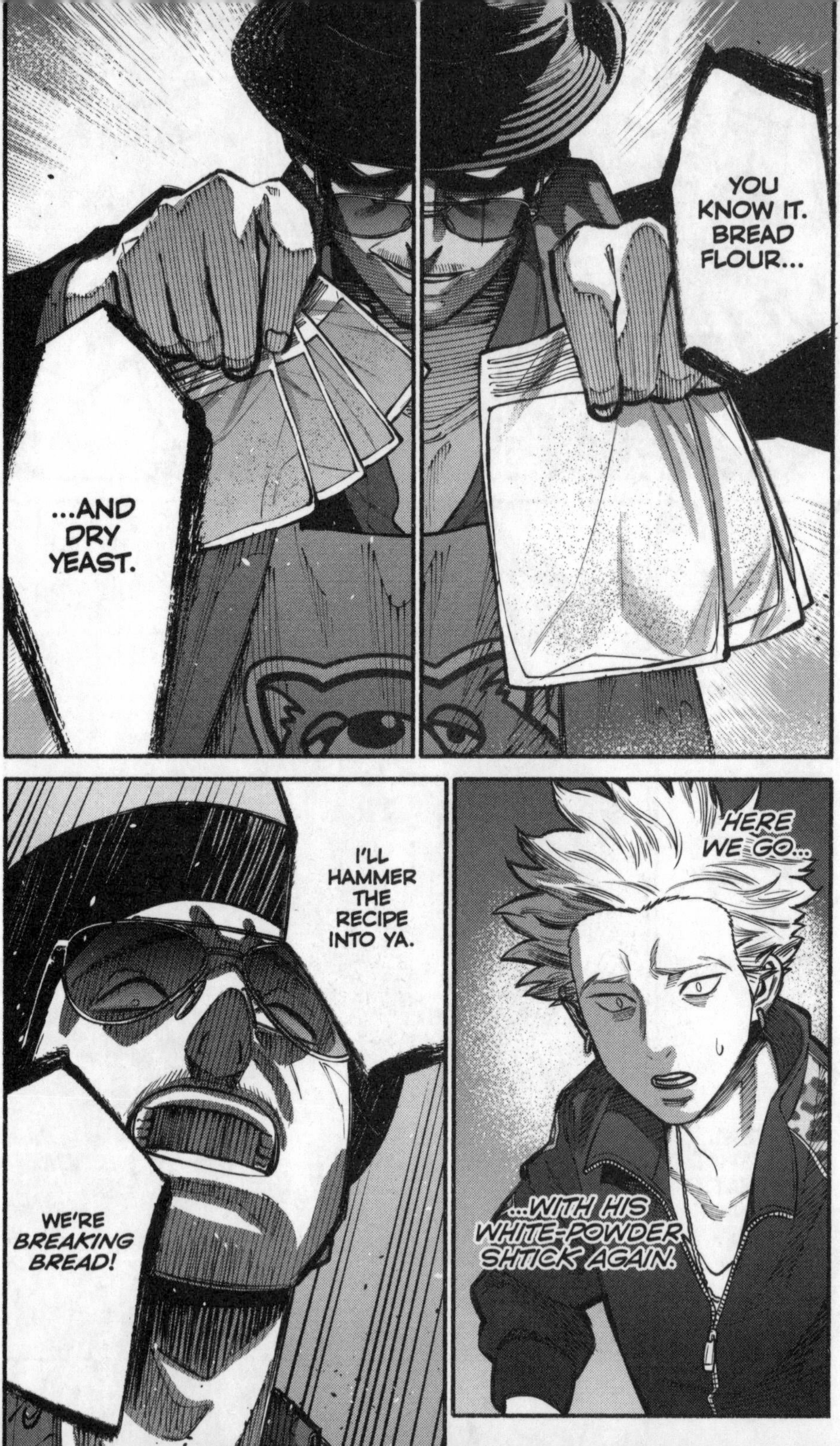
YOU KNOW IT. BREAD FLOUR...
...AND DRY YEAST.
HERE WE GO...
...WITH HIS WHITE-POWDER SHTICK AGAIN.
I'LL HAMMER THE RECIPE INTO YA.
WE'RE *BREAKING BREAD!*

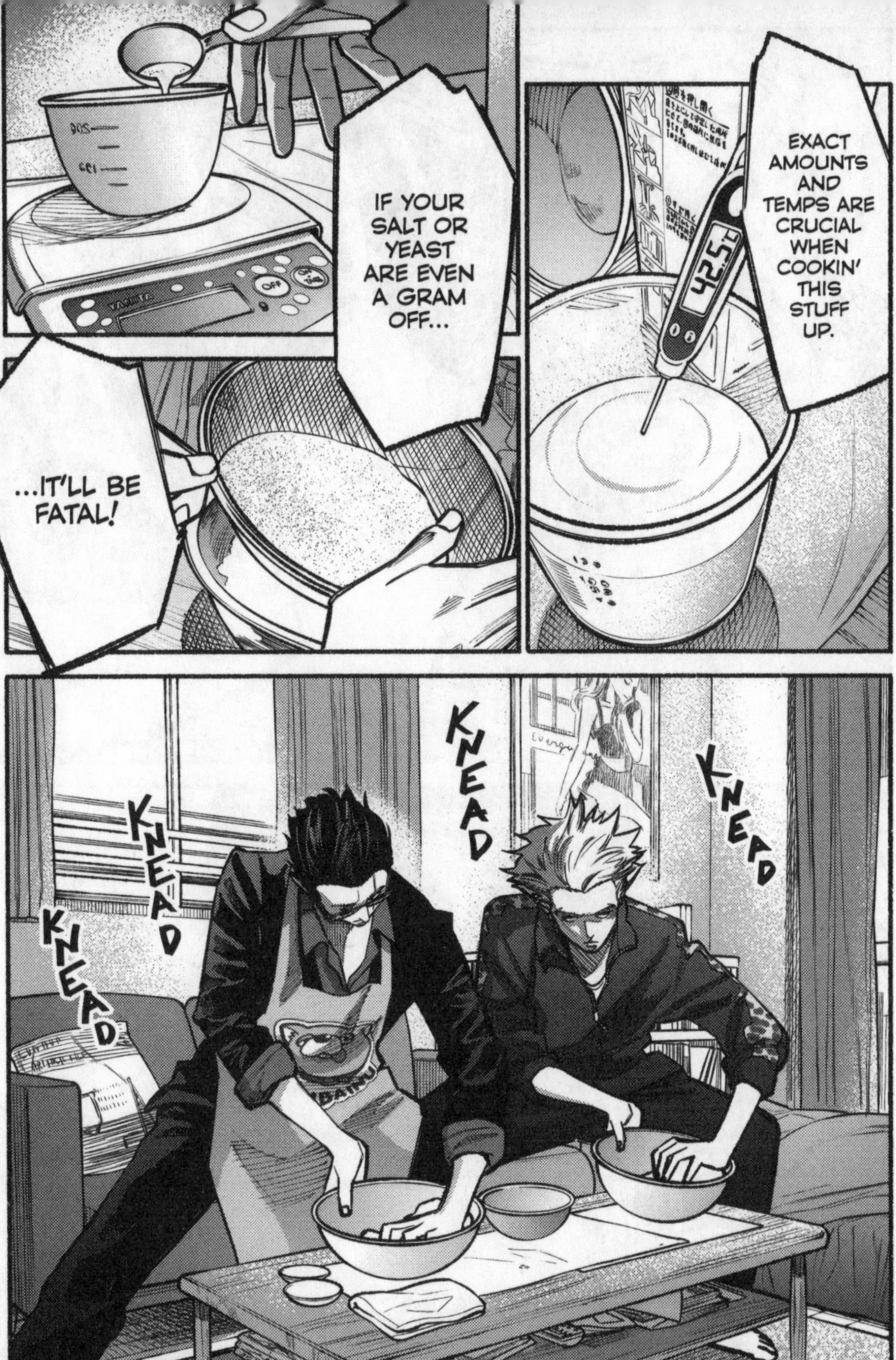
EXACT AMOUNTS AND TEMPS ARE CRUCIAL WHEN COOKIN' THIS STUFF UP.
IF YOUR SALT OR YEAST ARE EVEN A GRAM OFF...
...IT'LL BE FATAL!
KNEAD
KNEAD
KNEAD
KNEAD

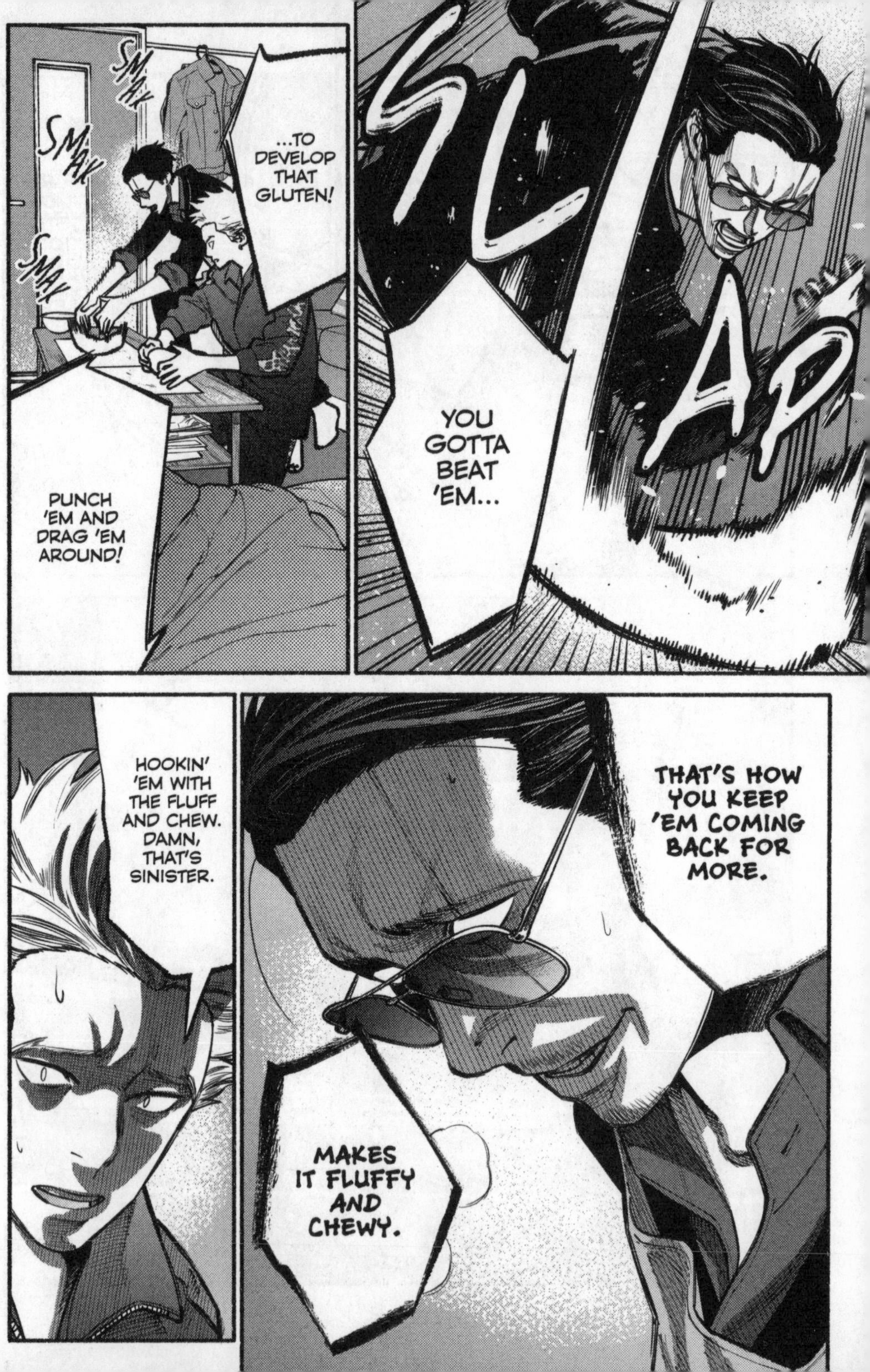
SLAP
YOU GOTTA BEAT 'EM...
...TO DEVELOP THAT GLUTEN!
SMAK
SMAK
SMAK
PUNCH 'EM AND DRAG 'EM AROUND!
THAT'S HOW YOU KEEP 'EM COMING BACK FOR MORE.
MAKES IT FLUFFY AND CHEWY.
HOOKIN' 'EM WITH THE FLUFF AND CHEW. DAMN, THAT'S SINISTER.

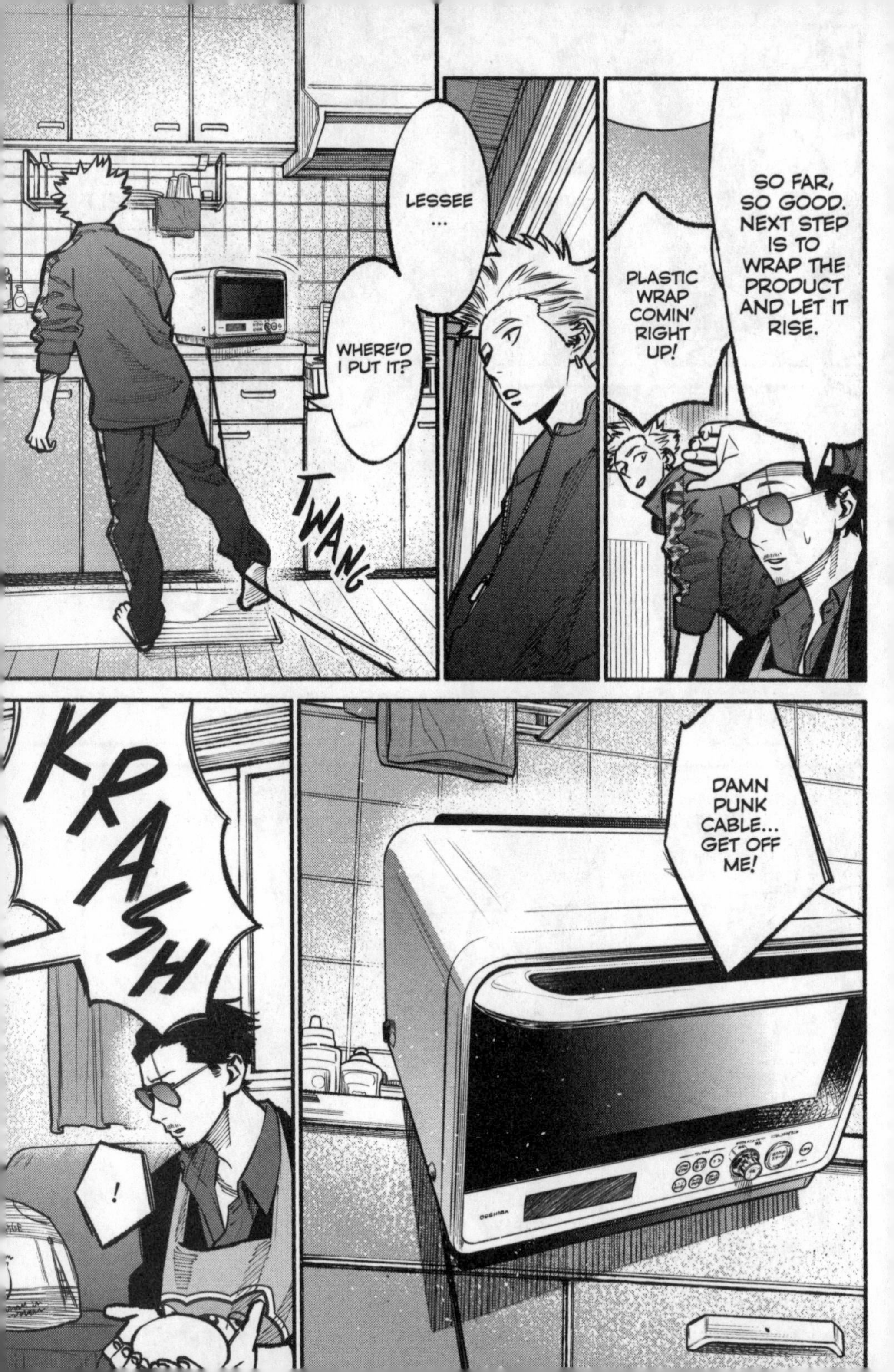
SO FAR, SO GOOD. NEXT STEP IS TO WRAP THE PRODUCT AND LET IT RISE.
PLASTIC WRAP COMIN' RIGHT UP!
LESSEE ...
WHERE'D I PUT IT?
TWANG
DAMN PUNK CABLE... GET OFF ME!
KRASH
!

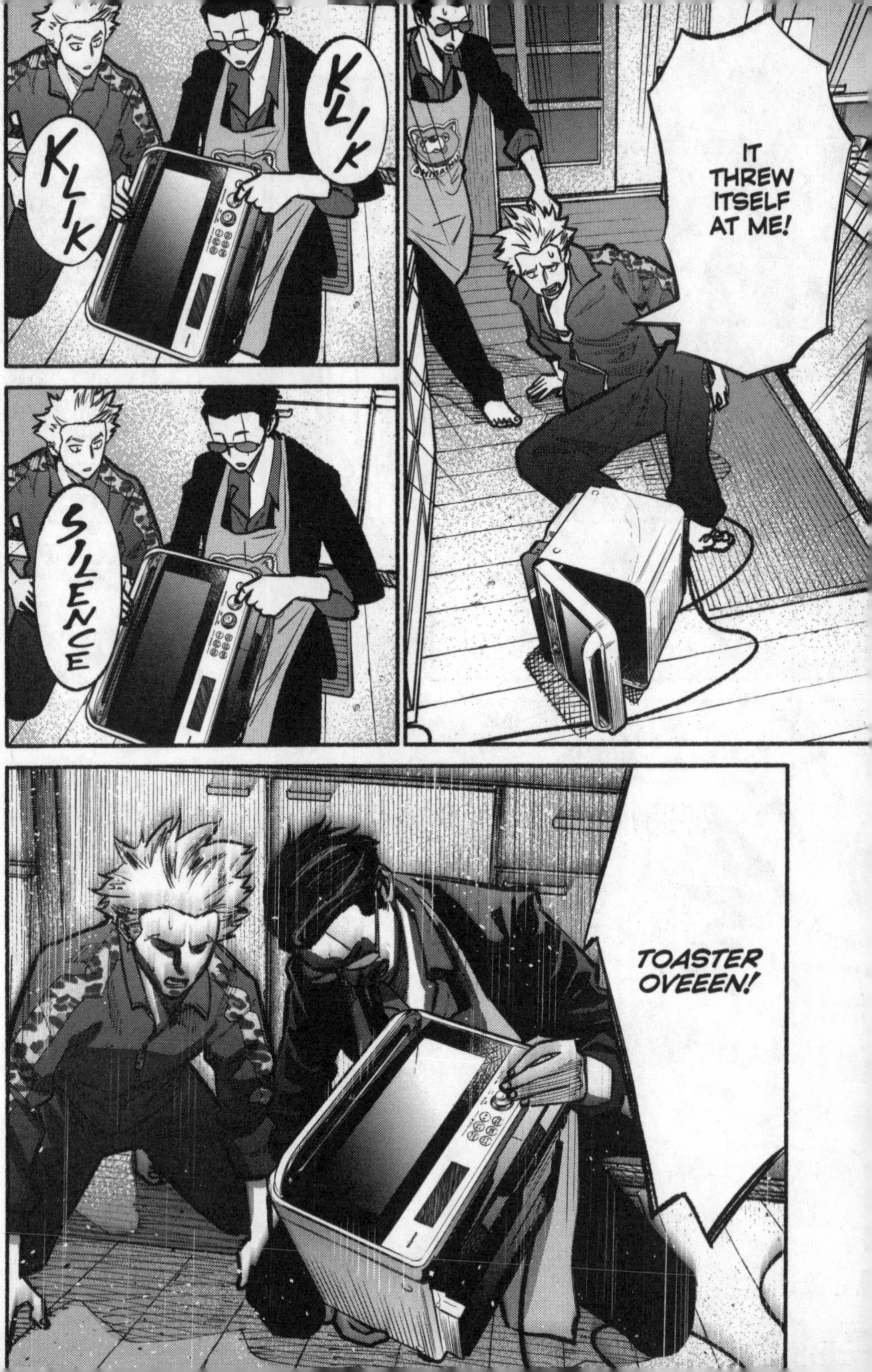
IT THREW ITSELF AT ME!
KLIK
KLIK
SILENCE
TOASTER OVEEEN!

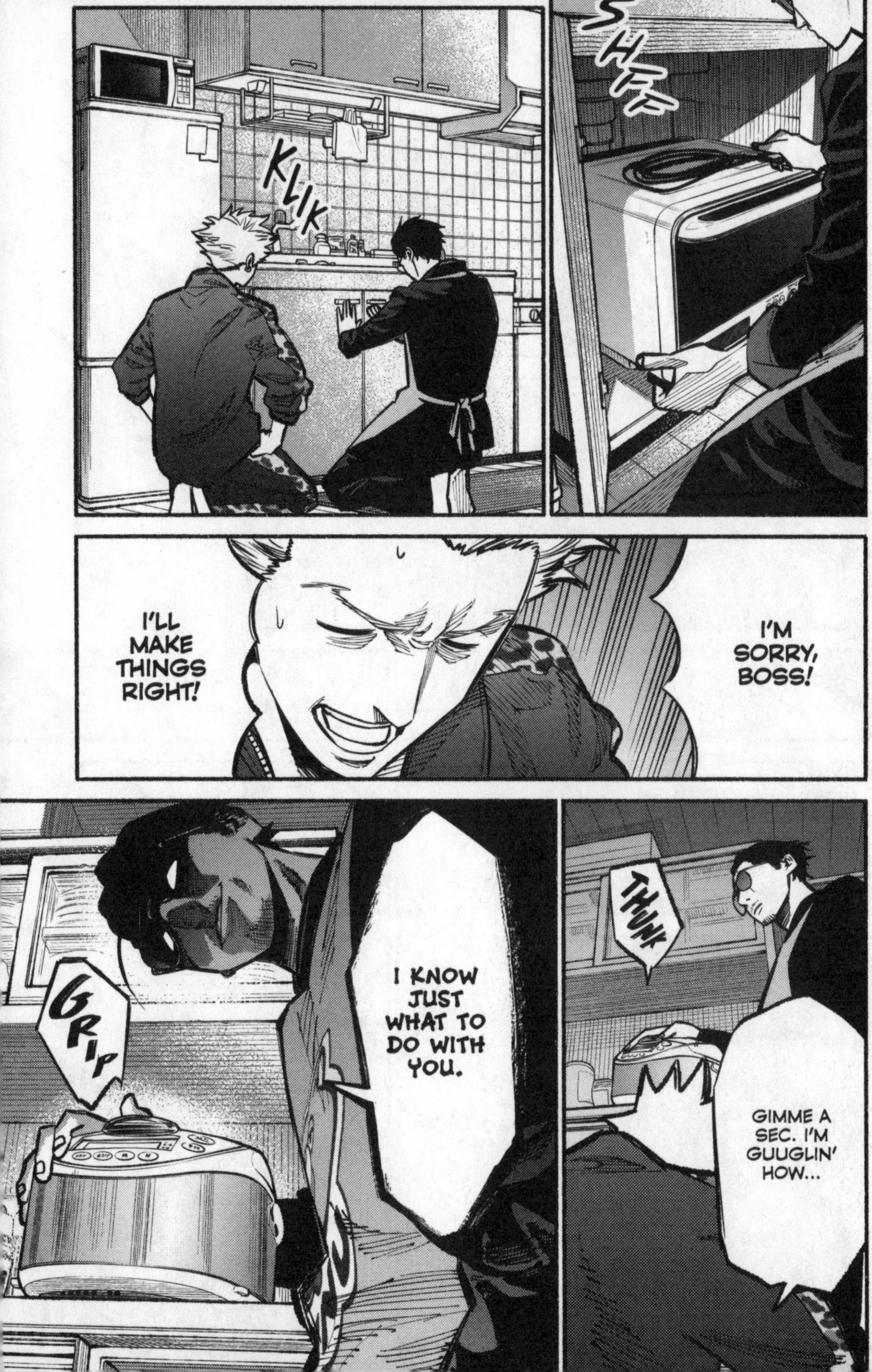
SHFF
KLIK
I'M SORRY, BOSS!
I'LL MAKE THINGS RIGHT!
THUNK
GIMME A SEC. I'M GUUGLIN' HOW...
I KNOW JUST WHAT TO DO WITH YOU.
GRIP

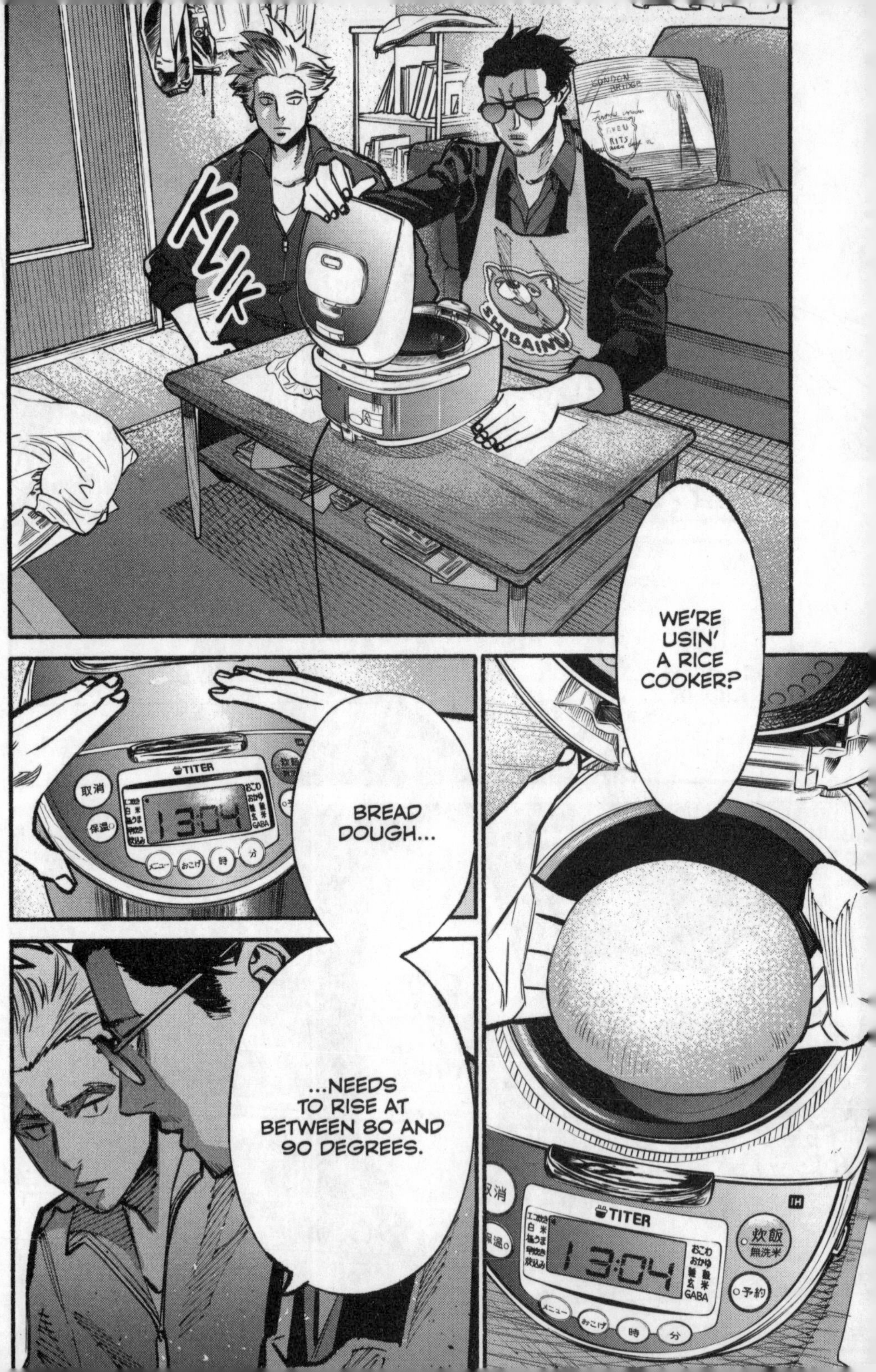
KLIK
SHIBAINU
WE'RE USIN' A RICE COOKER?
TITER
BREAD DOUGH...
...NEEDS TO RISE AT BETWEEN 80 AND 90 DEGREES.

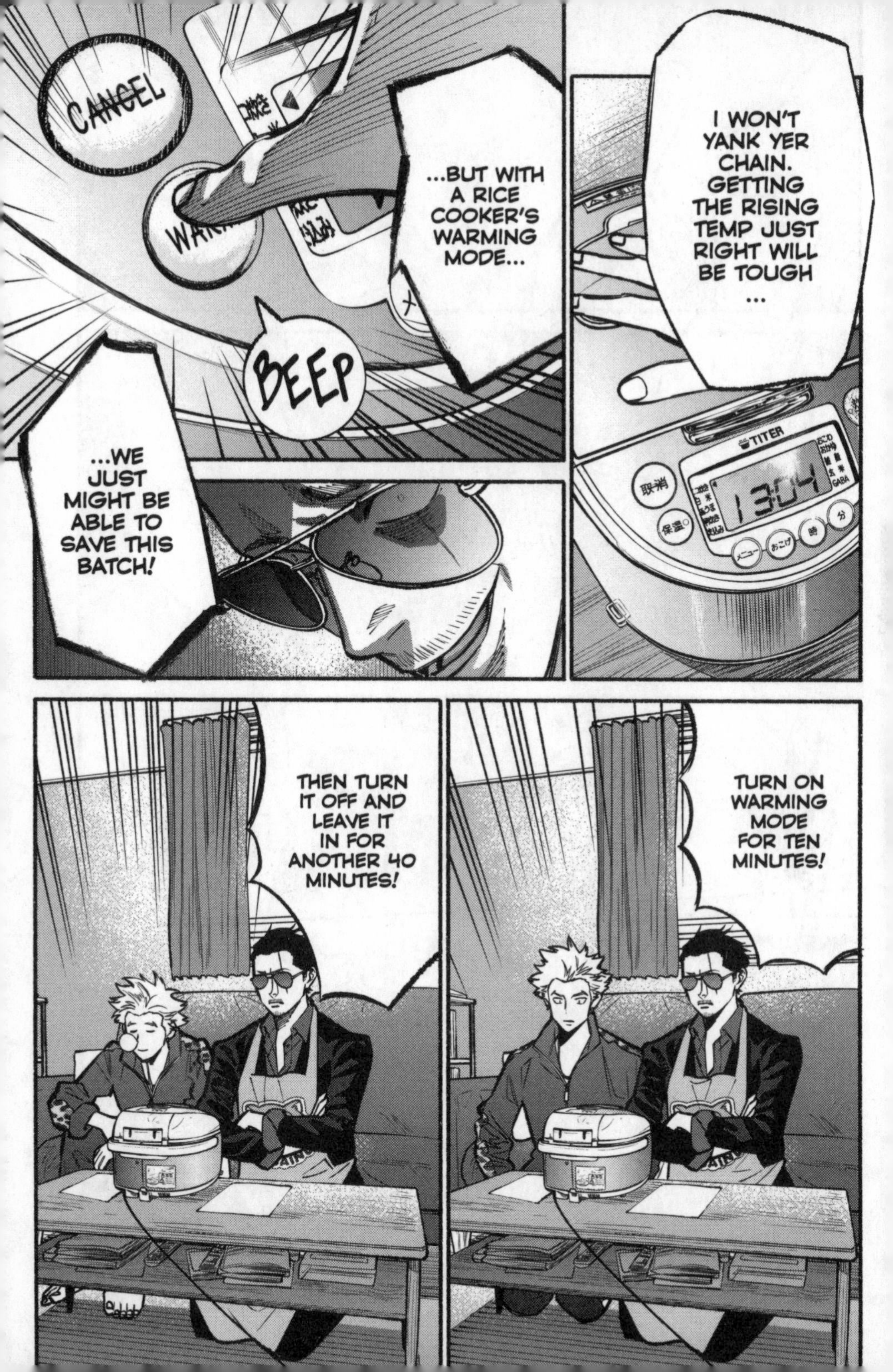
I WON'T YANK YER CHAIN. GETTING THE RISING TEMP JUST RIGHT WILL BE TOUGH ...
TITER
13:04
CANCEL
...BUT WITH A RICE COOKER'S WARMING MODE...
BEEP
...WE JUST MIGHT BE ABLE TO SAVE THIS BATCH!
TURN ON WARMING MODE FOR TEN MINUTES!
THEN TURN IT OFF AND LEAVE IT IN FOR ANOTHER 40 MINUTES!

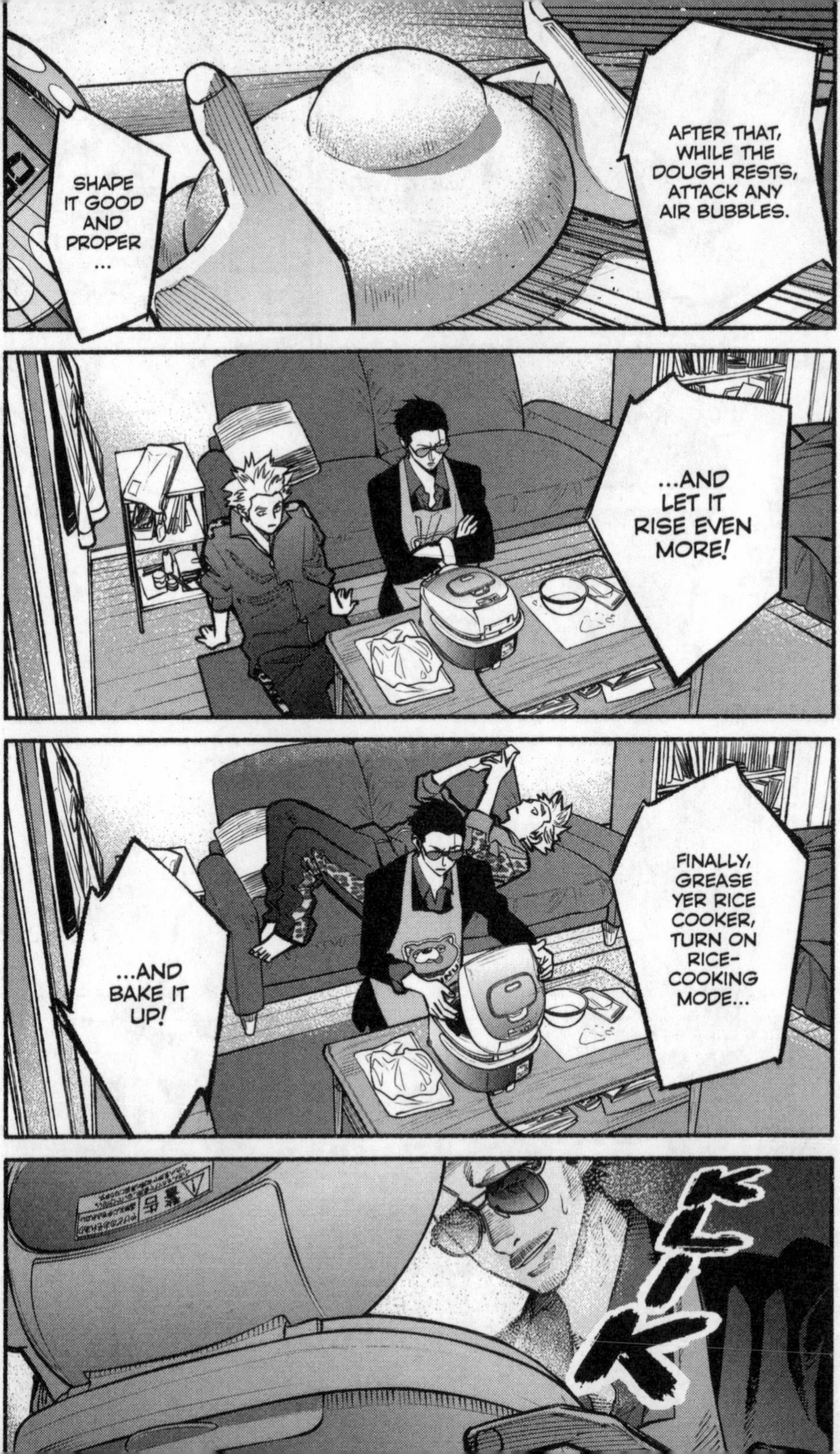
AFTER THAT, WHILE THE DOUGH RESTS, ATTACK ANY AIR BUBBLES.
SHAPE IT GOOD AND PROPER ...
...AND LET IT RISE EVEN MORE!
FINALLY, GREASE YER RICE COOKER, TURN ON RICE-COOKING MODE...
...AND BAKE IT UP!
KLIK

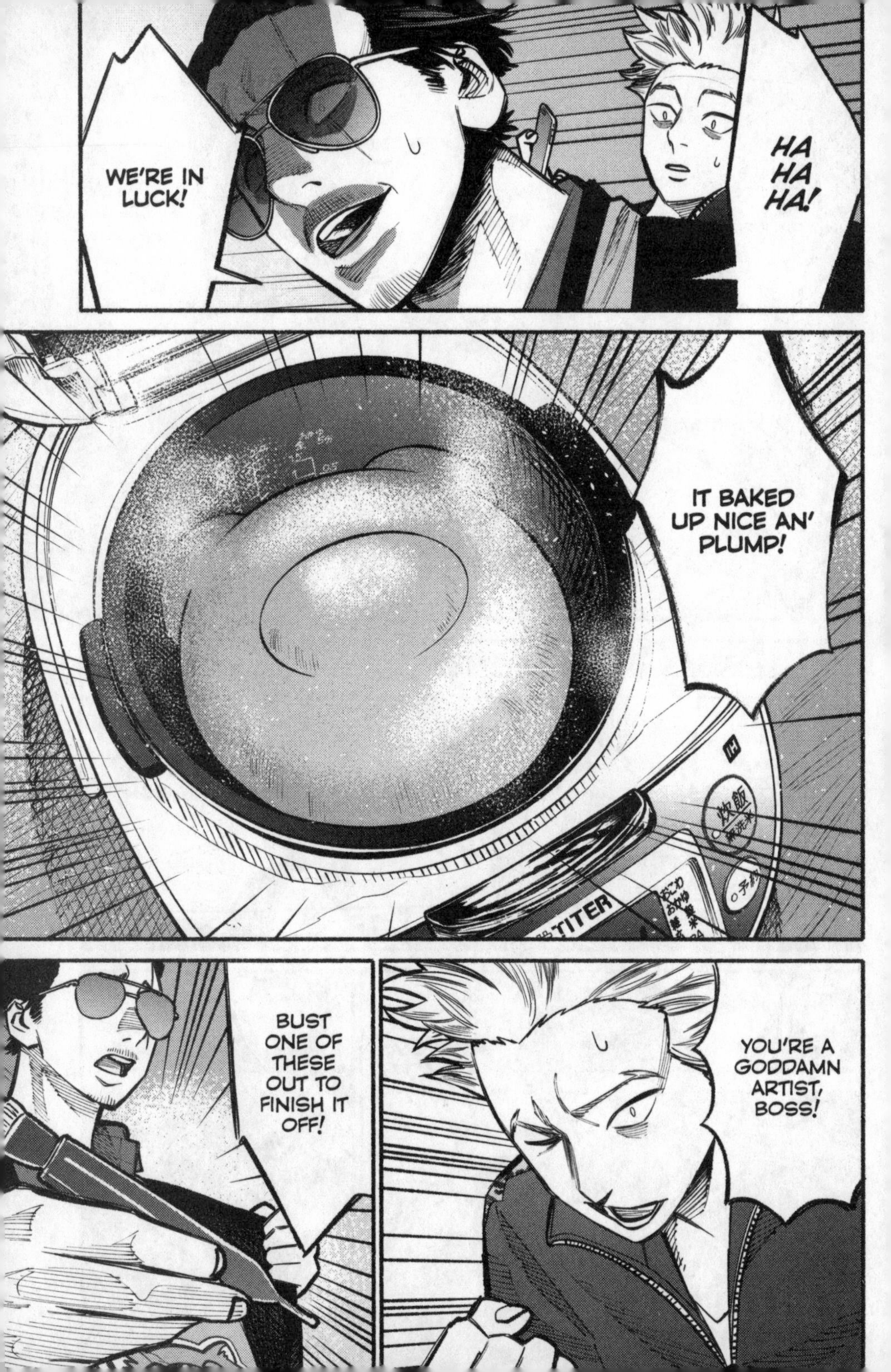
HA HA HA!
WE'RE IN LUCK!
IT BAKED UP NICE AN' PLUMP!
YOU'RE A GODDAMN ARTIST, BOSS!
BUST ONE OF THESE OUT TO FINISH IT OFF!

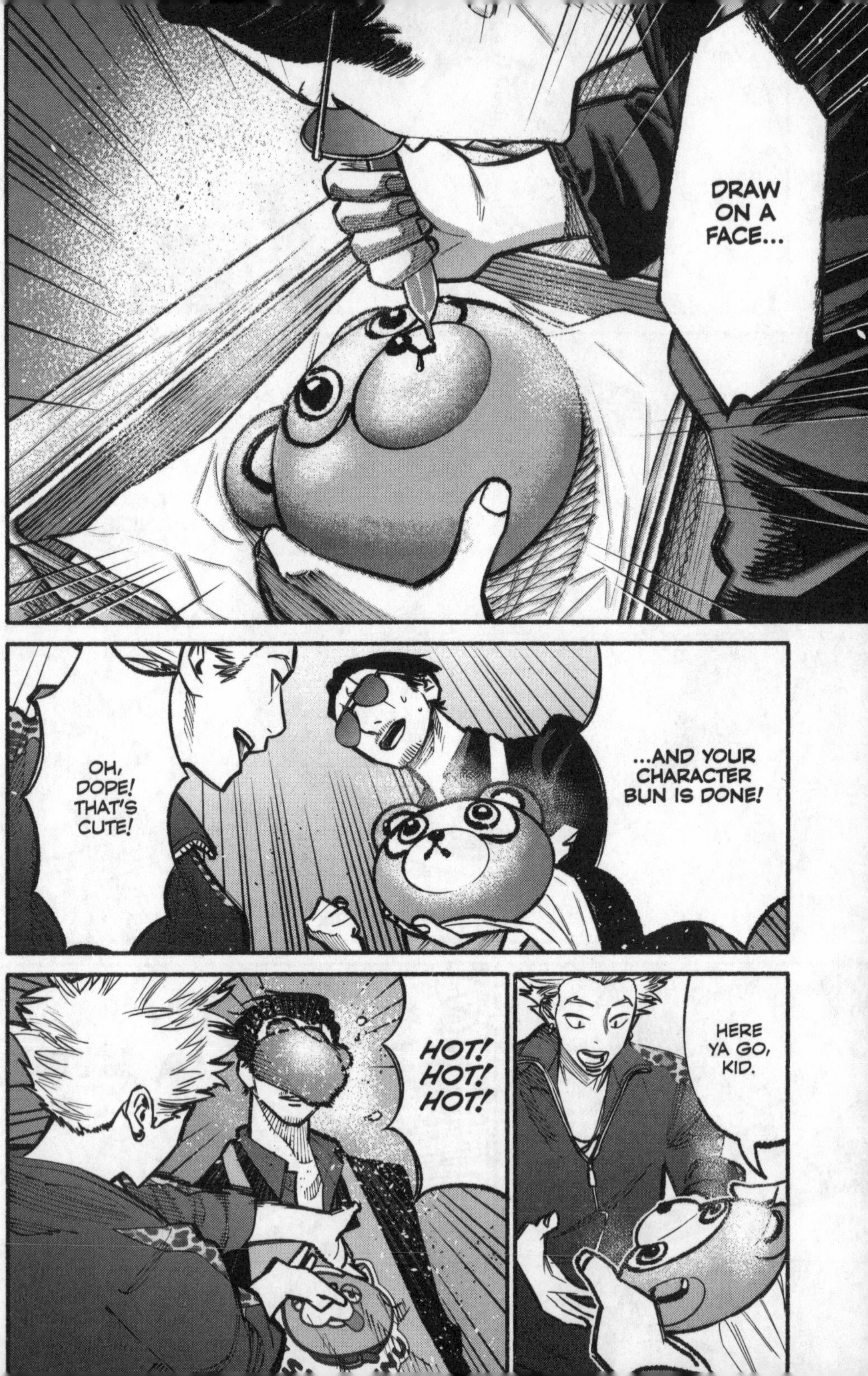
DRAW ON A FACE...
...AND YOUR CHARACTER BUN IS DONE!
OH, DOPE! THAT'S CUTE!
HERE YA GO, KID.
HOT! HOT! HOT!

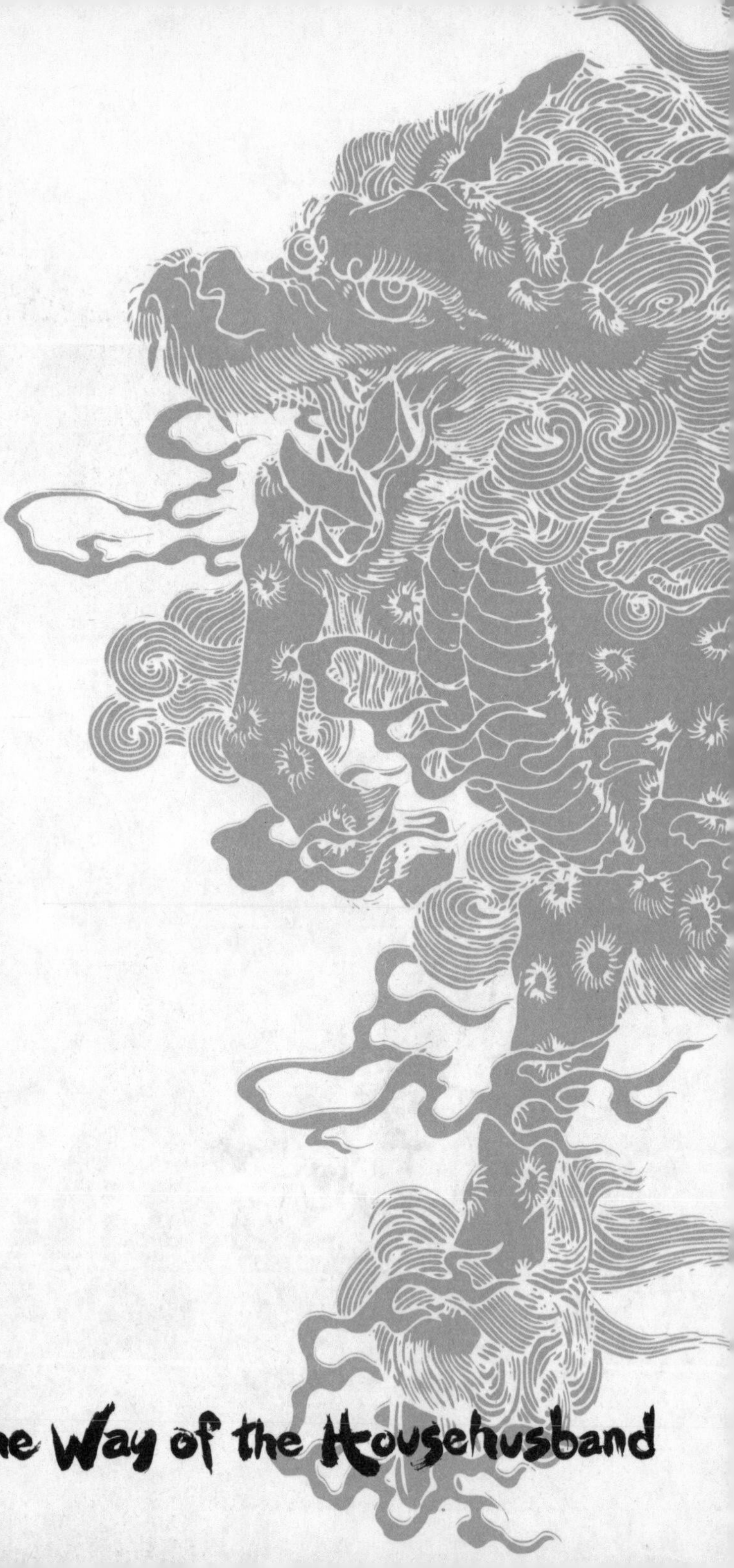

The Way of the Househusband

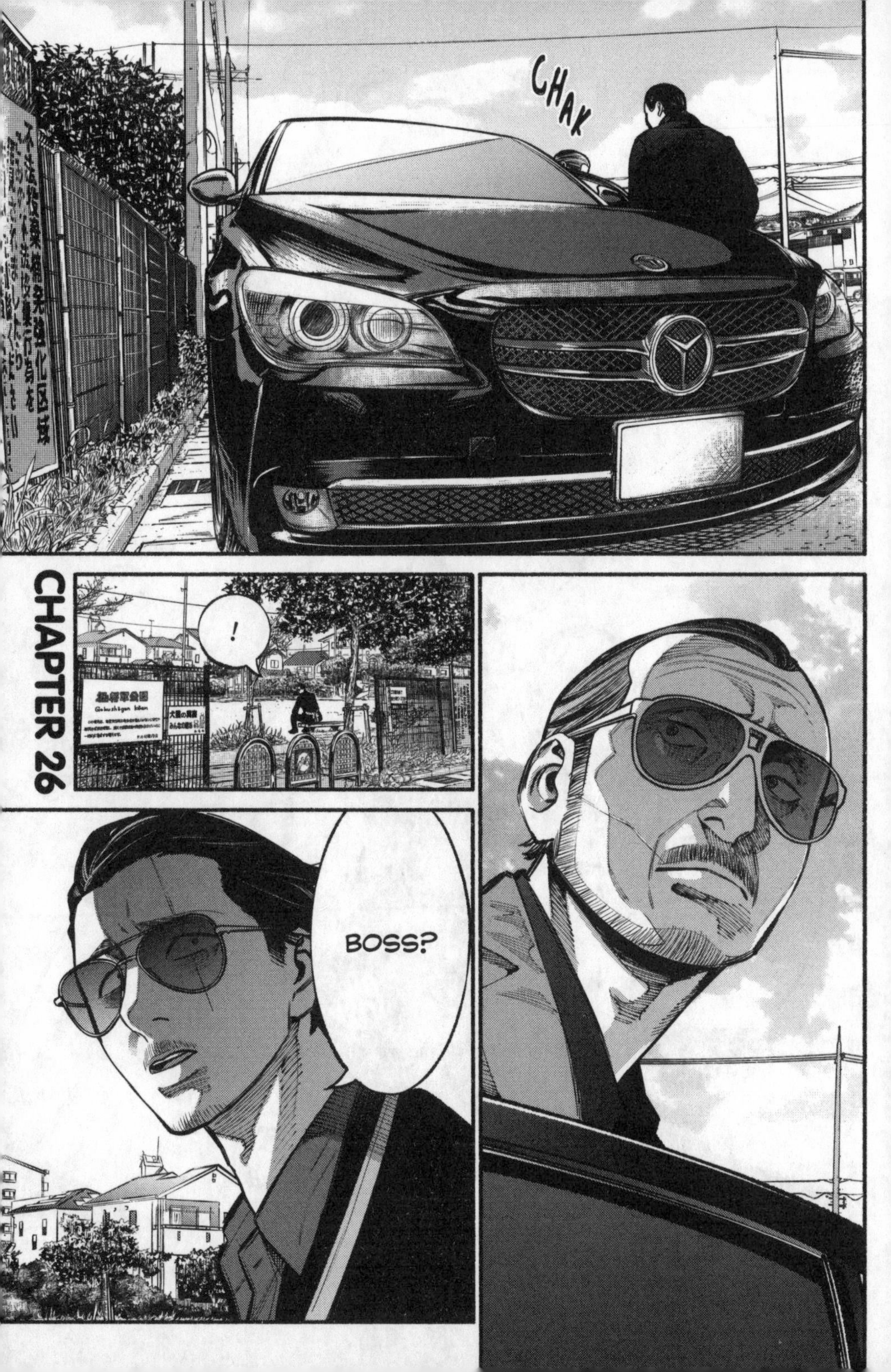
CHAK
CHAPTER 26
!
BOSS?

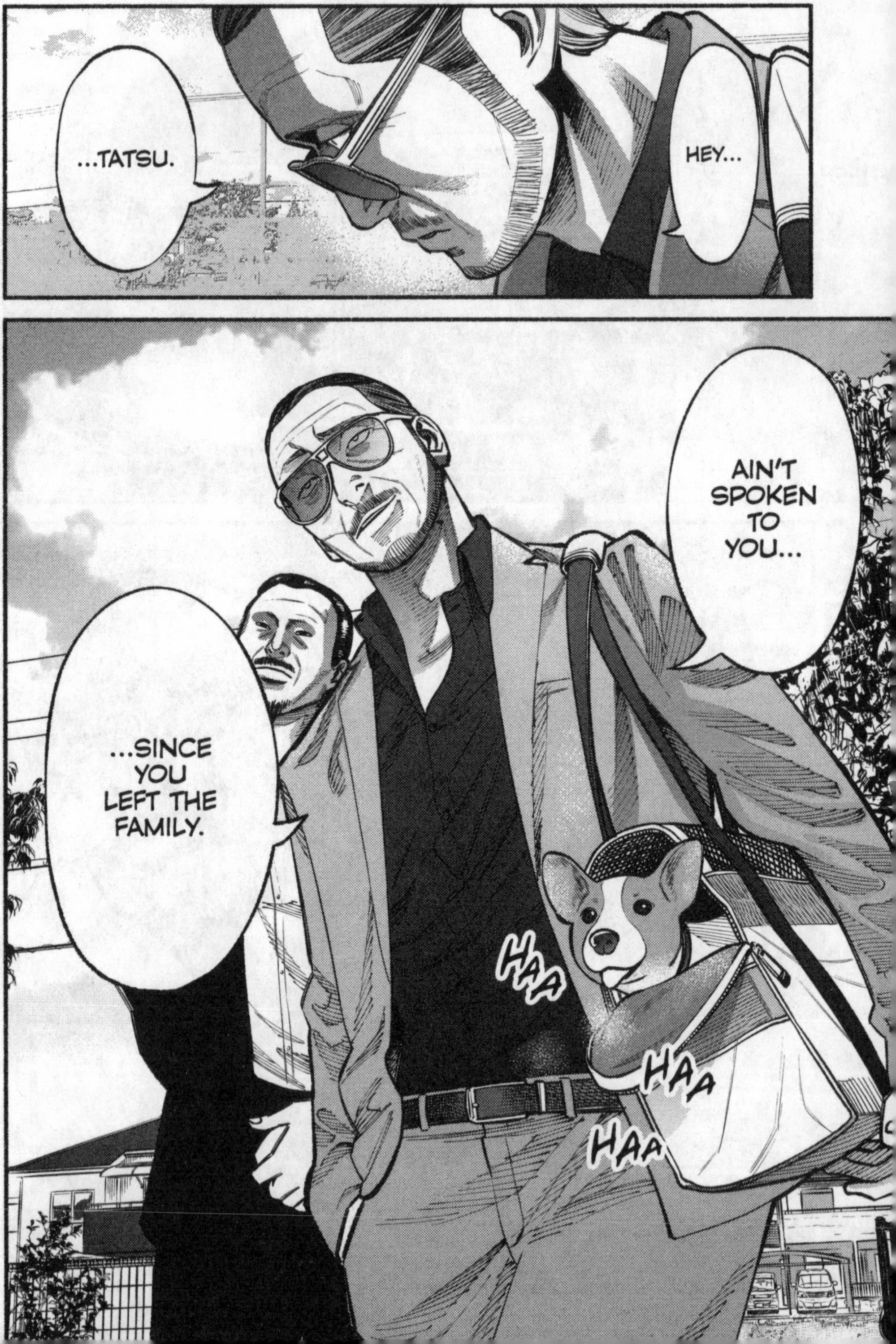
HEY...
...TATSU.
AIN'T SPOKEN TO YOU...
...SINCE YOU LEFT THE FAMILY.
HAA
HAA
HAA

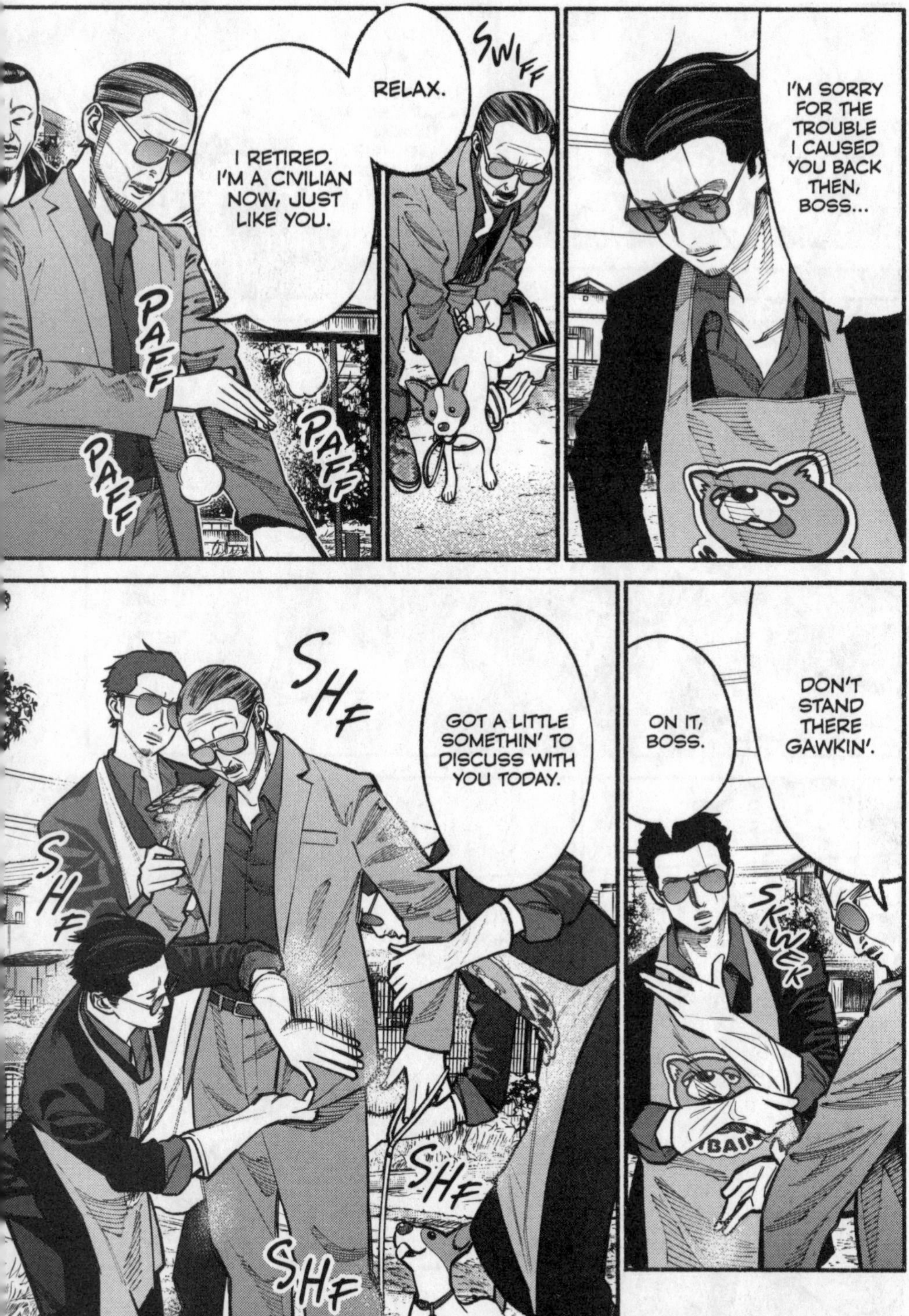
I'M SORRY FOR THE TROUBLE I CAUSED YOU BACK THEN, BOSS...
SWIFF
RELAX.
I RETIRED. I'M A CIVILIAN NOW, JUST LIKE YOU.
PAFF
PAFF
PAFF
DON'T STAND THERE GAWKIN'.
SKWEK
ON IT, BOSS.
GOT A LITTLE SOMETHIN' TO DISCUSS WITH YOU TODAY.
SHF
SHF
SHF
SHF

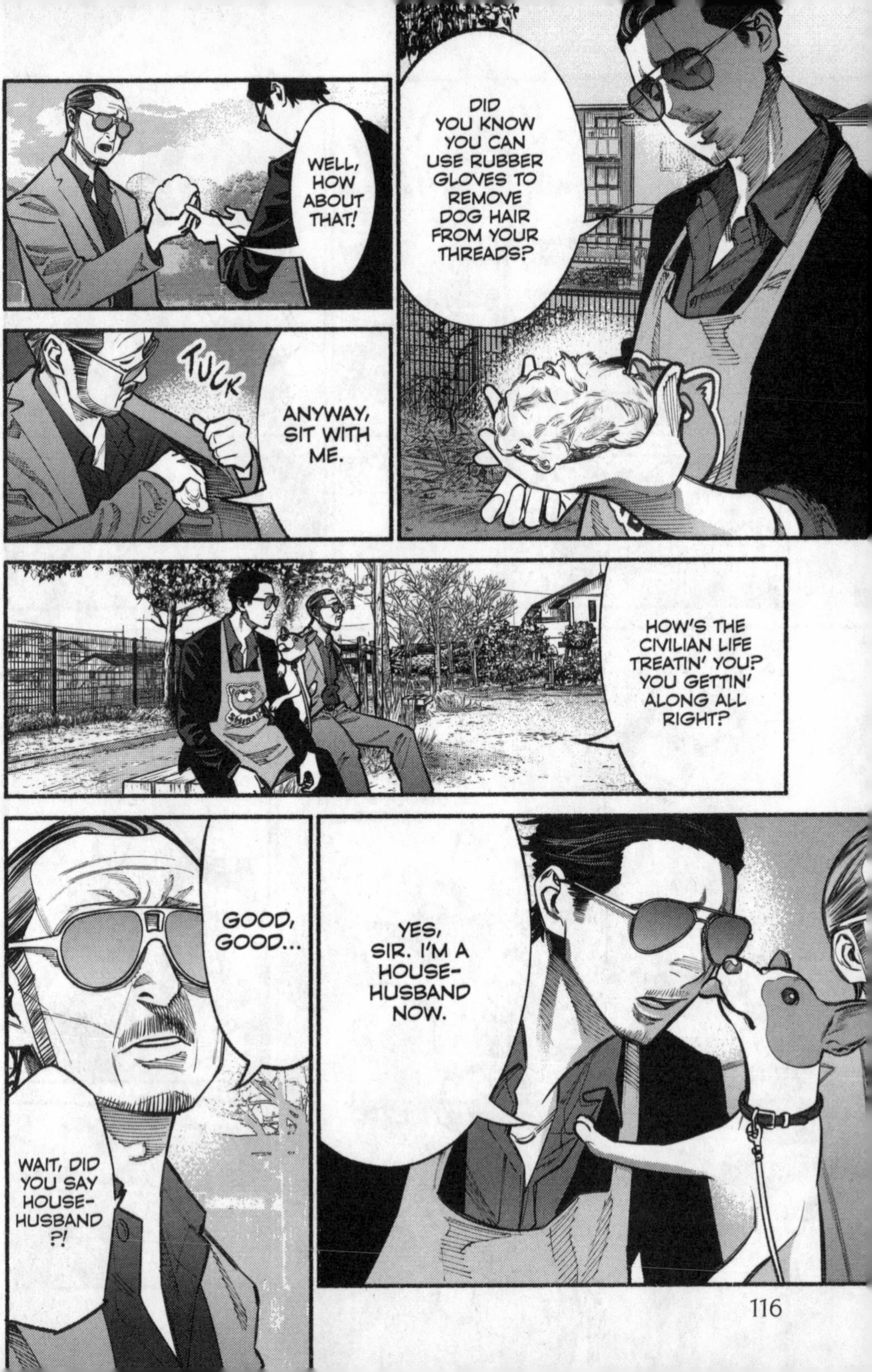
DID YOU KNOW YOU CAN USE RUBBER GLOVES TO REMOVE DOG HAIR FROM YOUR THREADS?
WELL, HOW ABOUT THAT!
TUCK
ANYWAY, SIT WITH ME.
HOW'S THE CIVILIAN LIFE TREATIN' YOU? YOU GETTIN' ALONG ALL RIGHT?
YES, SIR. I'M A HOUSE-HUSBAND NOW.
GOOD, GOOD...
WAIT, DID YOU SAY HOUSE-HUSBAND ?!

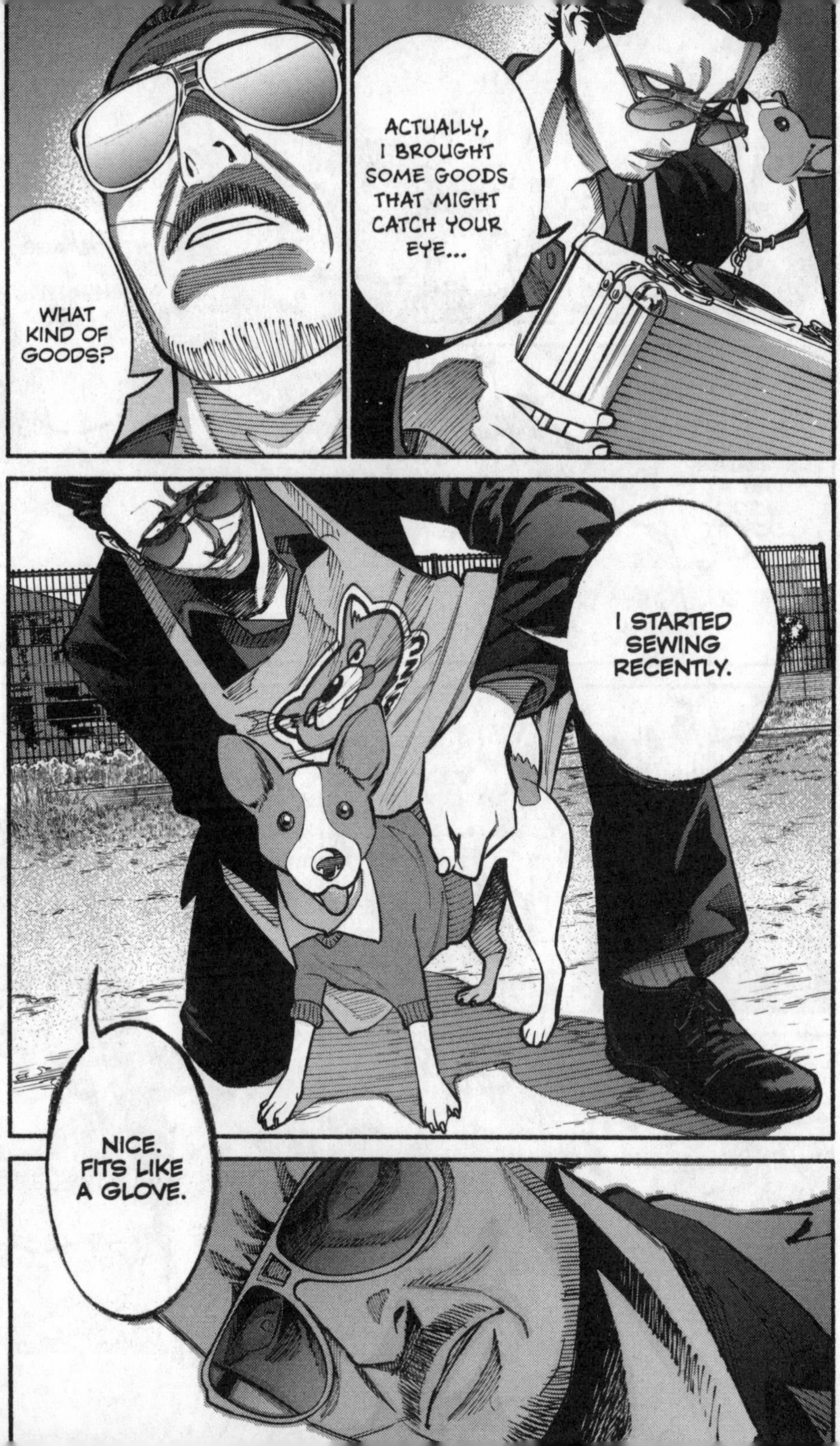
ACTUALLY, I BROUGHT SOME GOODS THAT MIGHT CATCH YOUR EYE...
WHAT KIND OF GOODS?
I STARTED SEWING RECENTLY.
NICE. FITS LIKE A GLOVE.

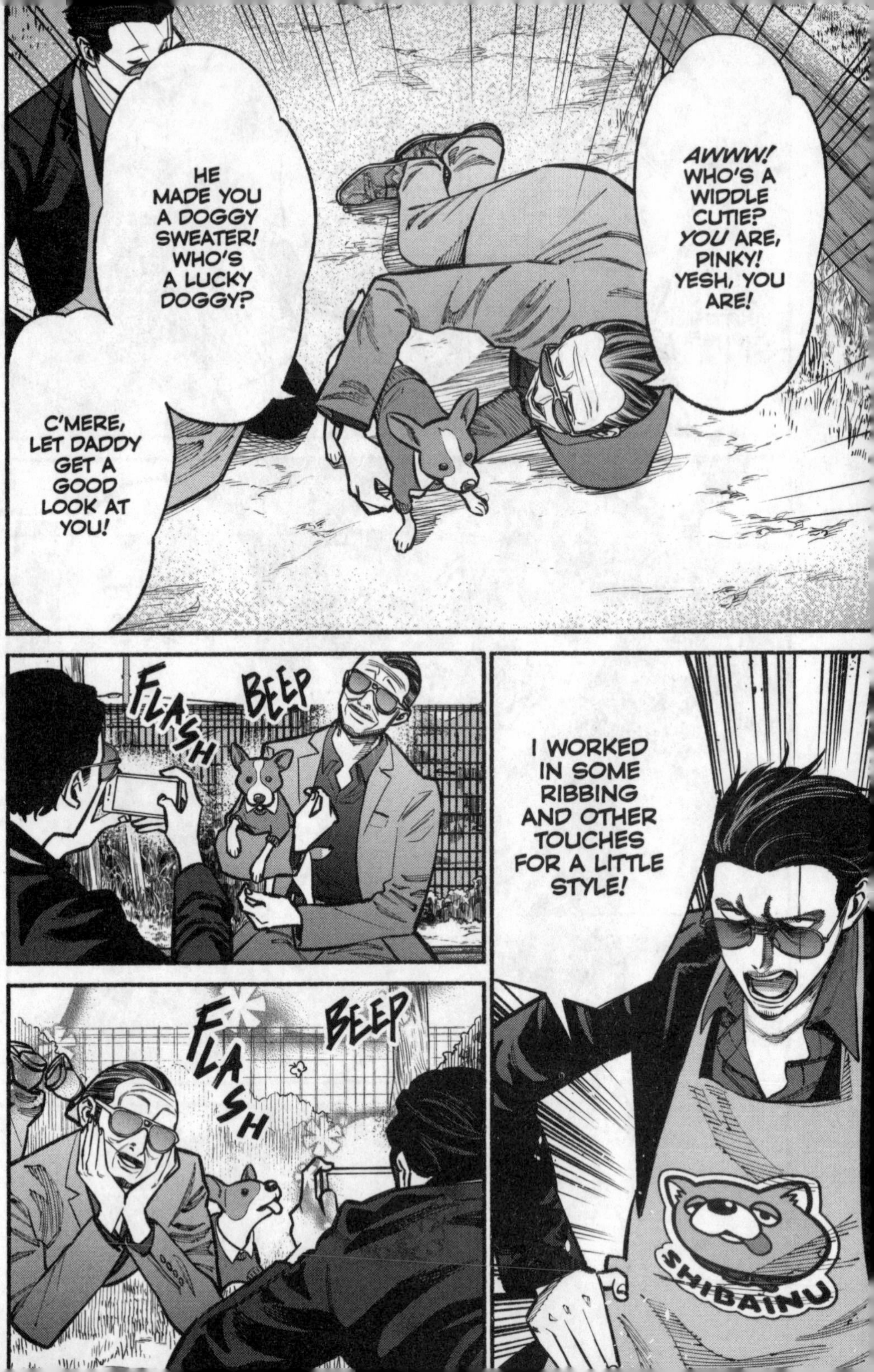
AWWW! WHO'S A WIDDLE CUTIE? YOU ARE, PINKY! YESH, YOU ARE!
HE MADE YOU A DOGGY SWEATER! WHO'S A LUCKY DOGGY?
C'MERE, LET DADDY GET A GOOD LOOK AT YOU!
I WORKED IN SOME RIBBING AND OTHER TOUCHES FOR A LITTLE STYLE!
SHIBAINU
BEEP
FLASH
BEEP
FLASH

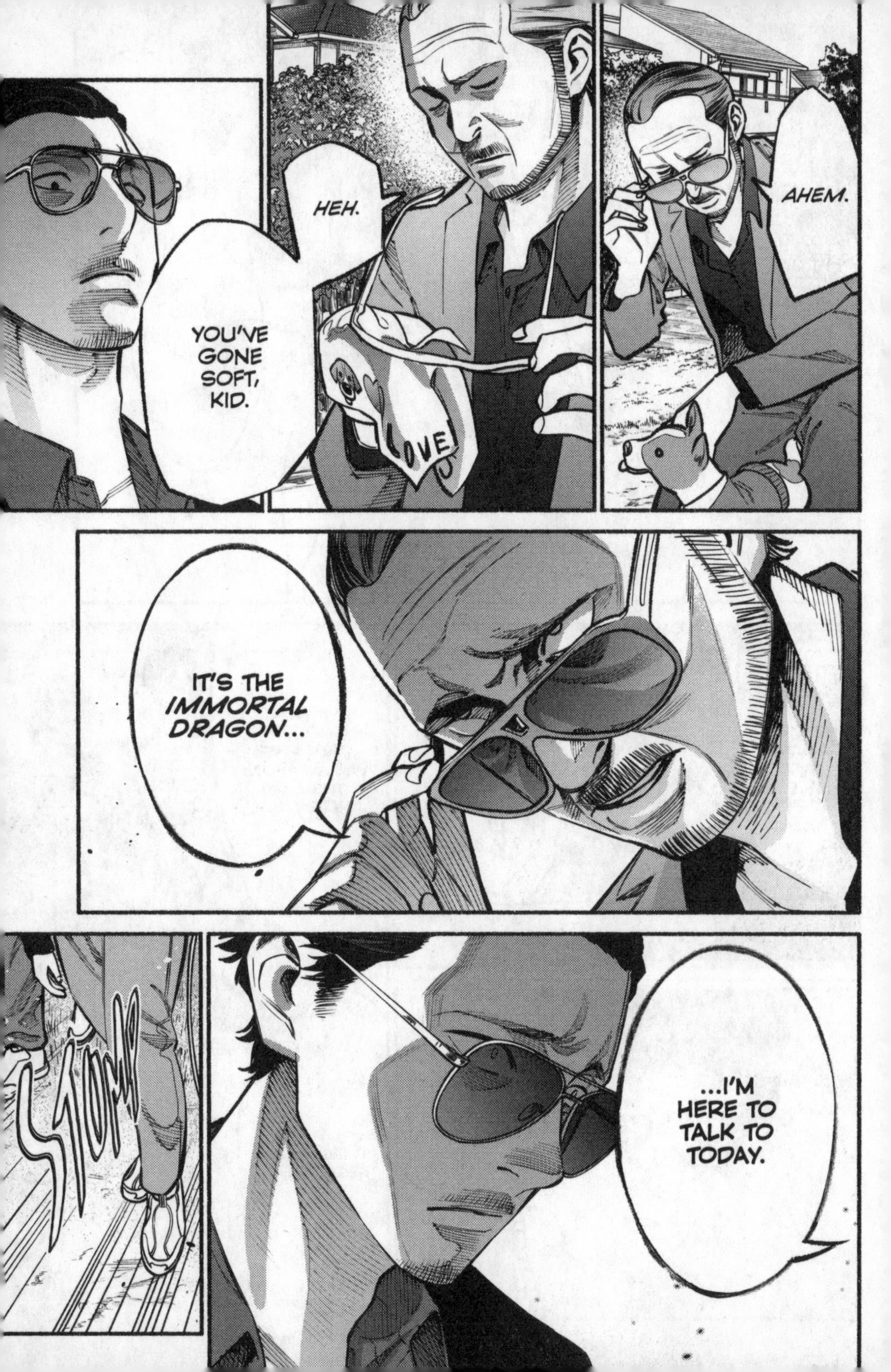
AHEM.
HEH.
LOVE
YOU'VE GONE SOFT, KID.
IT'S THE *IMMORTAL DRAGON*...
...I'M HERE TO TALK TO TODAY.
STOMP

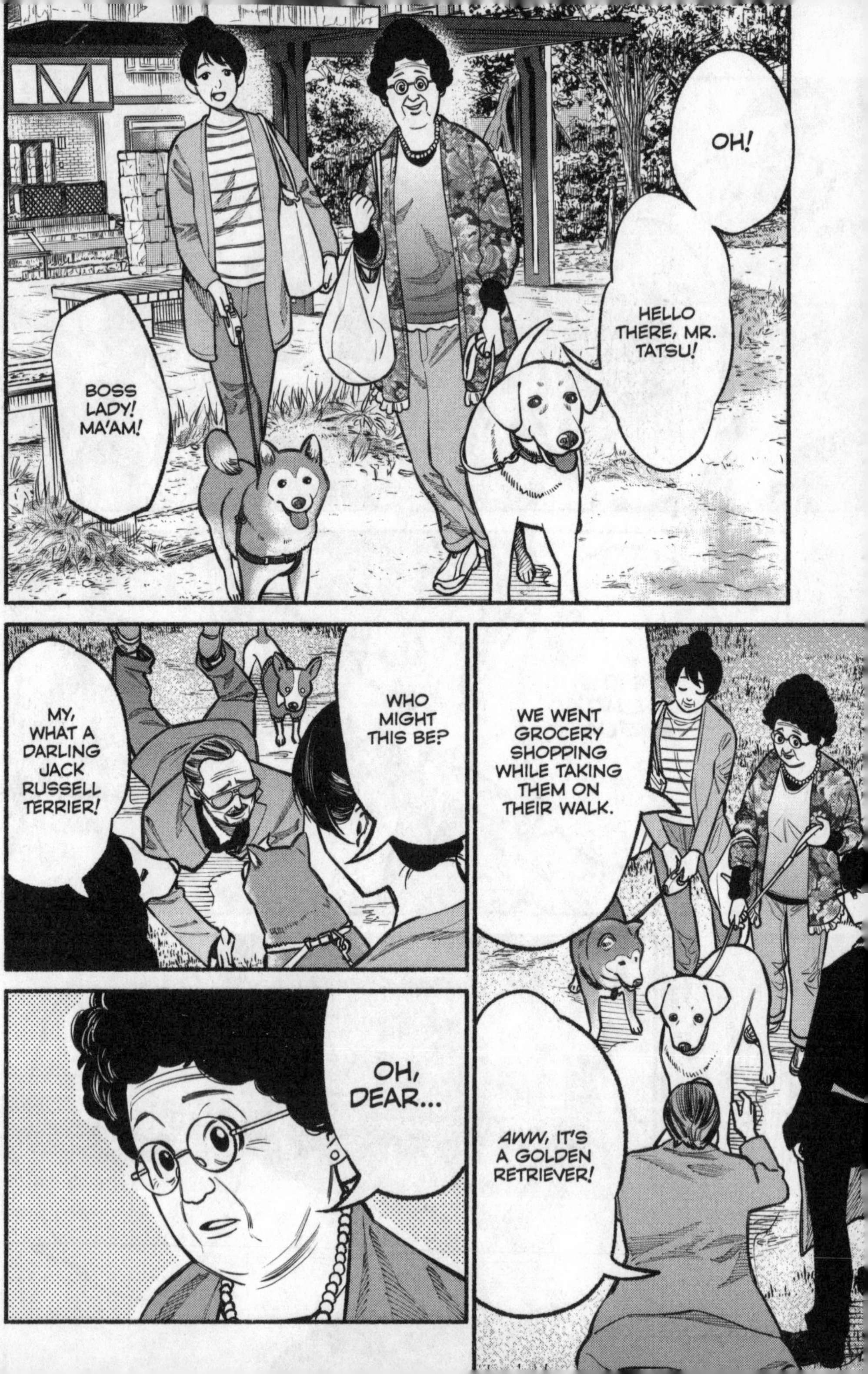
OH!
HELLO THERE, MR. TATSU!
BOSS LADY! MA'AM!
WE WENT GROCERY SHOPPING WHILE TAKING THEM ON THEIR WALK.
AWW, IT'S A GOLDEN RETRIEVER!
WHO MIGHT THIS BE?
MY, WHAT A DARLING JACK RUSSELL TERRIER!
OH, DEAR...

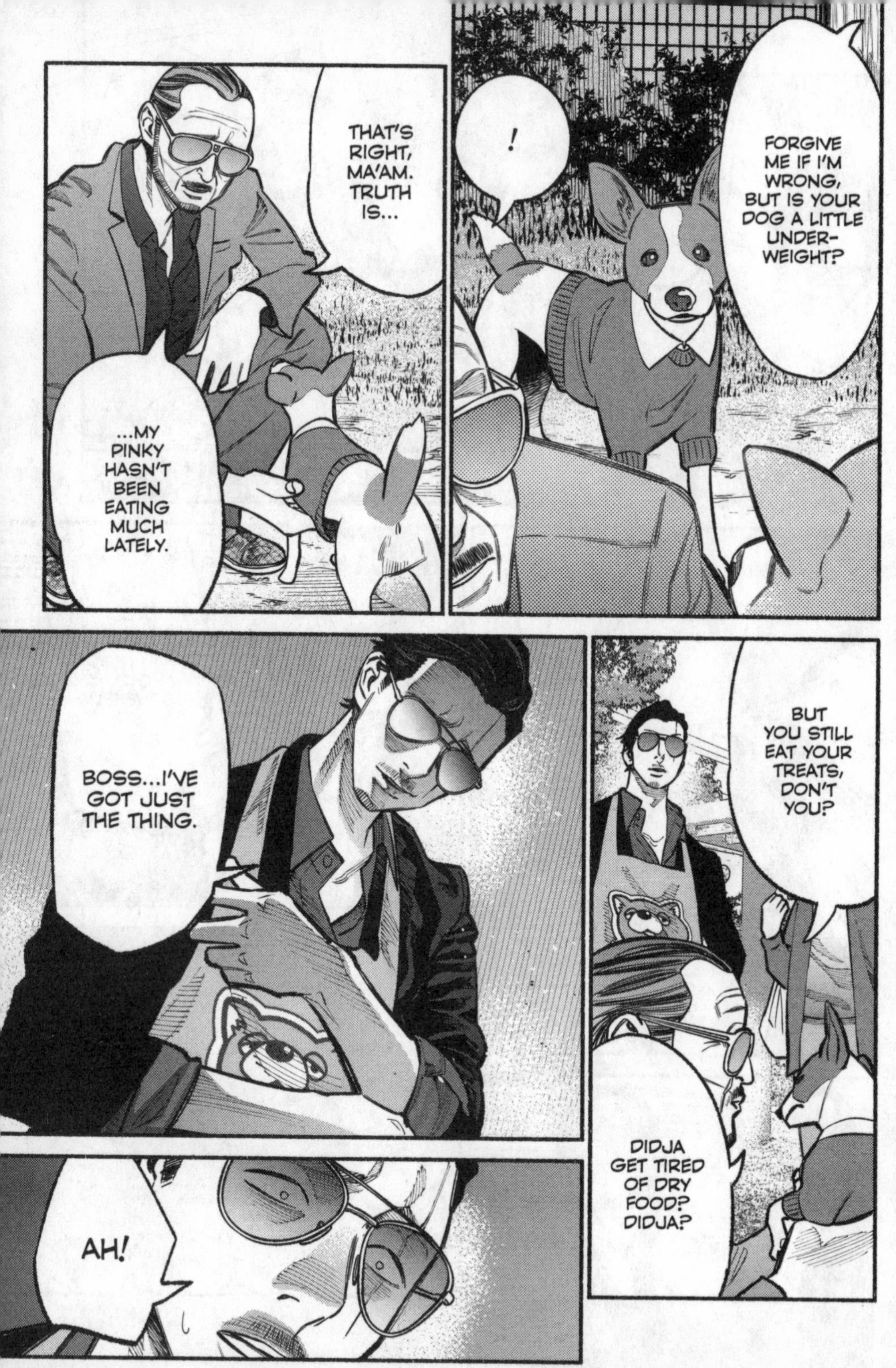
FORGIVE ME IF I'M WRONG, BUT IS YOUR DOG A LITTLE UNDER-WEIGHT?
!
THAT'S RIGHT, MA'AM. TRUTH IS...
...MY PINKY HASN'T BEEN EATING MUCH LATELY.
BUT YOU STILL EAT YOUR TREATS, DON'T YOU?
DIDJA GET TIRED OF DRY FOOD? DIDJA?
BOSS...I'VE GOT JUST THE THING.
AH!

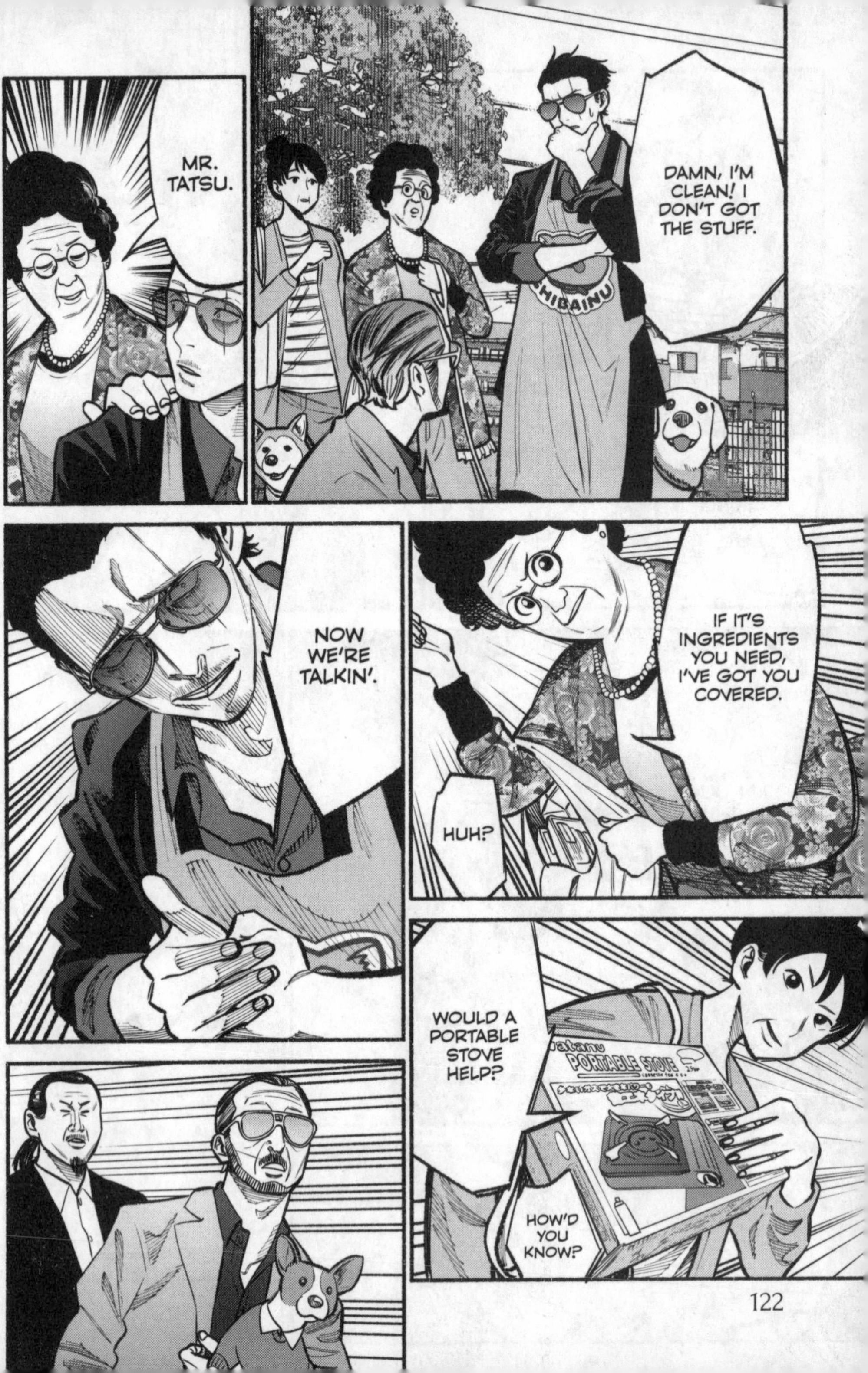
DAMN, I'M CLEAN! I DON'T GOT THE STUFF.
MR. TATSU.
IF IT'S INGREDIENTS YOU NEED, I'VE GOT YOU COVERED.
HUH?
NOW WE'RE TALKIN'.
WOULD A PORTABLE STOVE HELP?
PORTABLE STOVE
HOW'D YOU KNOW?

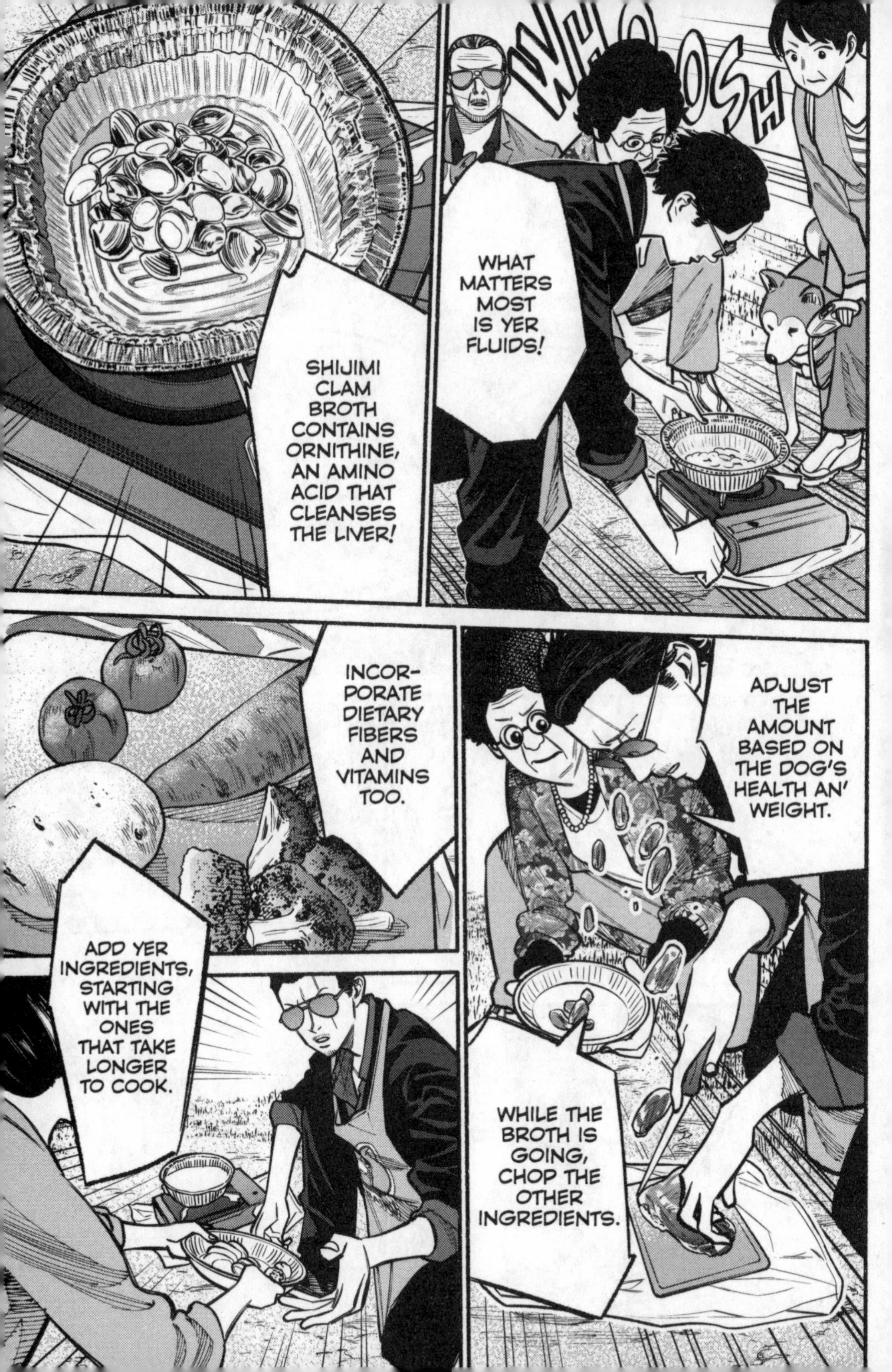
WHOOSH
WHAT MATTERS MOST IS YER FLUIDS!
SHIJIMI CLAM BROTH CONTAINS ORNITHINE, AN AMINO ACID THAT CLEANSES THE LIVER!
ADJUST THE AMOUNT BASED ON THE DOG'S HEALTH AN' WEIGHT.
WHILE THE BROTH IS GOING, CHOP THE OTHER INGREDIENTS.
INCORPORATE DIETARY FIBERS AND VITAMINS TOO.
ADD YER INGREDIENTS, STARTING WITH THE ONES THAT TAKE LONGER TO COOK.

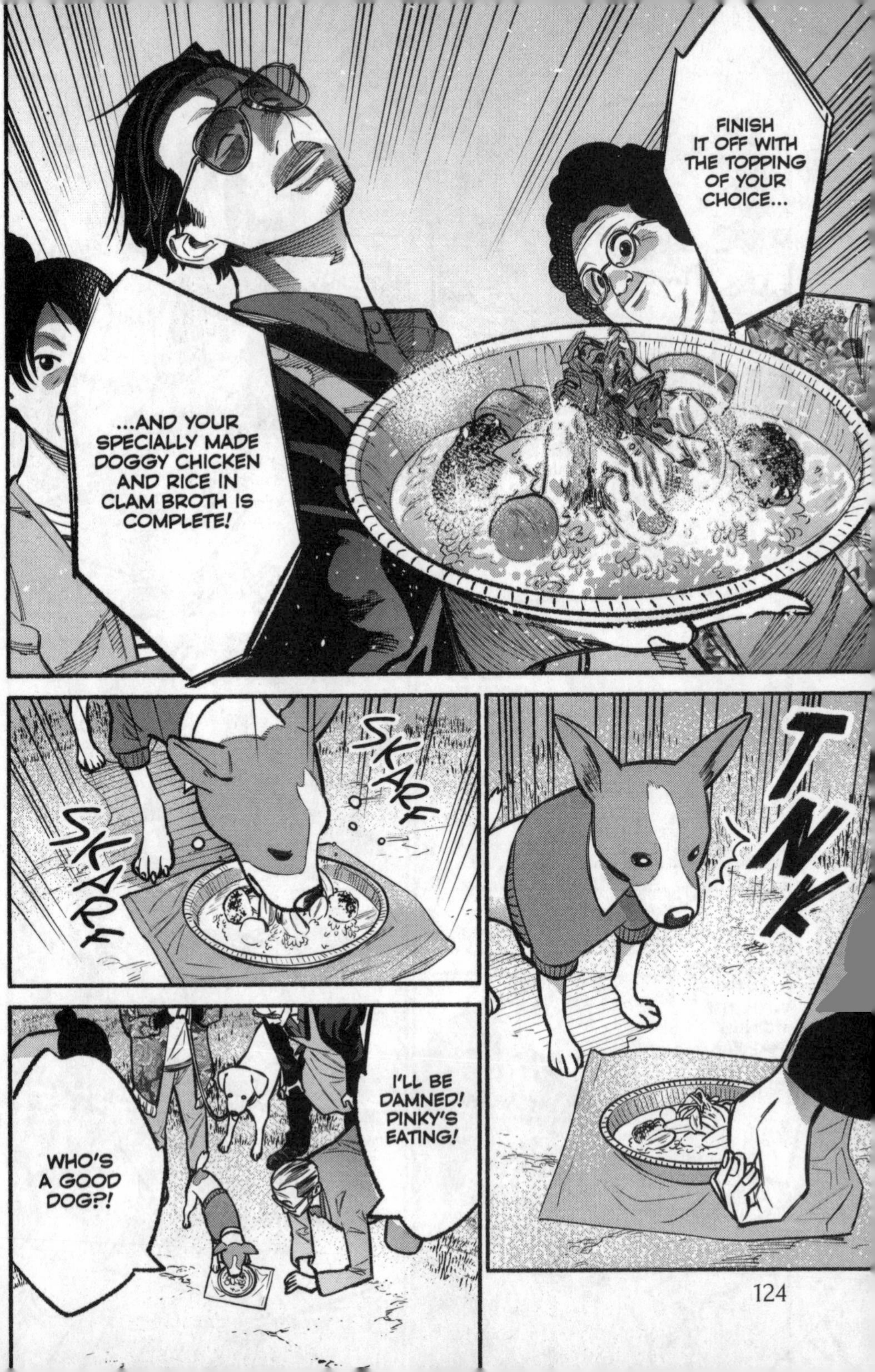
FINISH IT OFF WITH THE TOPPING OF YOUR CHOICE...
...AND YOUR SPECIALLY MADE DOGGY CHICKEN AND RICE IN CLAM BROTH IS COMPLETE!
TNK
SKARF
SKARF
I'LL BE DAMNED! PINKY'S EATING!
WHO'S A GOOD DOG?!

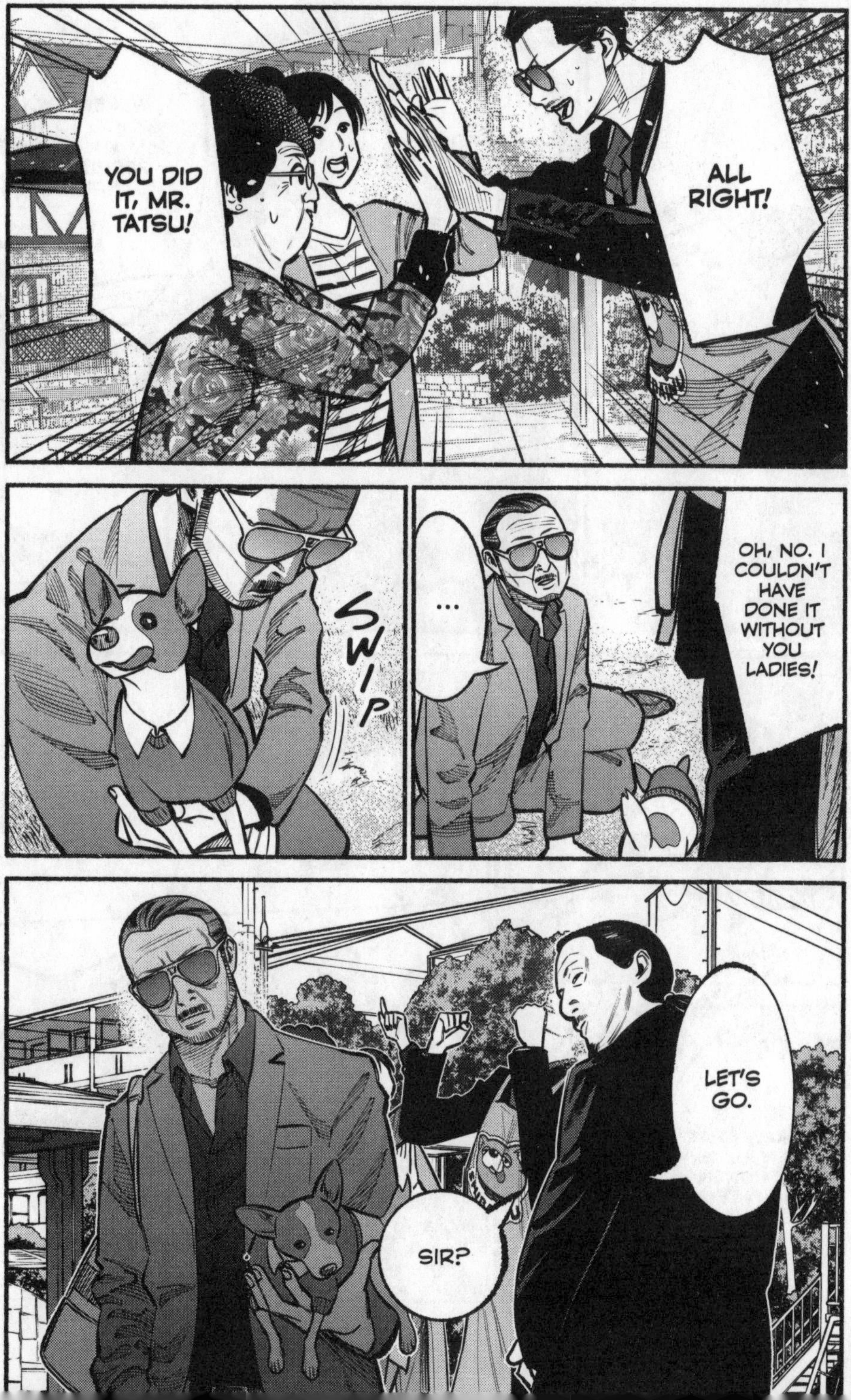
ALL RIGHT!
YOU DID IT, MR. TATSU!
OH, NO. I COULDN'T HAVE DONE IT WITHOUT YOU LADIES!
...
SWIP
LET'S GO.
SIR?

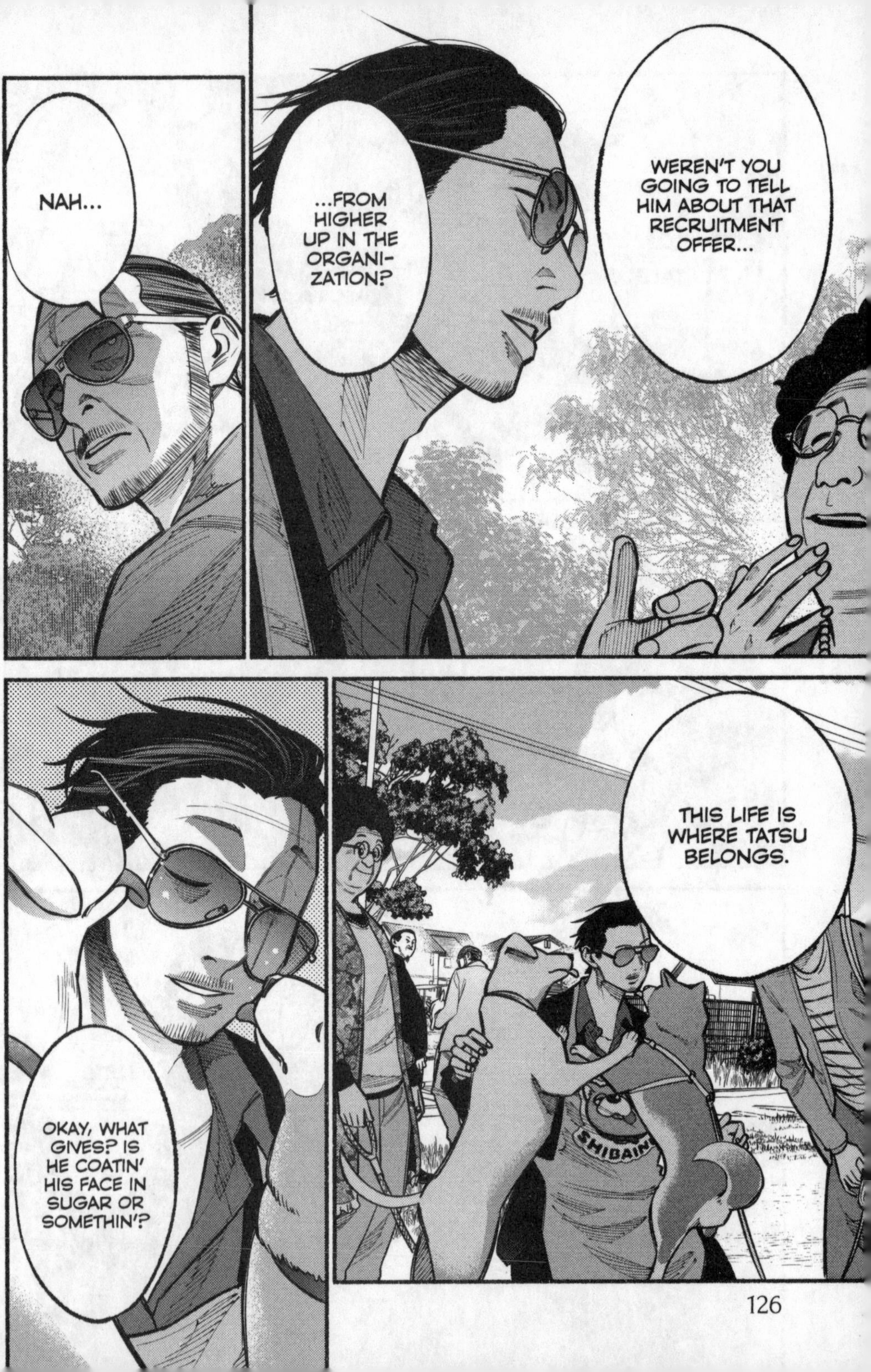
WEREN'T YOU GOING TO TELL HIM ABOUT THAT RECRUITMENT OFFER...
...FROM HIGHER UP IN THE ORGANI-ZATION?
NAH...
THIS LIFE IS WHERE TATSU BELONGS.
OKAY, WHAT GIVES? IS HE COATIN' HIS FACE IN SUGAR OR SOMETHIN'?
SHIBAIN

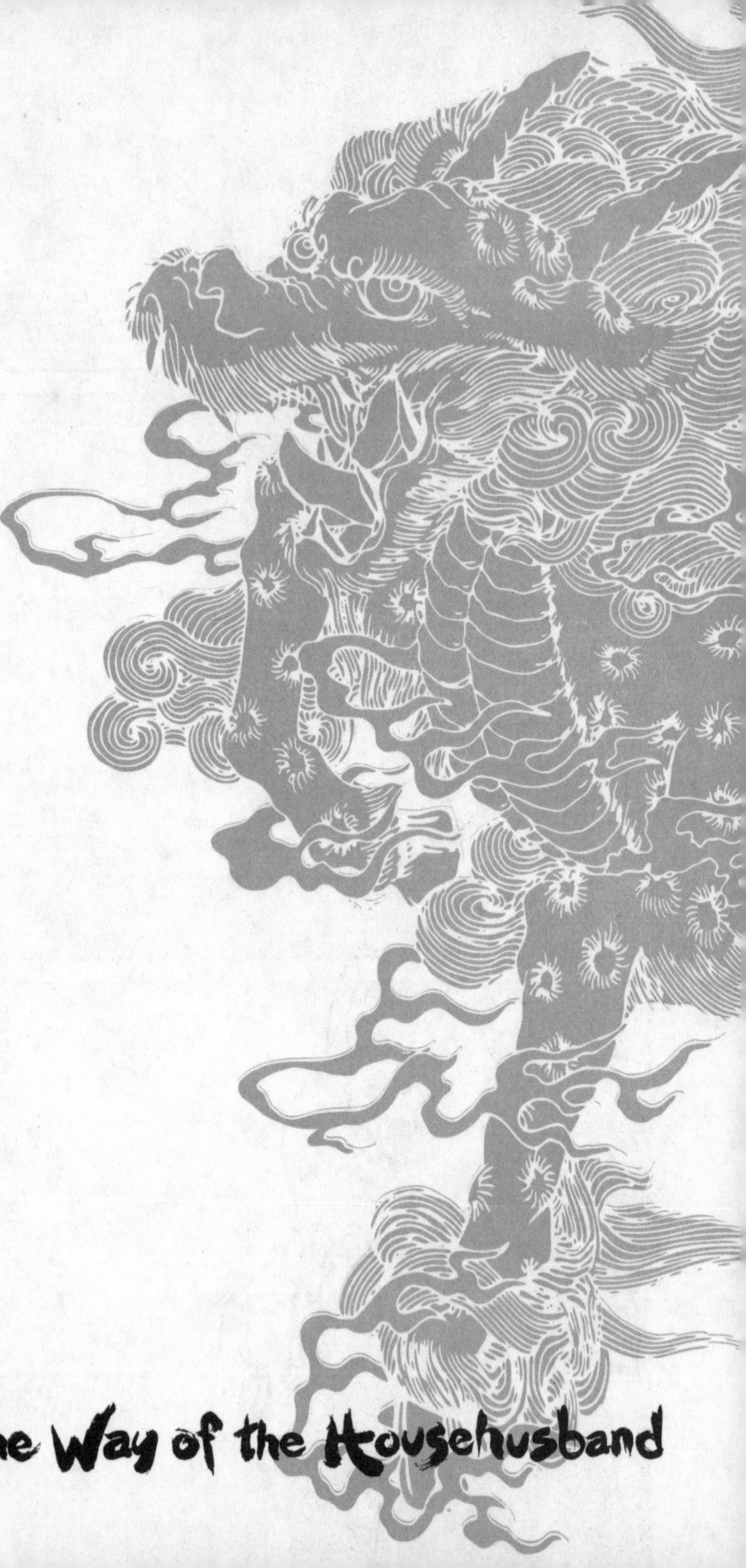

The Way of the Househusband

DING DONG

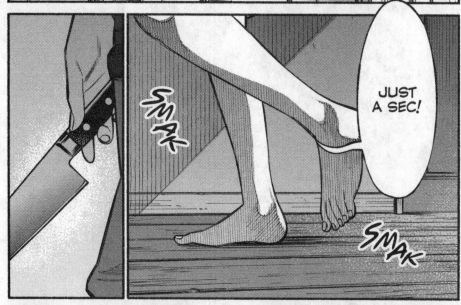

SMAK

SMAK

JUST A SEC!

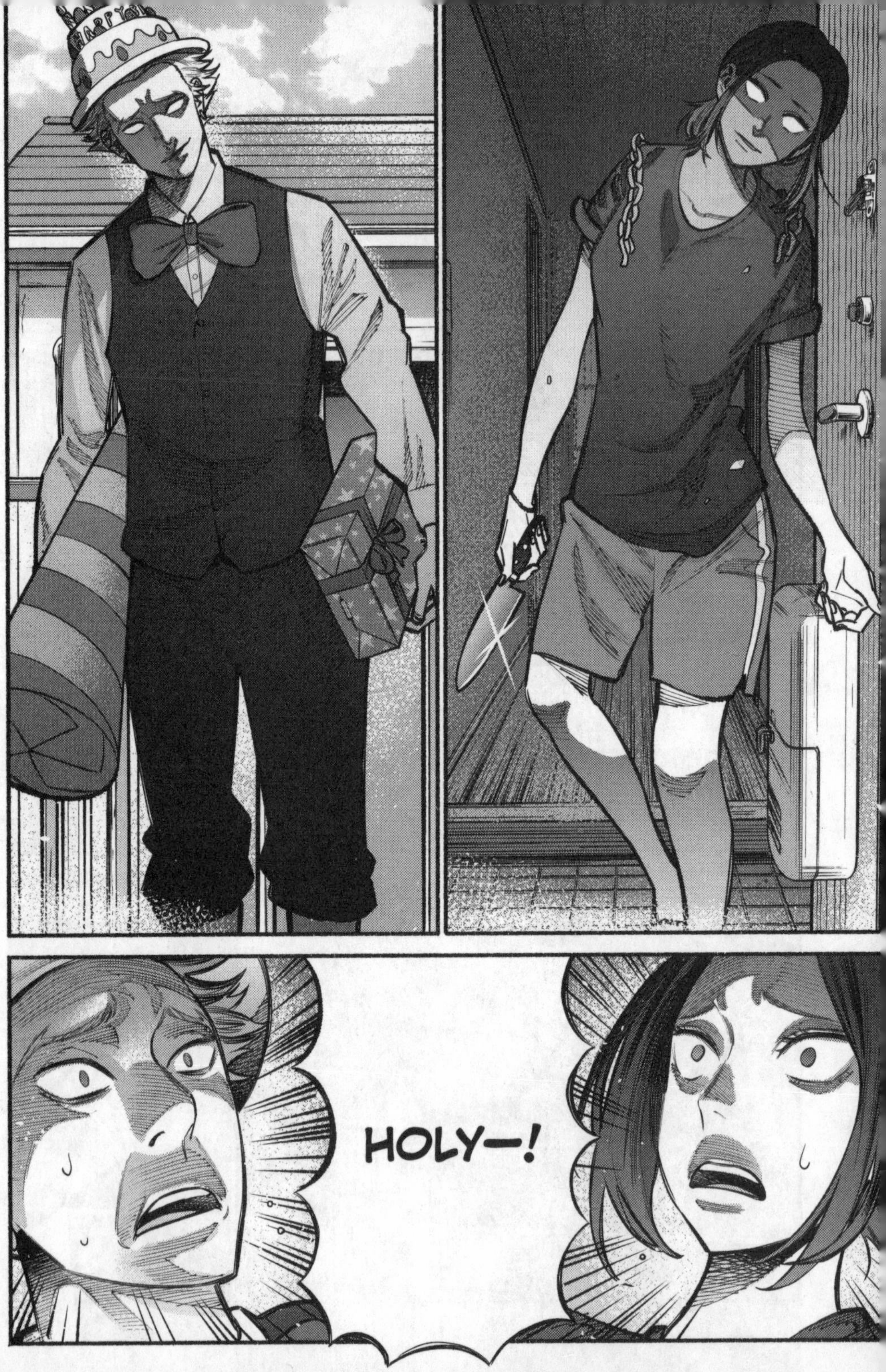
HOLY—!

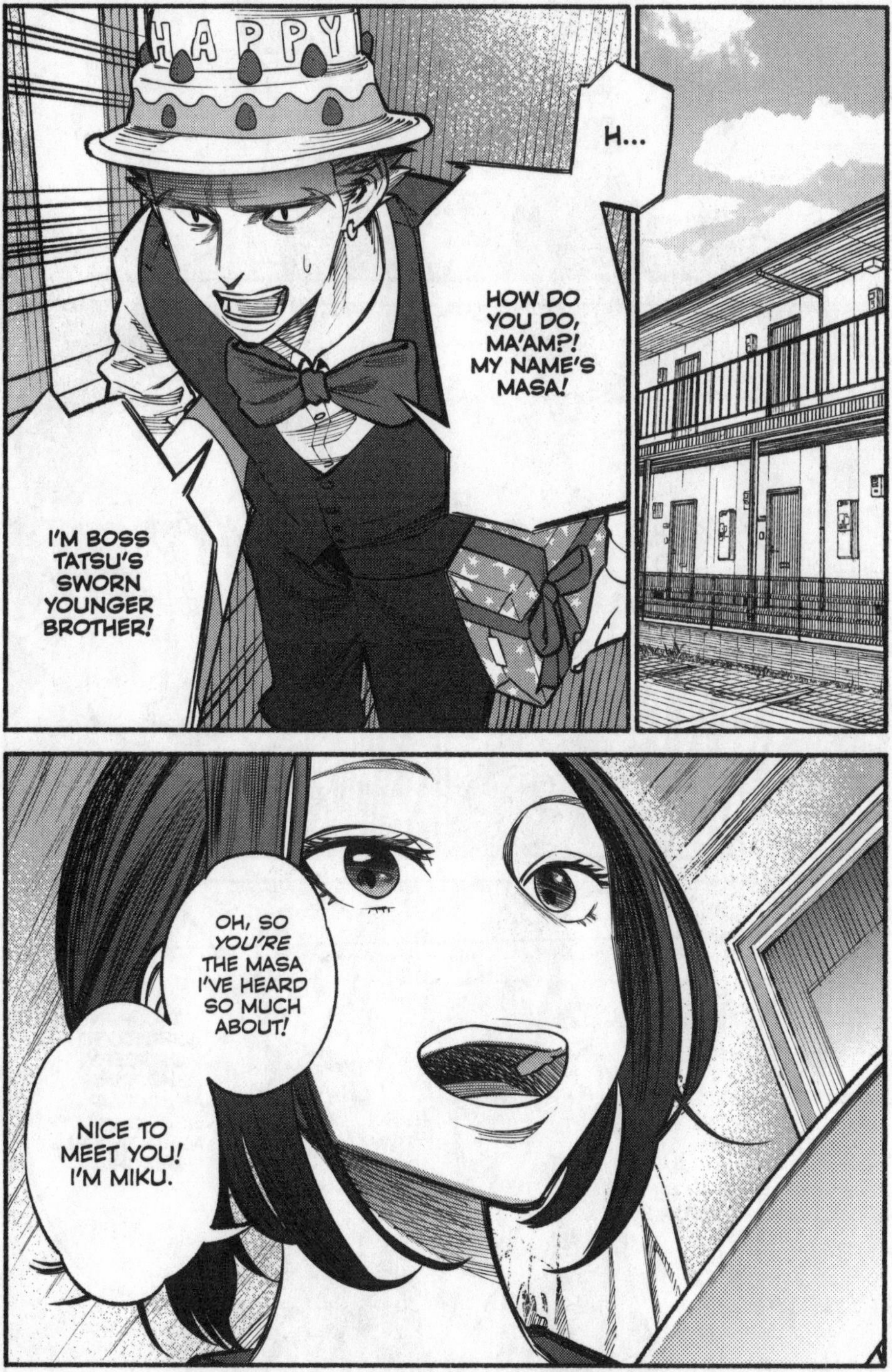
H...
HOW DO YOU DO, MA'AM?! MY NAME'S MASA!
I'M BOSS TATSU'S SWORN YOUNGER BROTHER!
OH, SO *YOU'RE* THE MASA I'VE HEARD SO MUCH ABOUT!
NICE TO MEET YOU! I'M MIKU.

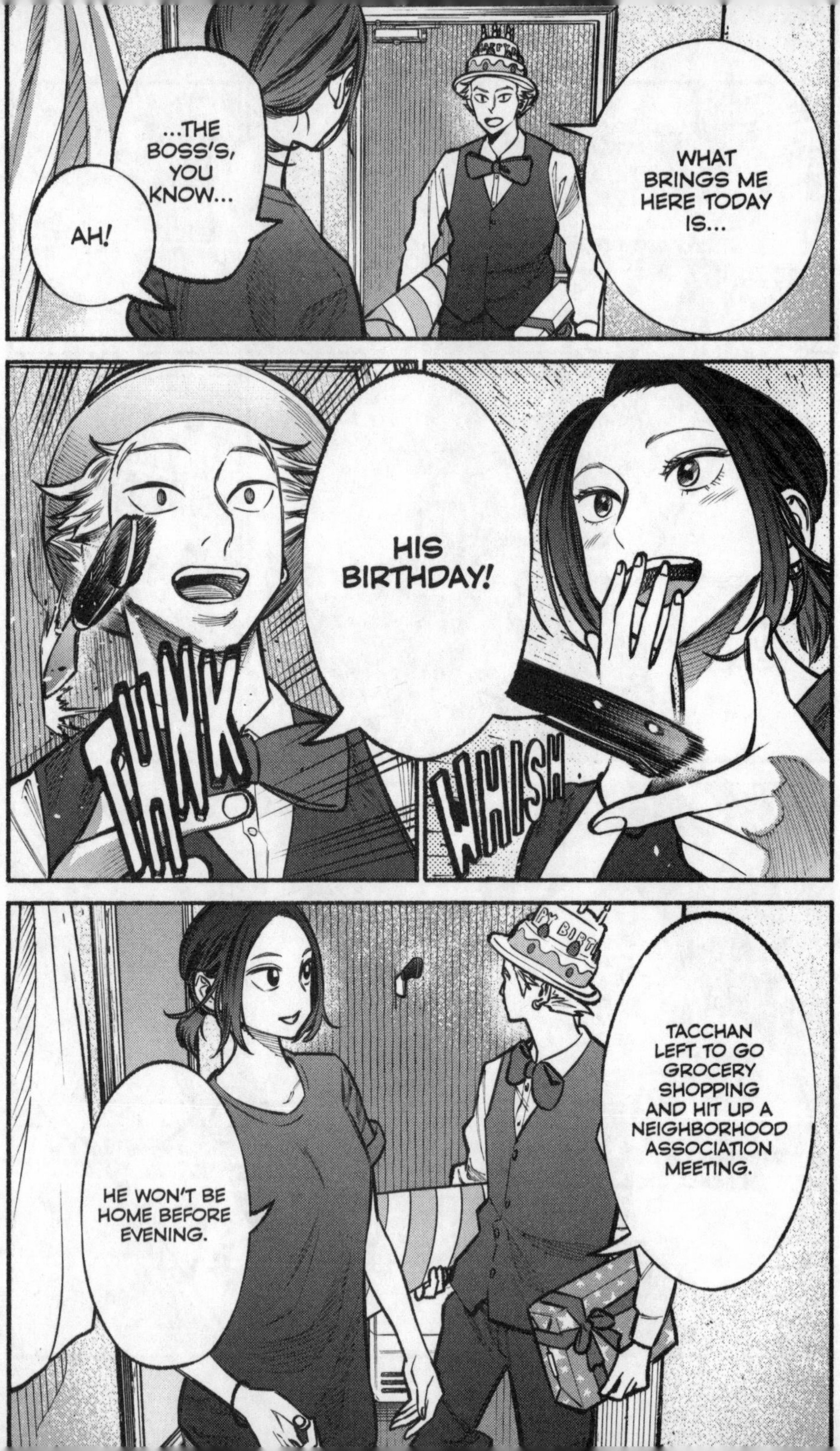
WHAT BRINGS ME HERE TODAY IS...
...THE BOSS'S, YOU KNOW...
AH!
WHISH
HIS BIRTHDAY!
THWK
TACCHAN LEFT TO GO GROCERY SHOPPING AND HIT UP A NEIGHBORHOOD ASSOCIATION MEETING.
HE WON'T BE HOME BEFORE EVENING.

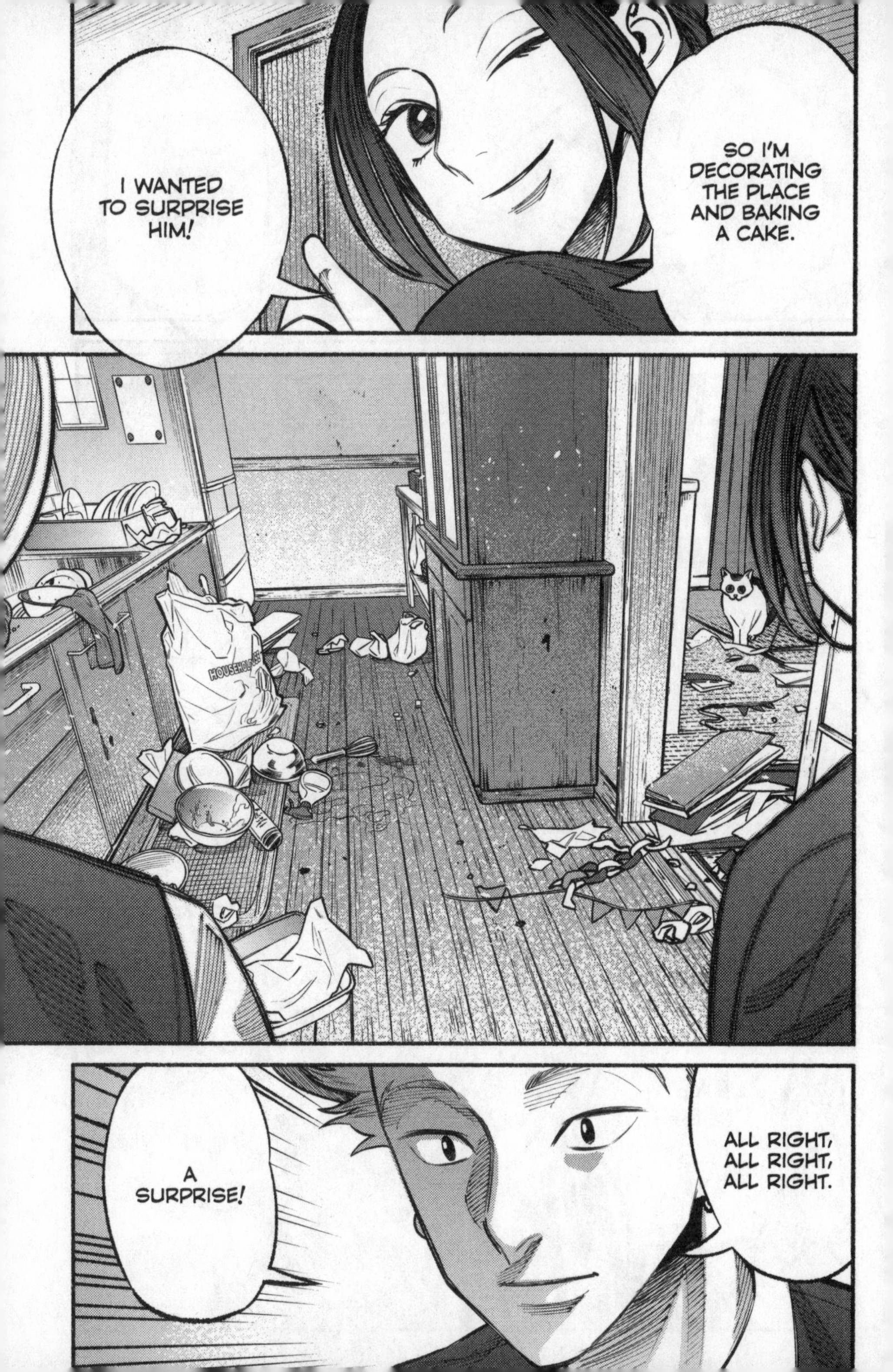
SO I'M DECORATING THE PLACE AND BAKING A CAKE.
I WANTED TO SURPRISE HIM!
ALL RIGHT, ALL RIGHT, ALL RIGHT.
A SURPRISE!

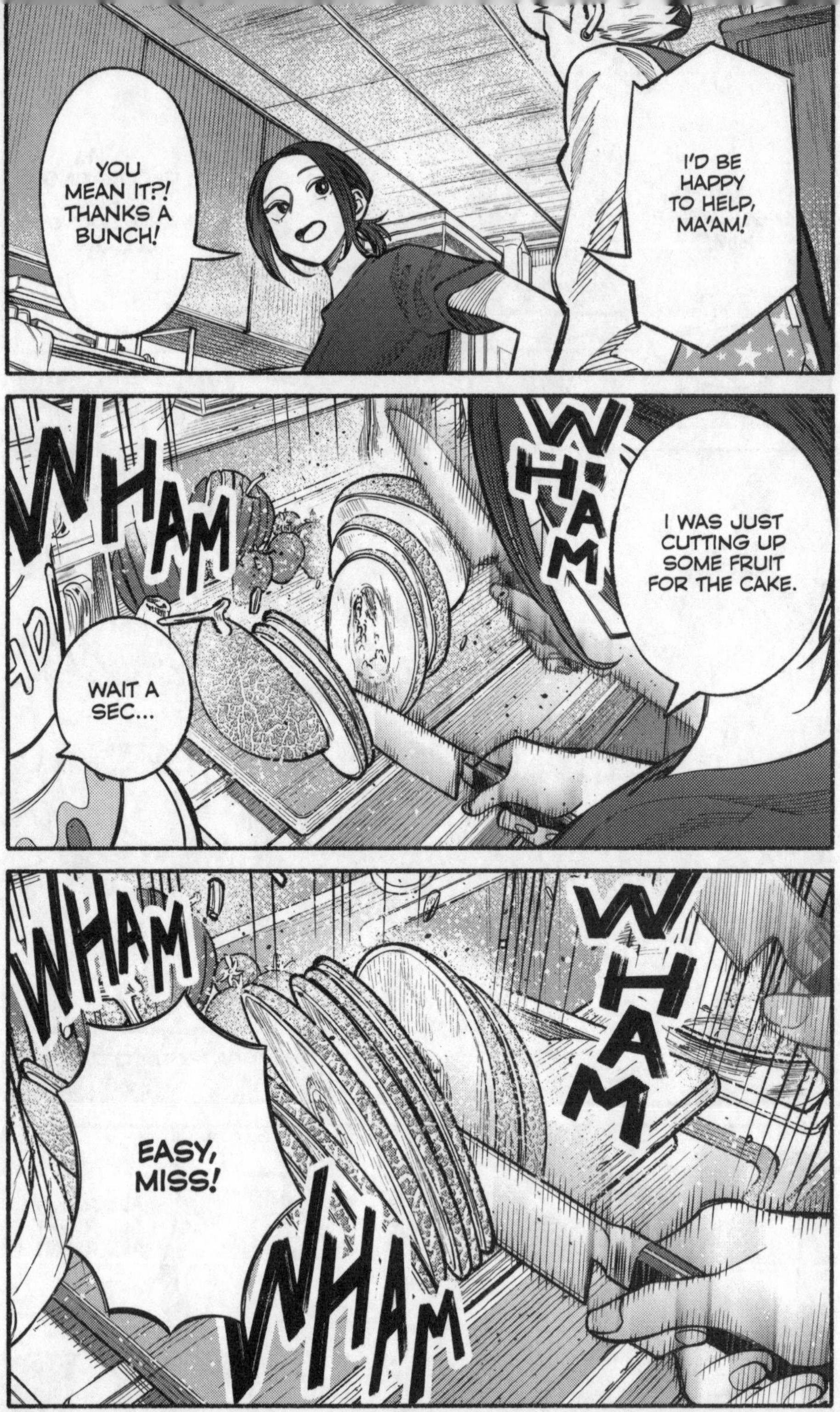
I'D BE HAPPY TO HELP, MA'AM!
YOU MEAN IT?! THANKS A BUNCH!
WHAM
I WAS JUST CUTTING UP SOME FRUIT FOR THE CAKE.
WHAM
WAIT A SEC...
WHAM
WHAM
EASY, MISS!
WHAM

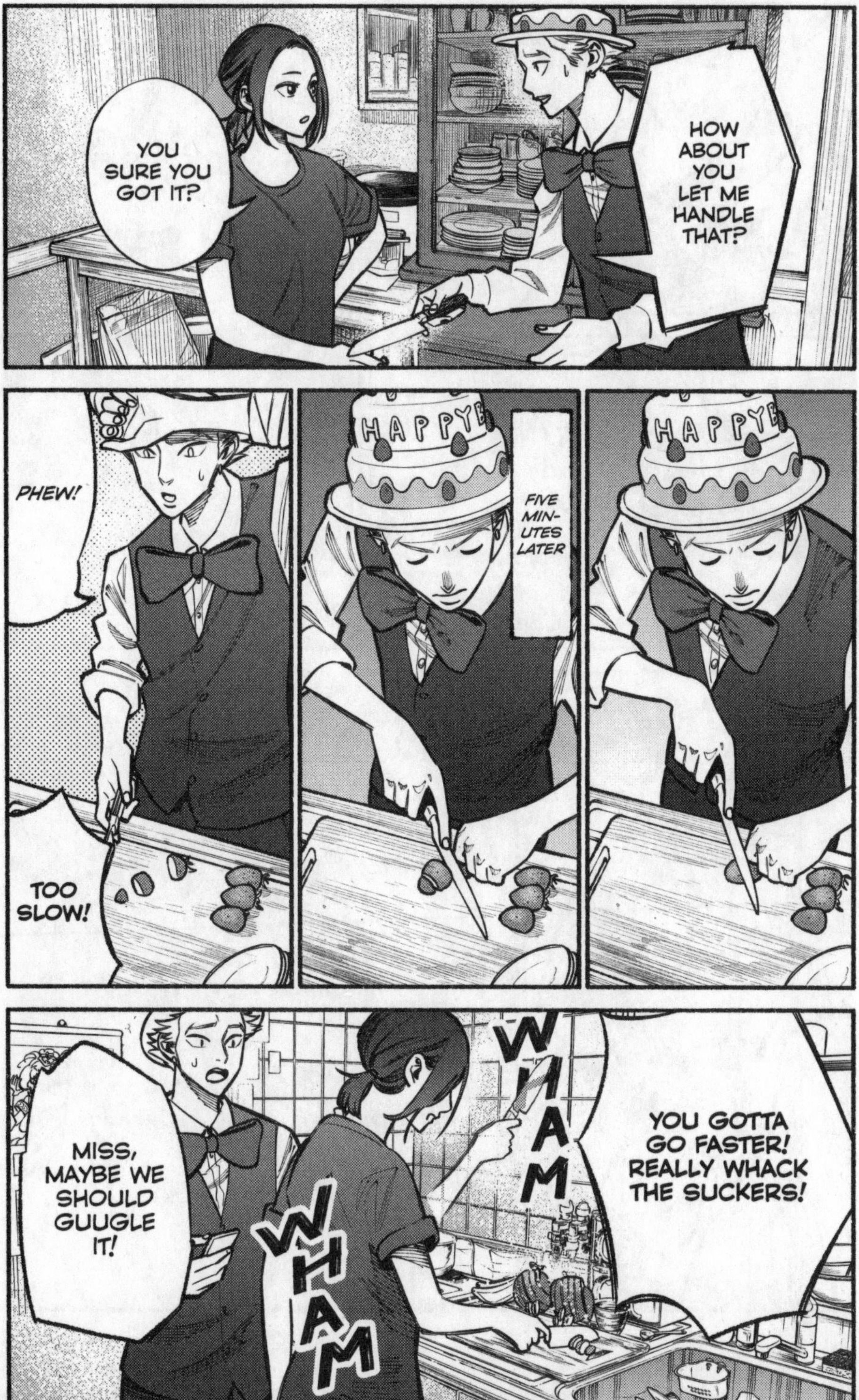
HOW ABOUT YOU LET ME HANDLE THAT?
YOU SURE YOU GOT IT?
FIVE MINUTES LATER
PHEW!
TOO SLOW!
WHAM
YOU GOTTA GO FASTER! REALLY WHACK THE SUCKERS!
WHAM
MISS, MAYBE WE SHOULD GUUGLE IT!

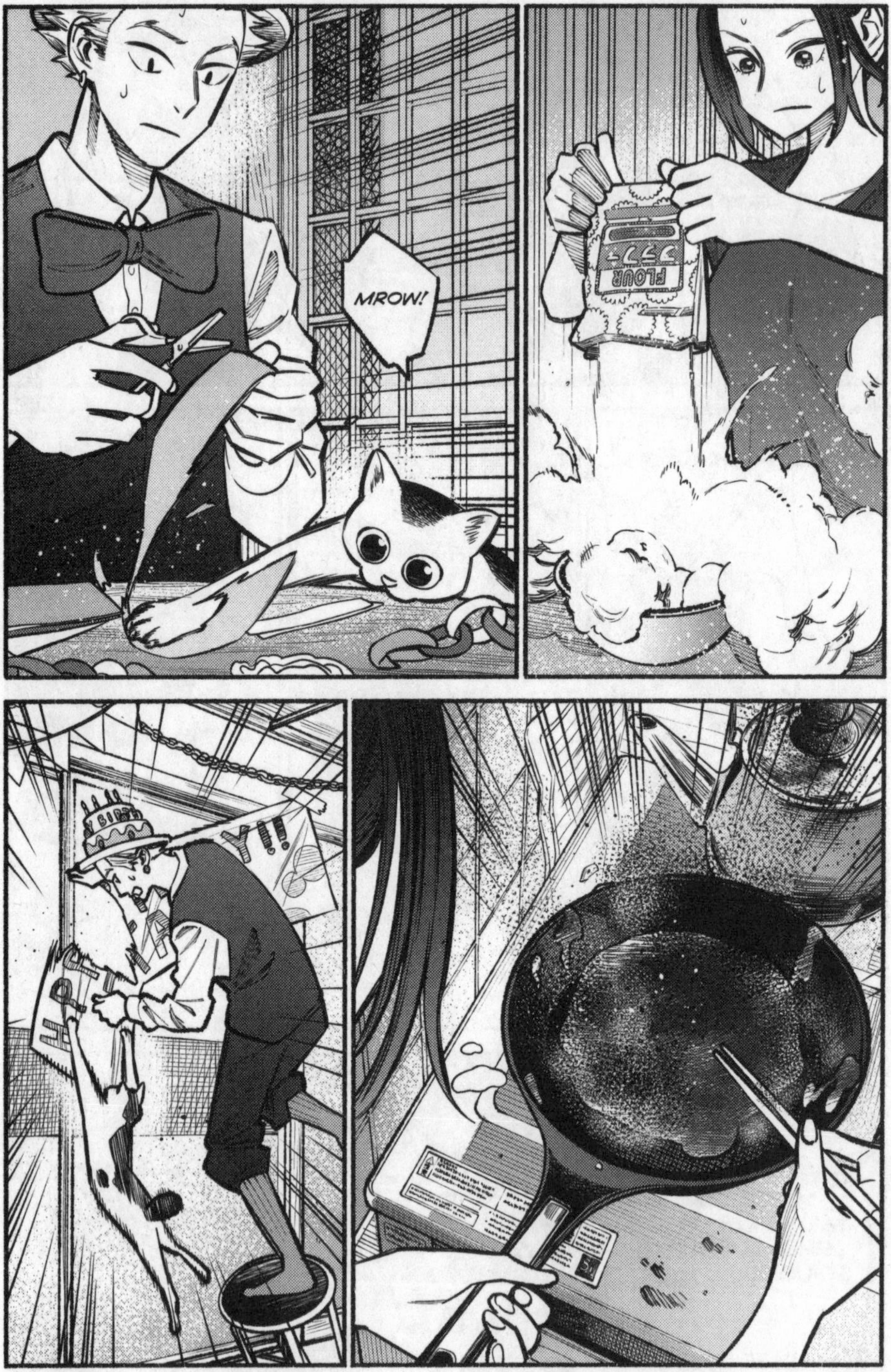
FLOUR
MROW!

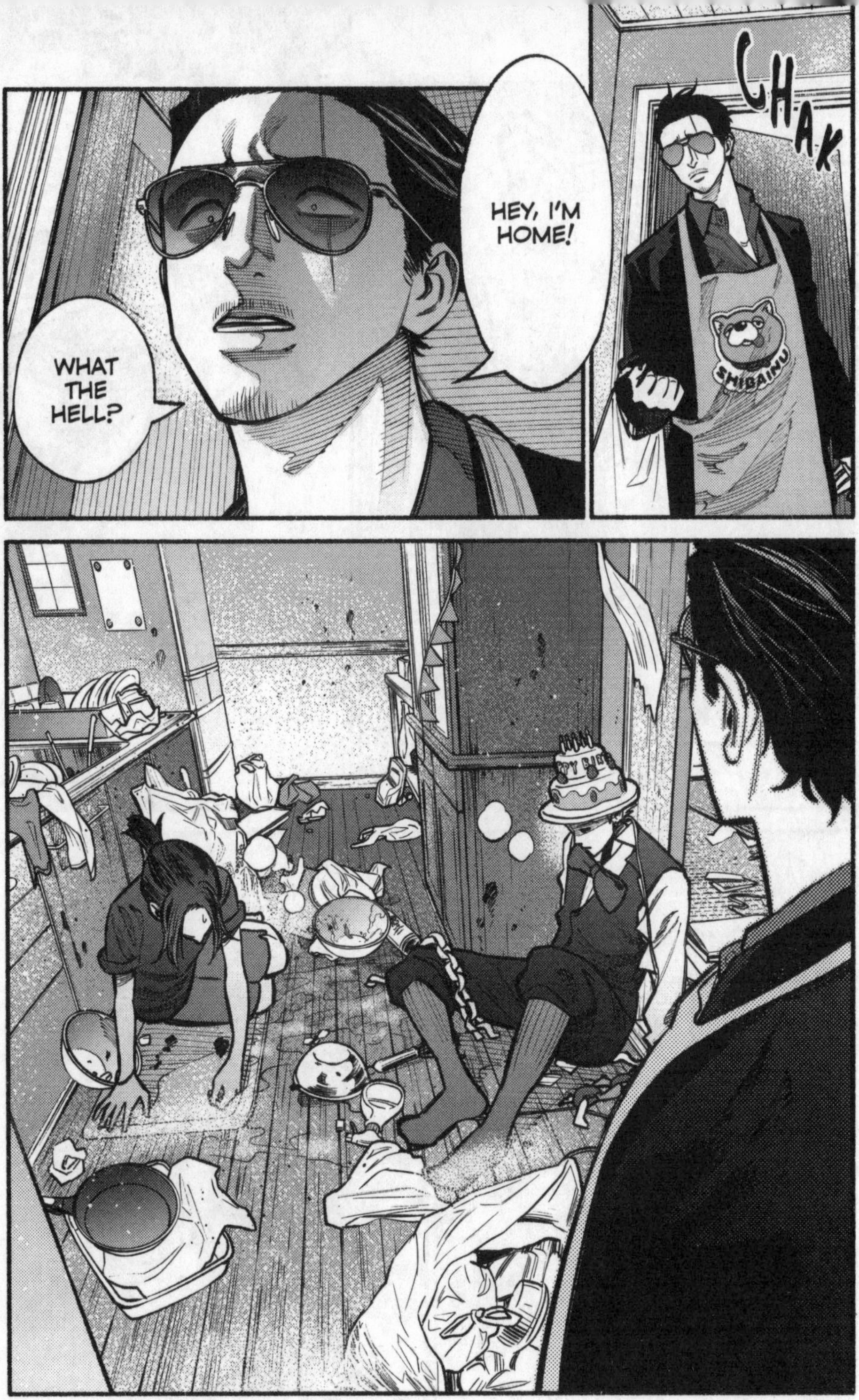
CHAK
SHIBAINU
HEY, I'M HOME!
WHAT THE HELL?

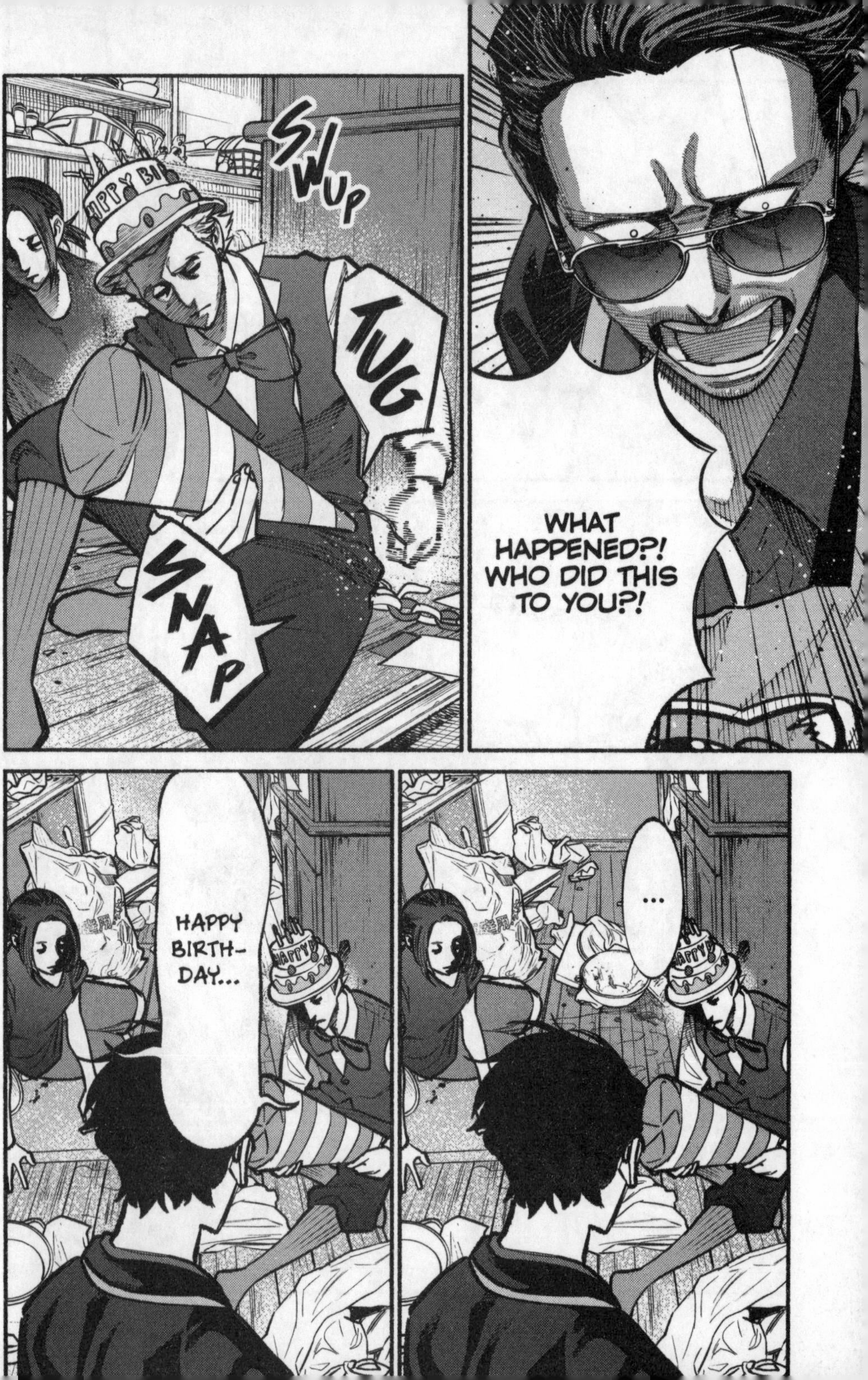
WHAT HAPPENED?! WHO DID THIS TO YOU?!
SWUP
TUG
SNAP
...
HAPPY BIRTH-DAY...

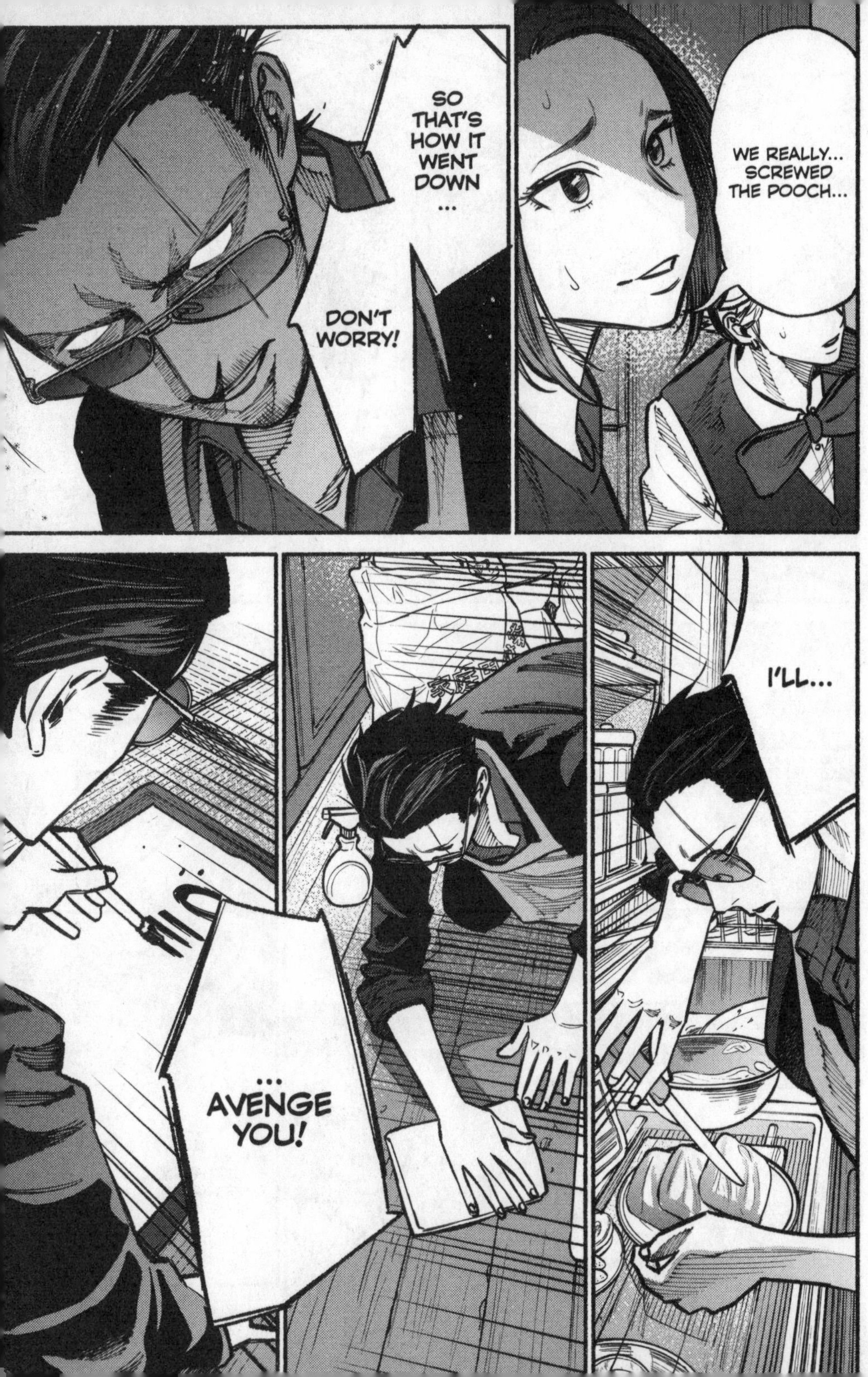
WE REALLY... SCREWED THE POOCH...
SO THAT'S HOW IT WENT DOWN ...
DON'T WORRY!
I'LL...
... AVENGE YOU!

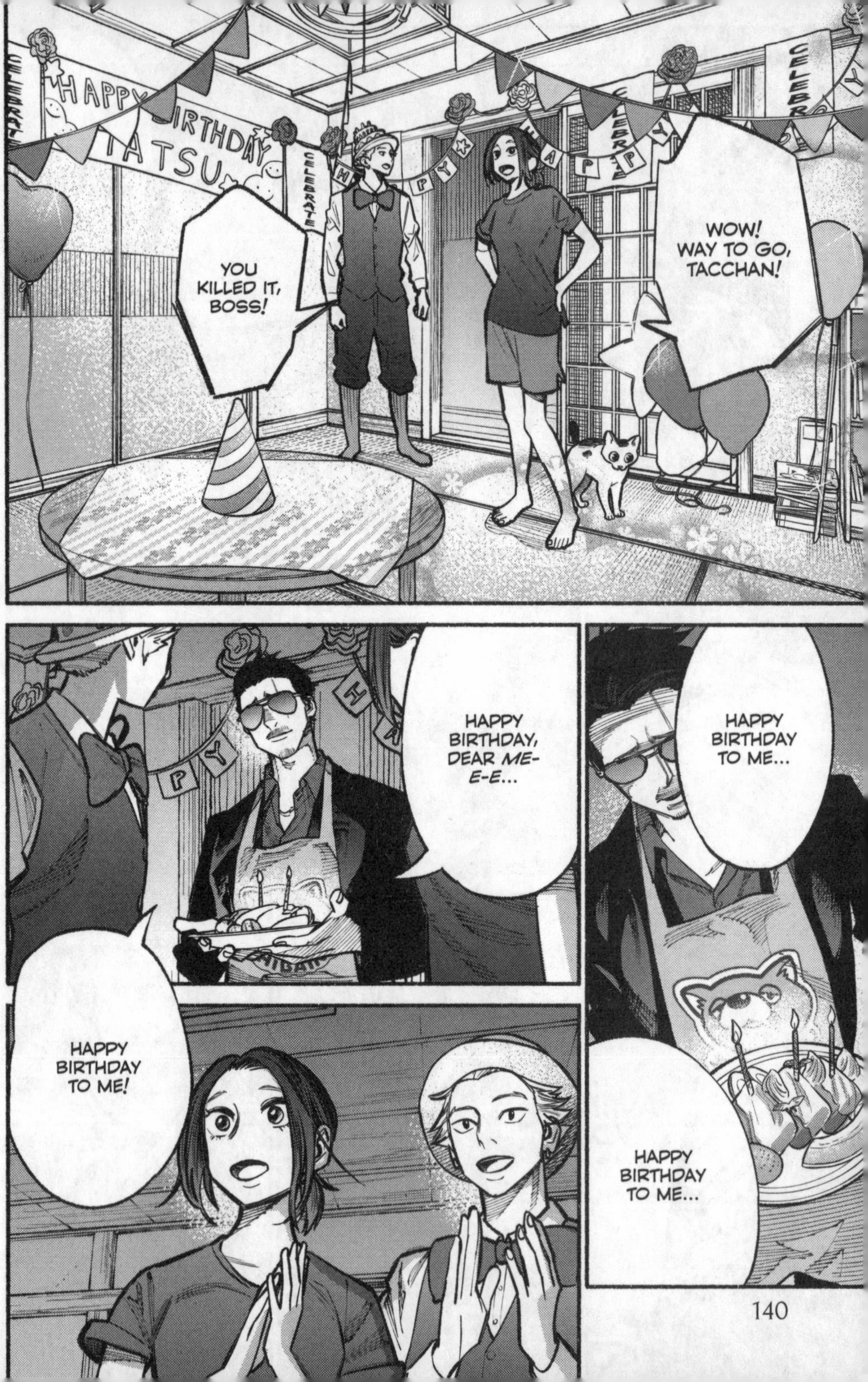
HAPPY BIRTHDAY TATSU
WOW! WAY TO GO, TACCHAN!
YOU KILLED IT, BOSS!
HAPPY BIRTHDAY TO ME...
HAPPY BIRTHDAY TO ME...
HAPPY BIRTHDAY, DEAR ME-E-E...
HAPPY BIRTHDAY TO ME!

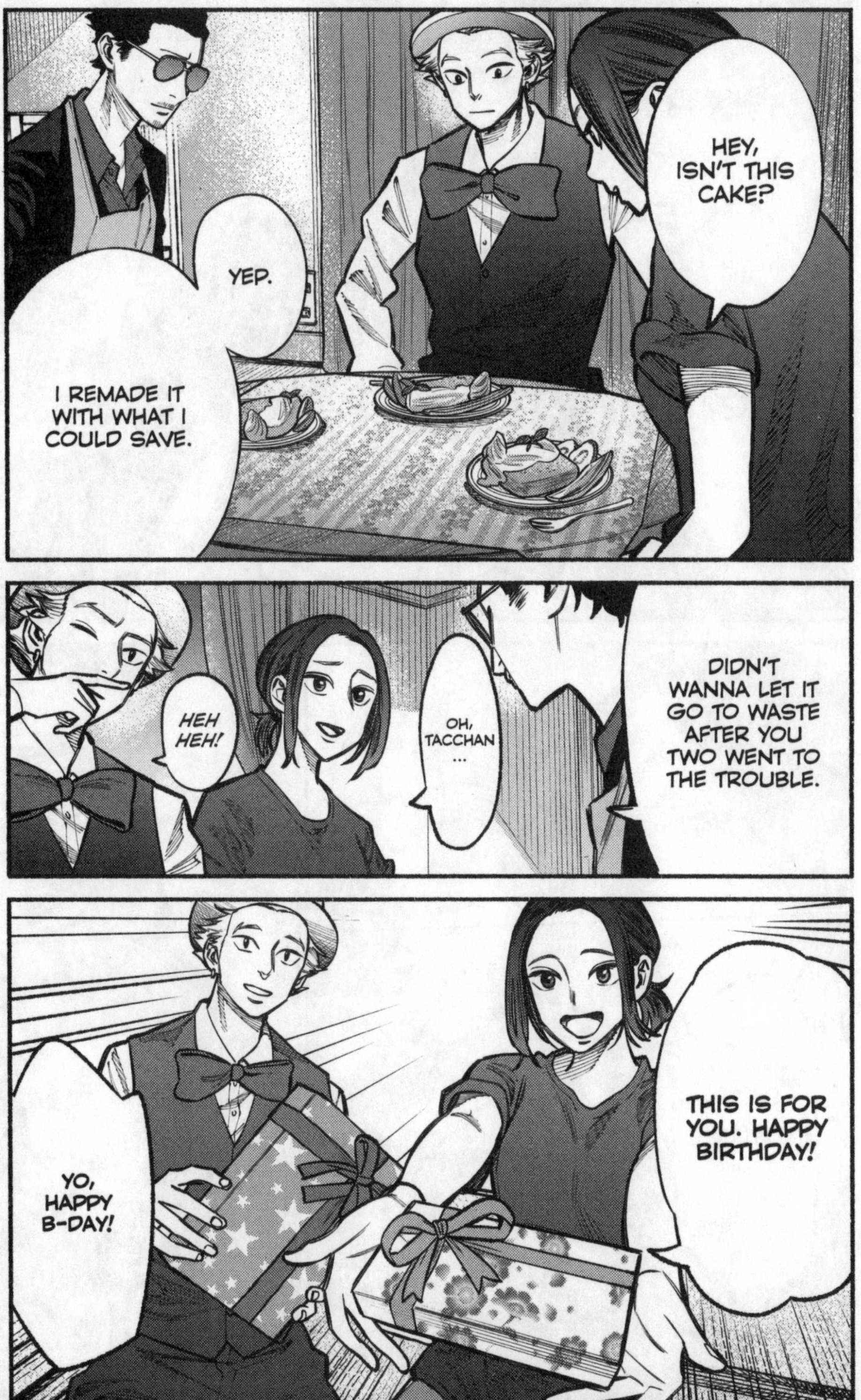
HEY, ISN'T THIS CAKE?
YEP.
I REMADE IT WITH WHAT I COULD SAVE.
DIDN'T WANNA LET IT GO TO WASTE AFTER YOU TWO WENT TO THE TROUBLE.
OH, TACCHAN...
HEH HEH!
THIS IS FOR YOU. HAPPY BIRTHDAY!
YO, HAPPY B-DAY!

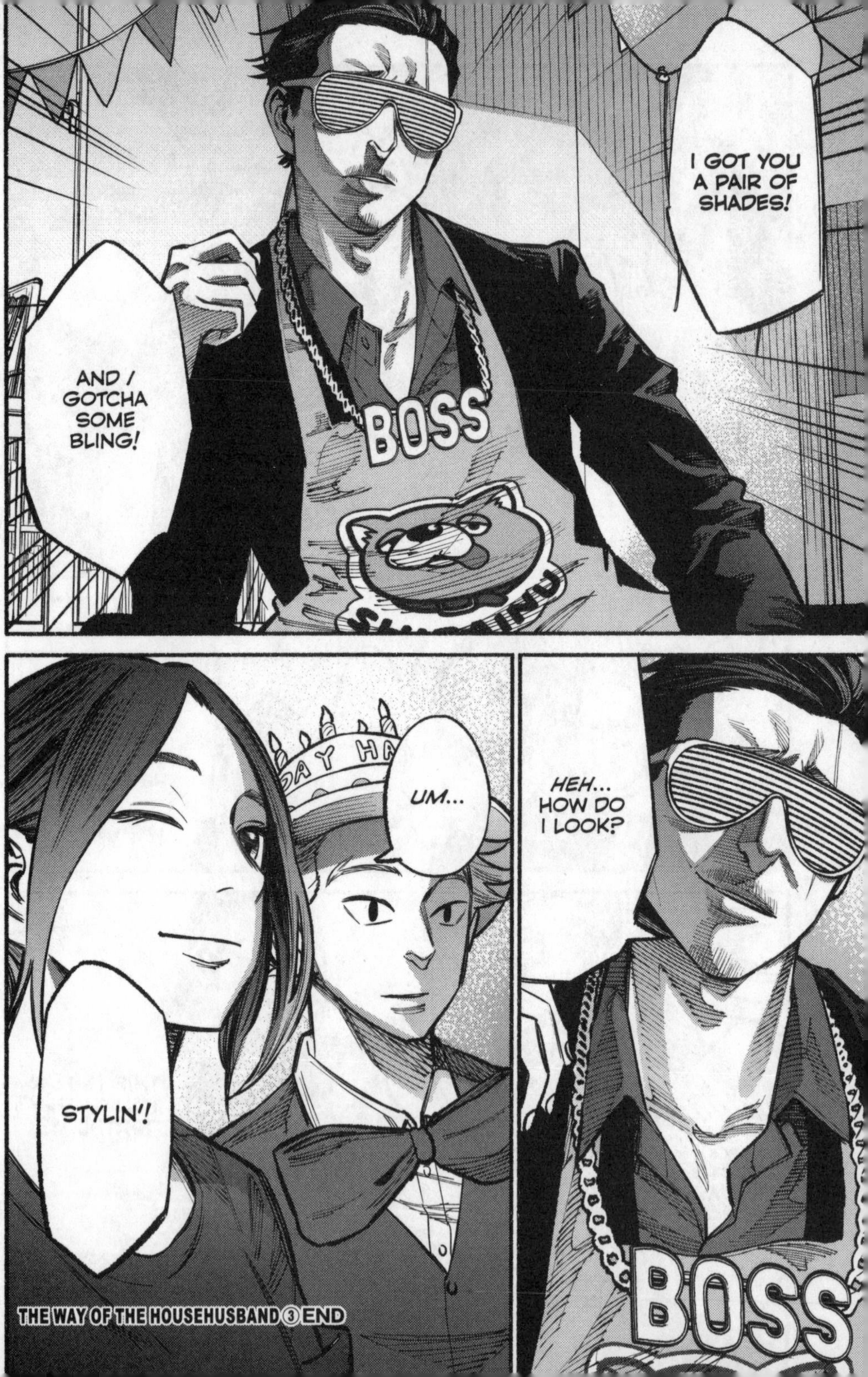
I GOT YOU A PAIR OF SHADES!
AND I GOTCHA SOME BLING!
BOSS
HEH... HOW DO I LOOK?
BOSS
UM...
STYLIN'!
THE WAY OF THE HOUSEHUSBAND 3 END

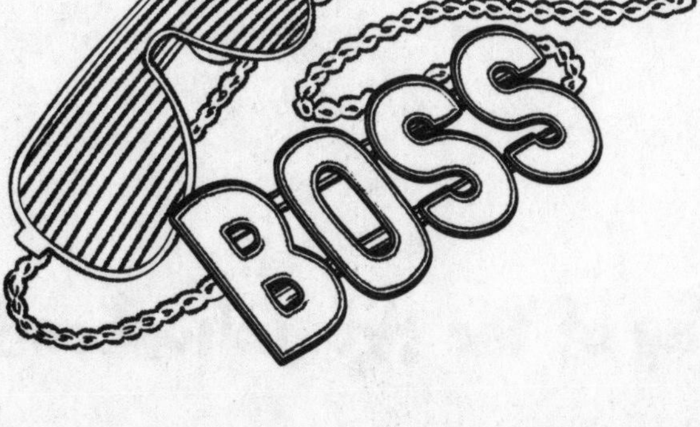
BOSS

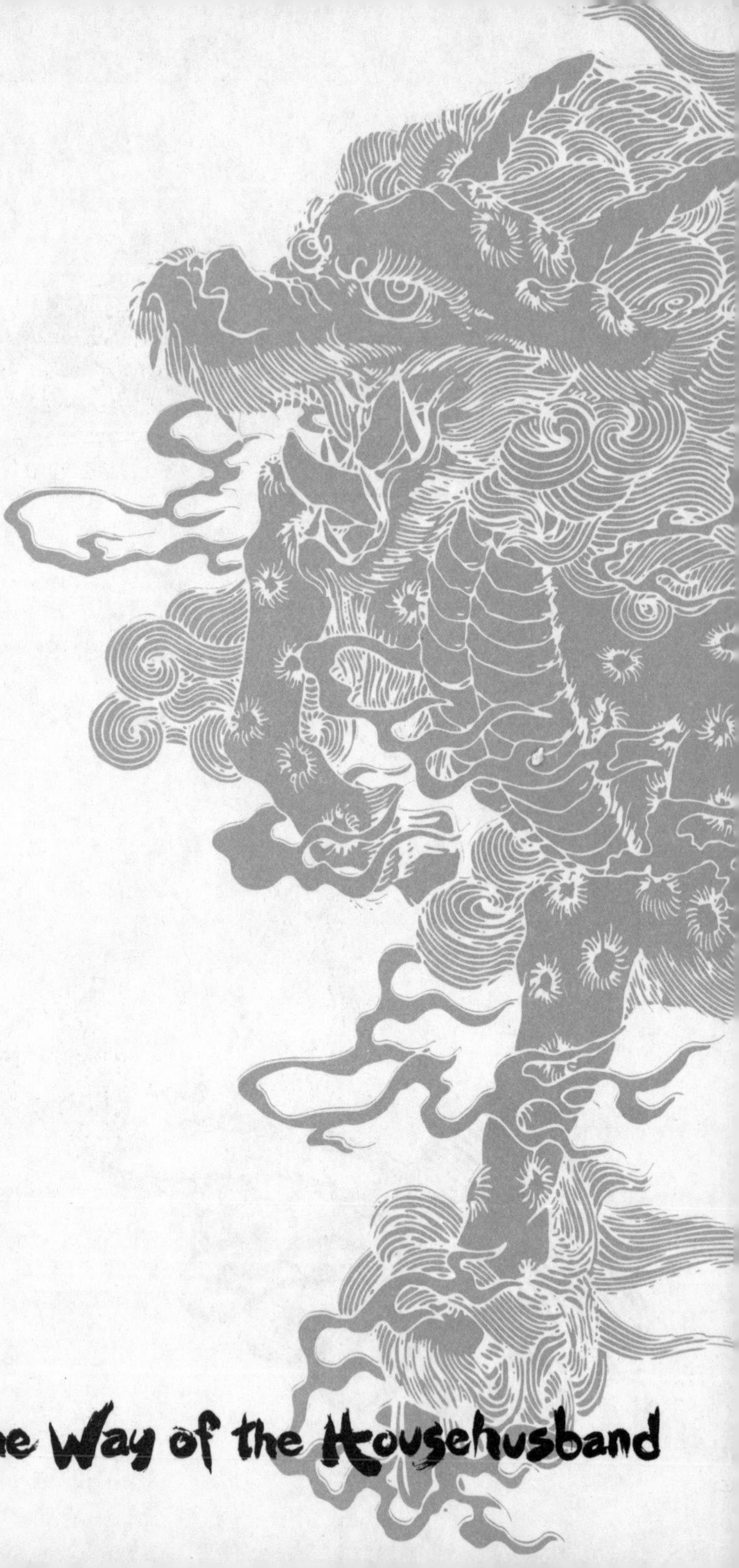

The Way of the Househusband

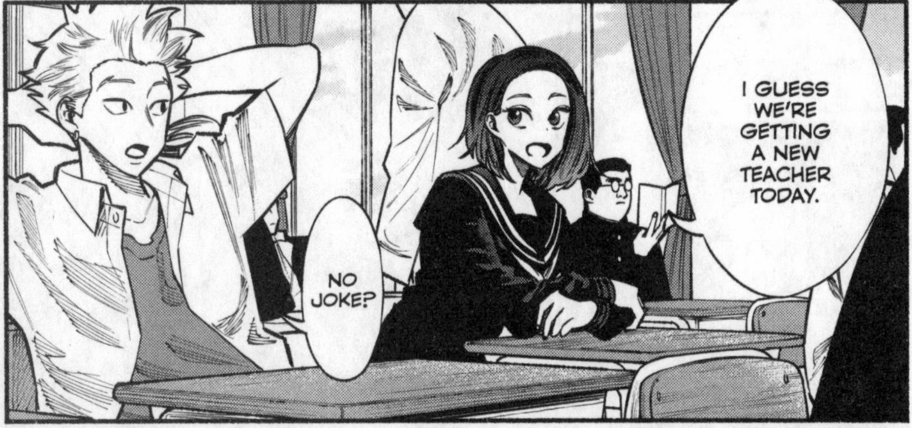
I GUESS WE'RE GETTING A NEW TEACHER TODAY.
NO JOKE?

THIRD-YEAR DRAGON CLASS

HOUSEHUSBAND SENSEI

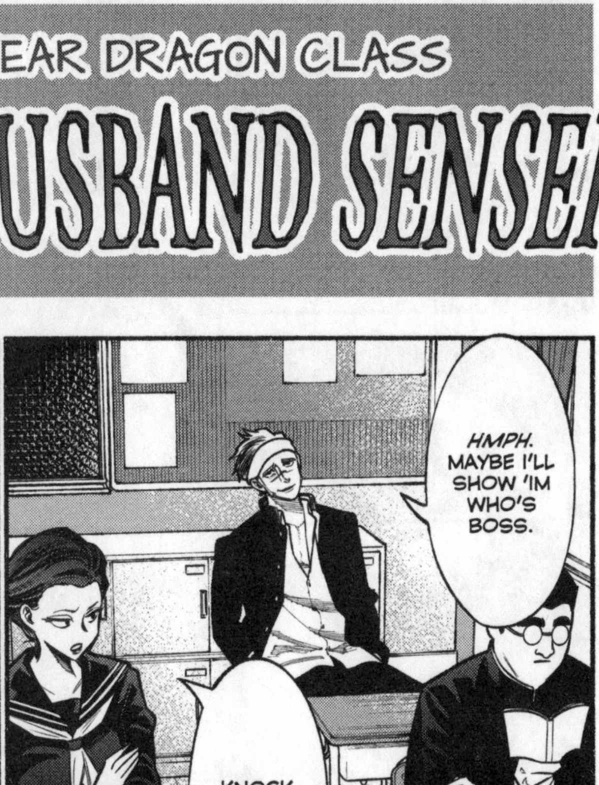
HMPH. MAYBE I'LL SHOW 'IM WHO'S BOSS.
KNOCK IT OFF.

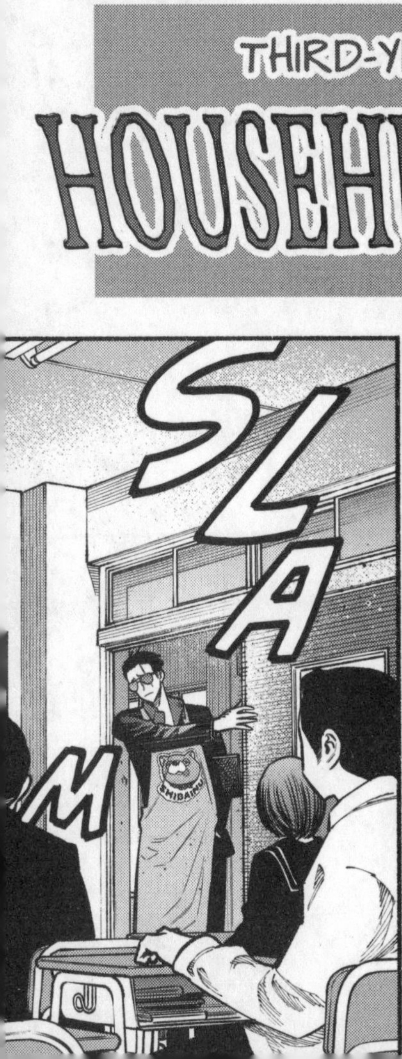
SLAM

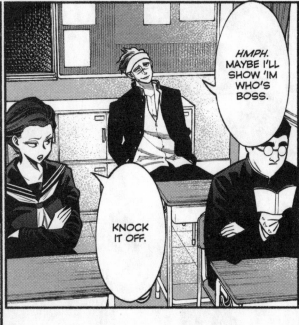

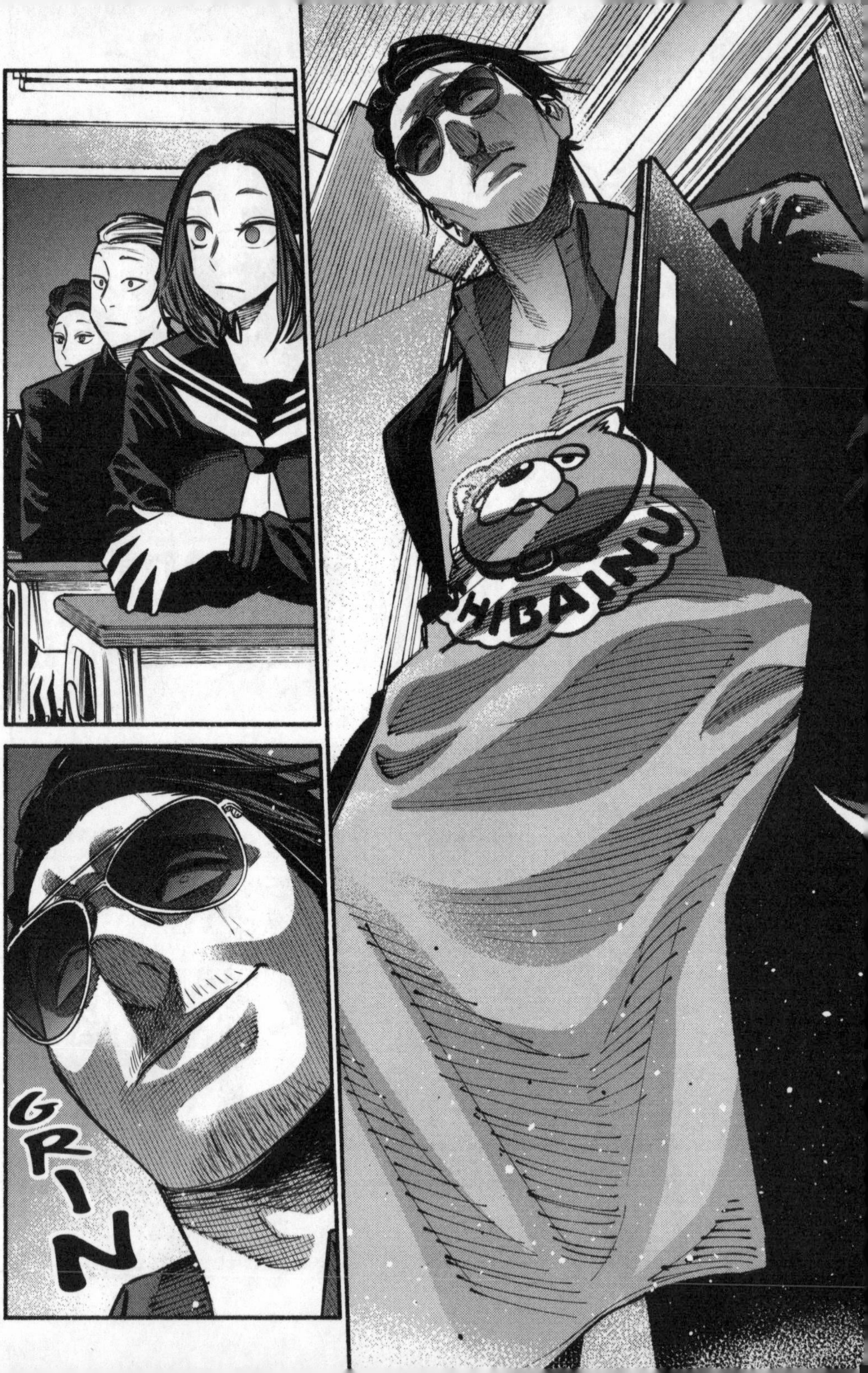
SHIBAINU
GRIN

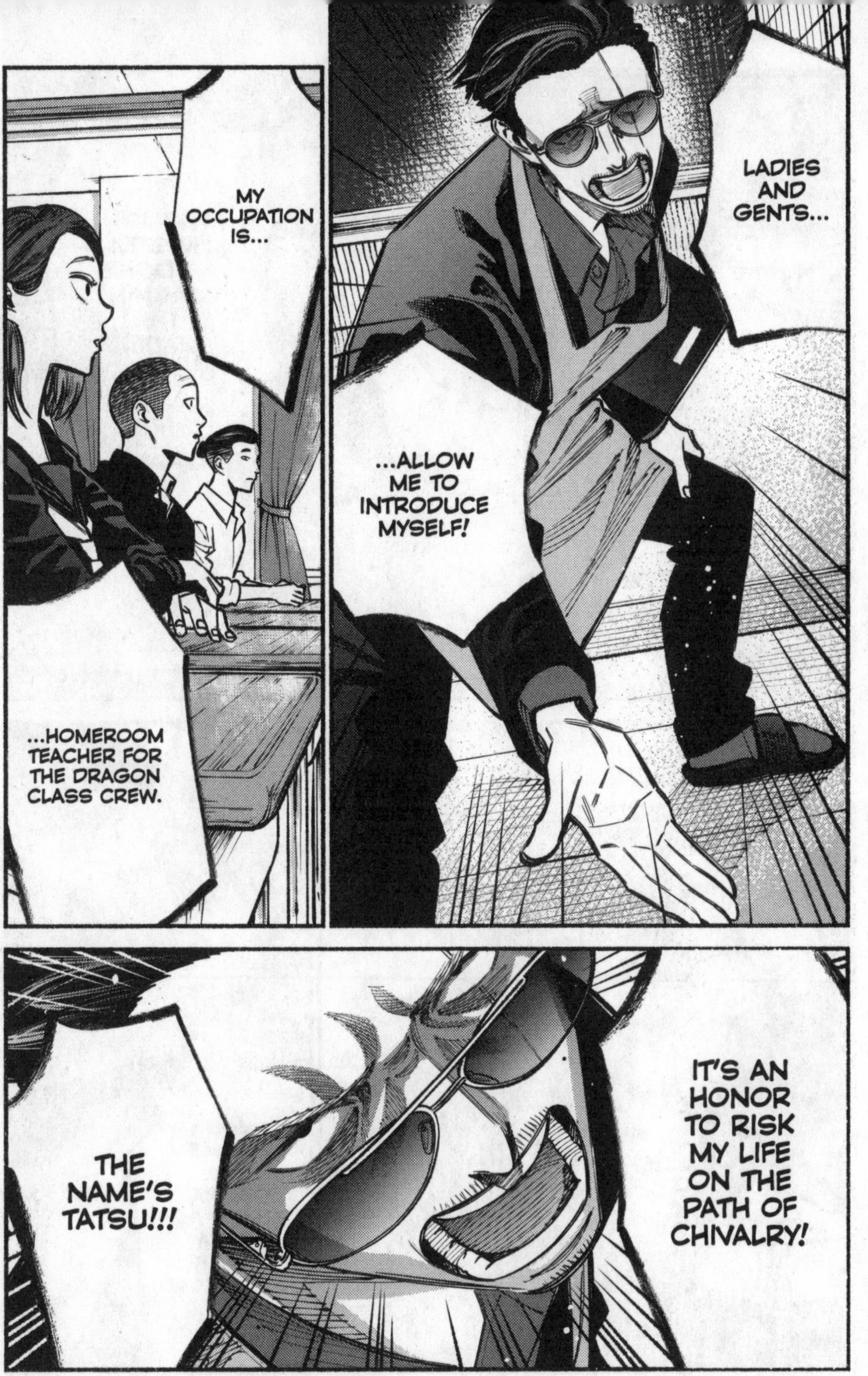
LADIES AND GENTS...
...ALLOW ME TO INTRODUCE MYSELF!
MY OCCUPATION IS...
...HOMEROOM TEACHER FOR THE DRAGON CLASS CREW.
IT'S AN HONOR TO RISK MY LIFE ON THE PATH OF CHIVALRY!
THE NAME'S TATSU!!!

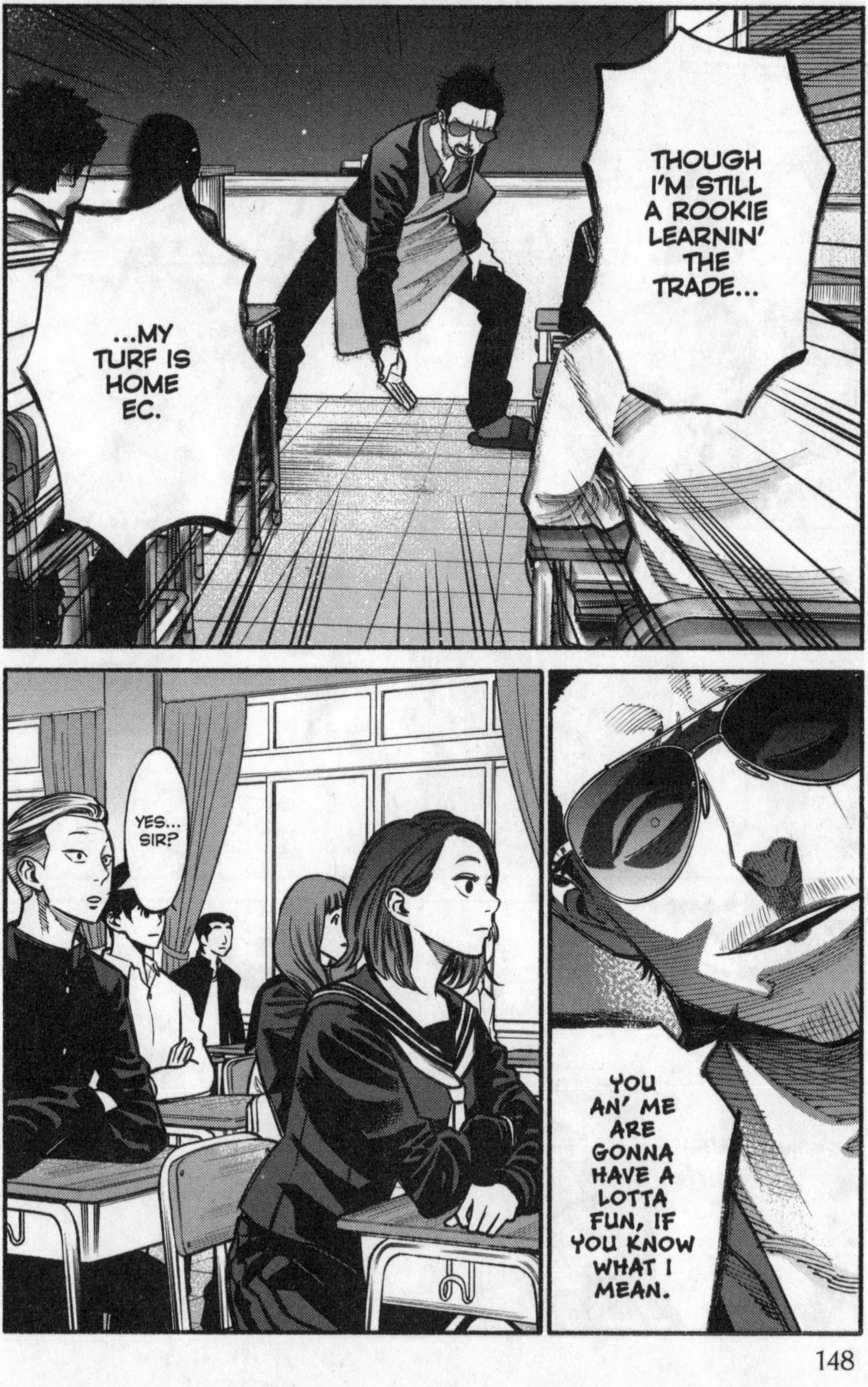
THOUGH I'M STILL A ROOKIE LEARNIN' THE TRADE...
...MY TURF IS HOME EC.
YOU AN' ME ARE GONNA HAVE A LOTTA FUN, IF YOU KNOW WHAT I MEAN.
YES... SIR?

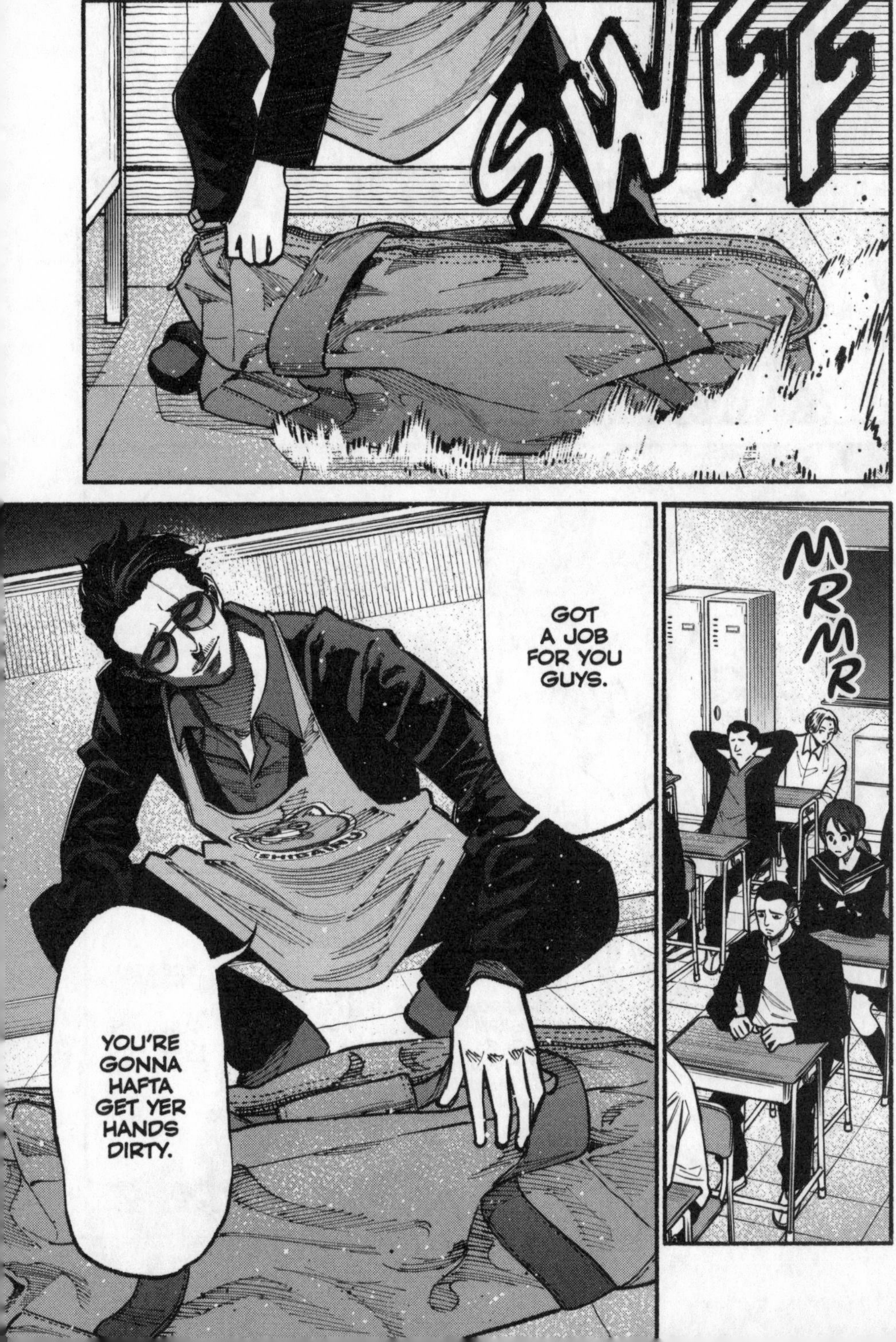
SWFF
MRMR
GOT A JOB FOR YOU GUYS.
YOU'RE GONNA HAFTA GET YER HANDS DIRTY.

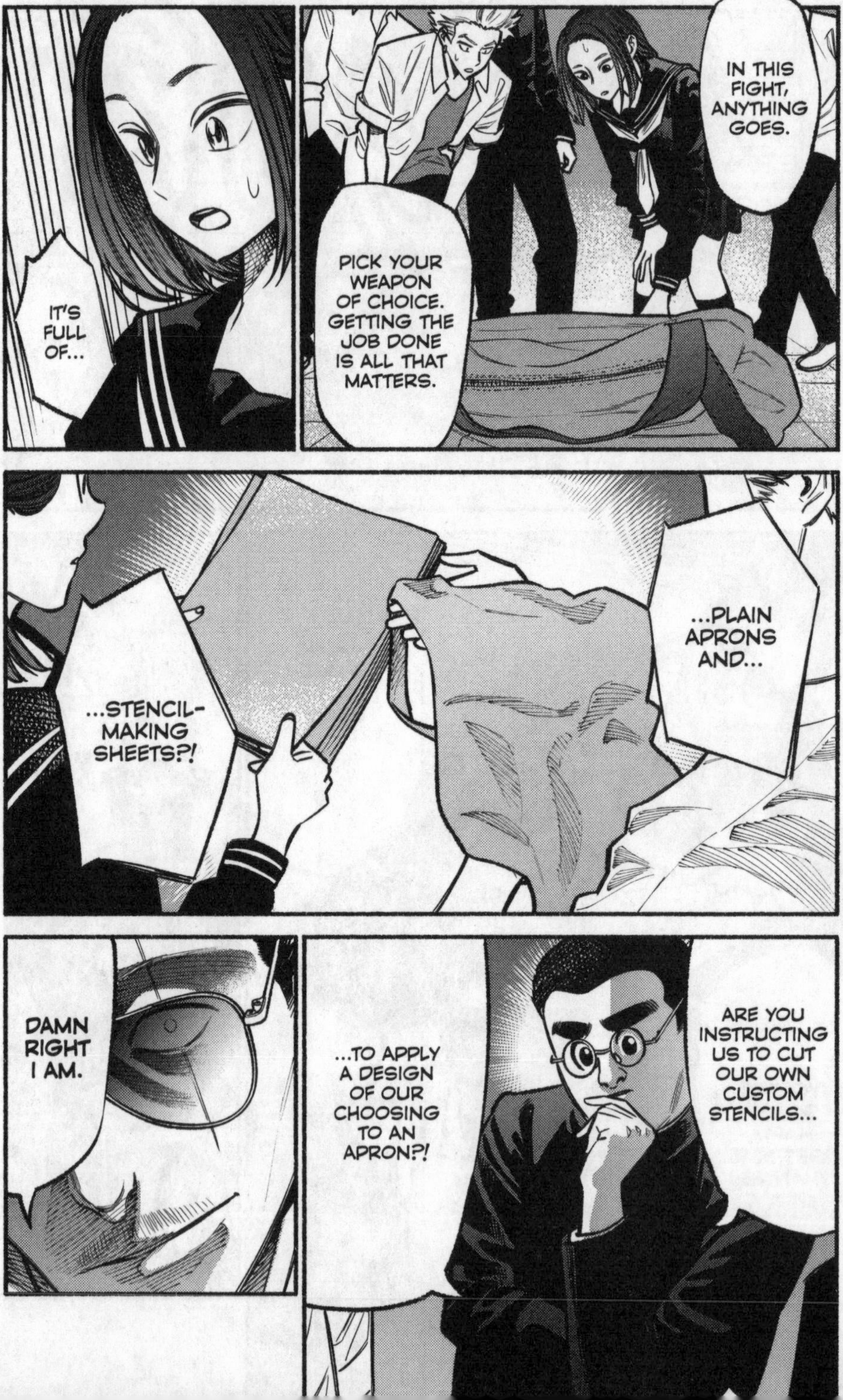
IN THIS FIGHT, ANYTHING GOES.
PICK YOUR WEAPON OF CHOICE. GETTING THE JOB DONE IS ALL THAT MATTERS.
IT'S FULL OF...
...PLAIN APRONS AND...
...STENCIL-MAKING SHEETS?!
ARE YOU INSTRUCTING US TO CUT OUR OWN CUSTOM STENCILS...
...TO APPLY A DESIGN OF OUR CHOOSING TO AN APRON?!
DAMN RIGHT I AM.

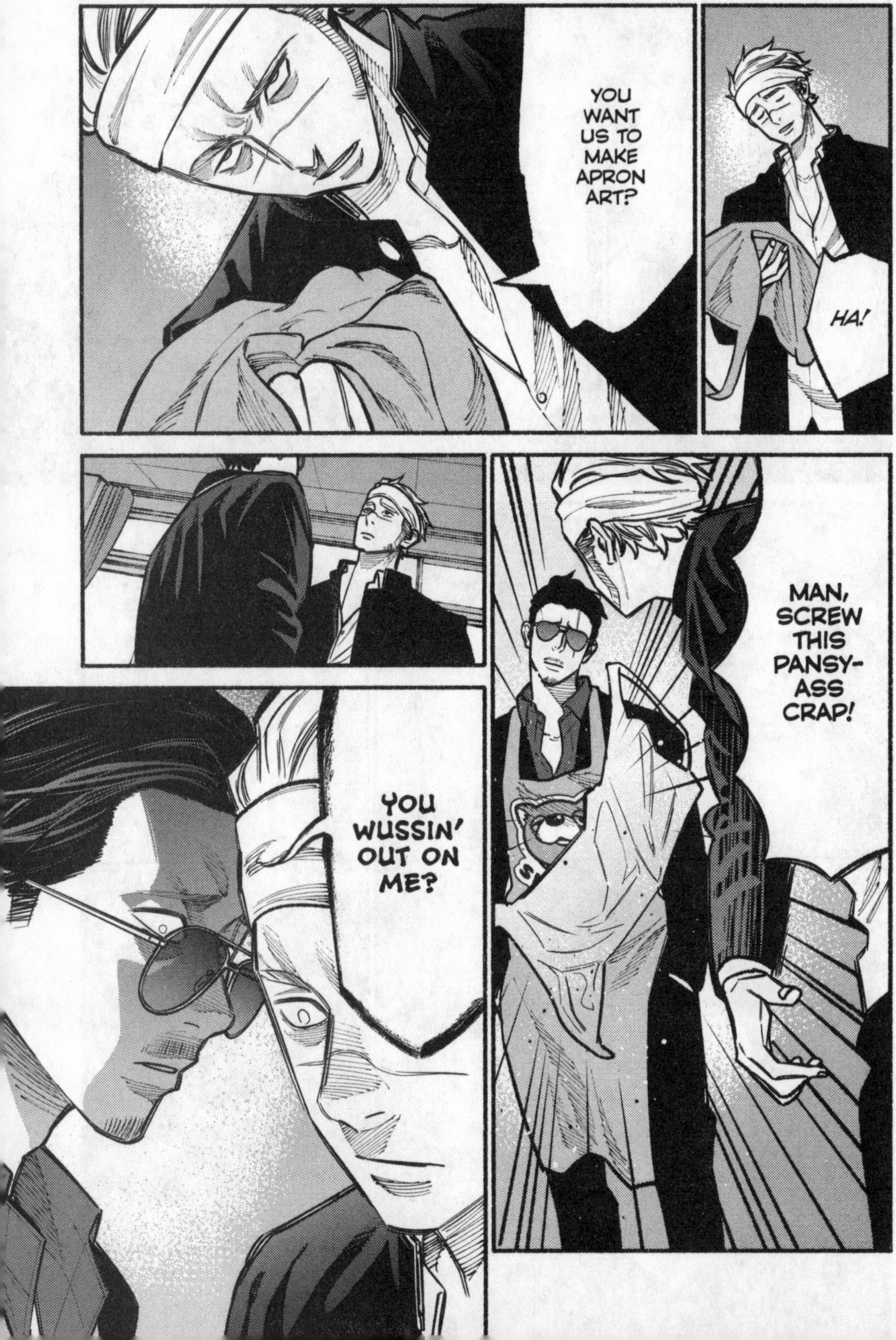
HA!
YOU WANT US TO MAKE APRON ART?
MAN, SCREW THIS PANSY-ASS CRAP!
YOU WUSSIN' OUT ON ME?

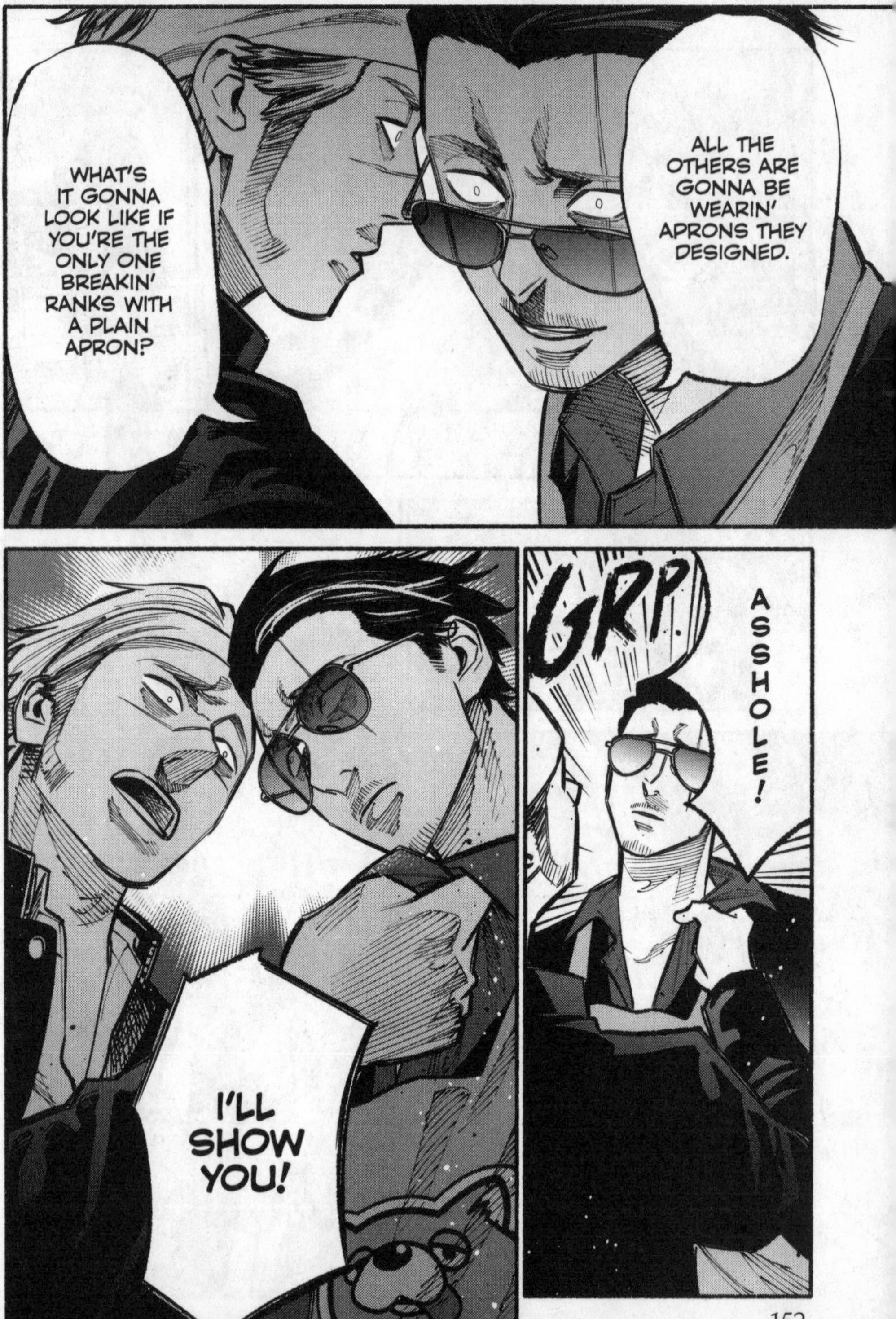
ALL THE OTHERS ARE GONNA BE WEARIN' APRONS THEY DESIGNED.
WHAT'S IT GONNA LOOK LIKE IF YOU'RE THE ONLY ONE BREAKIN' RANKS WITH A PLAIN APRON?
GRP.
ASSHOLE!
I'LL SHOW YOU!

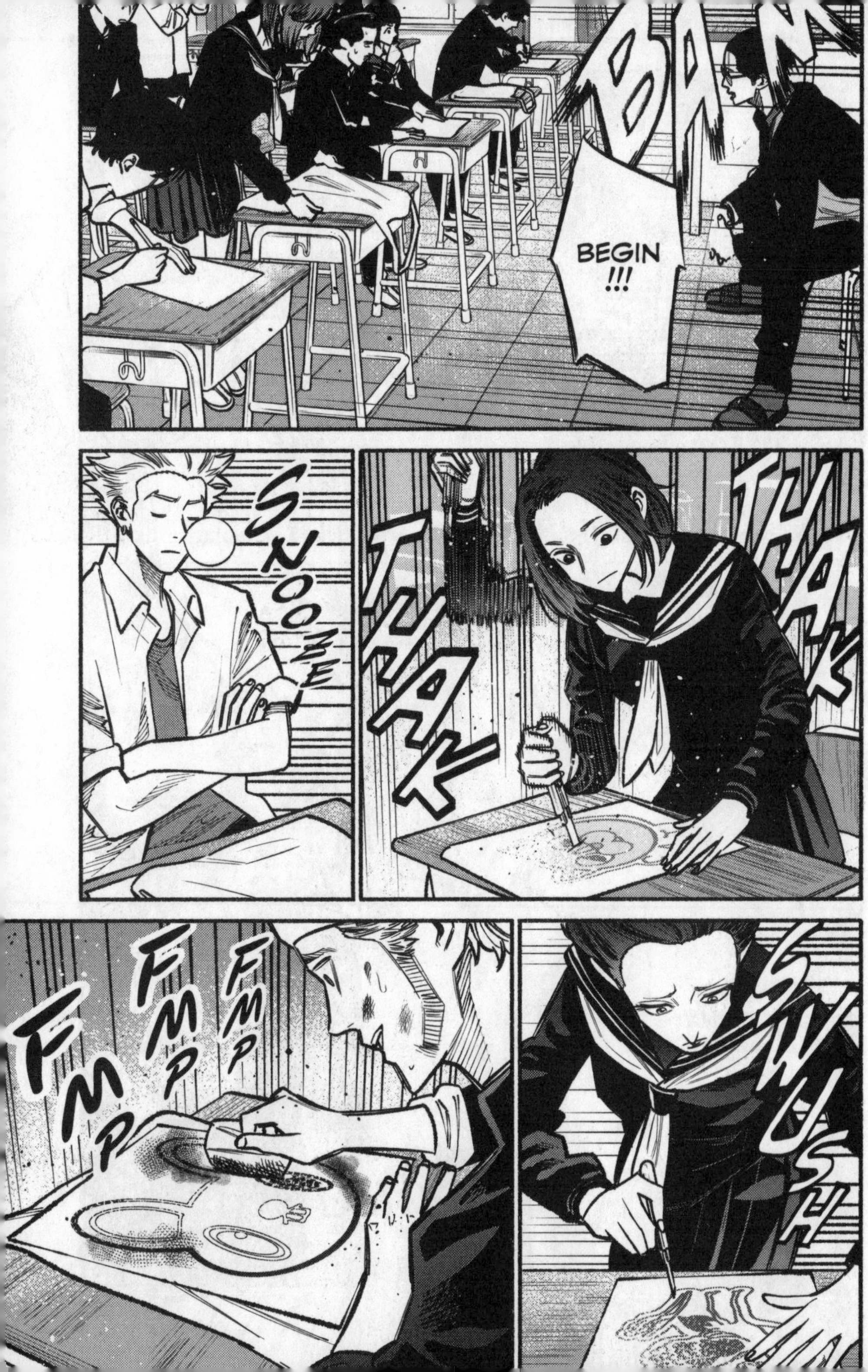
BAM
BEGIN!!!
THAK
THAK
SNOOZE
SWUSH
FMP
FMP
FMP

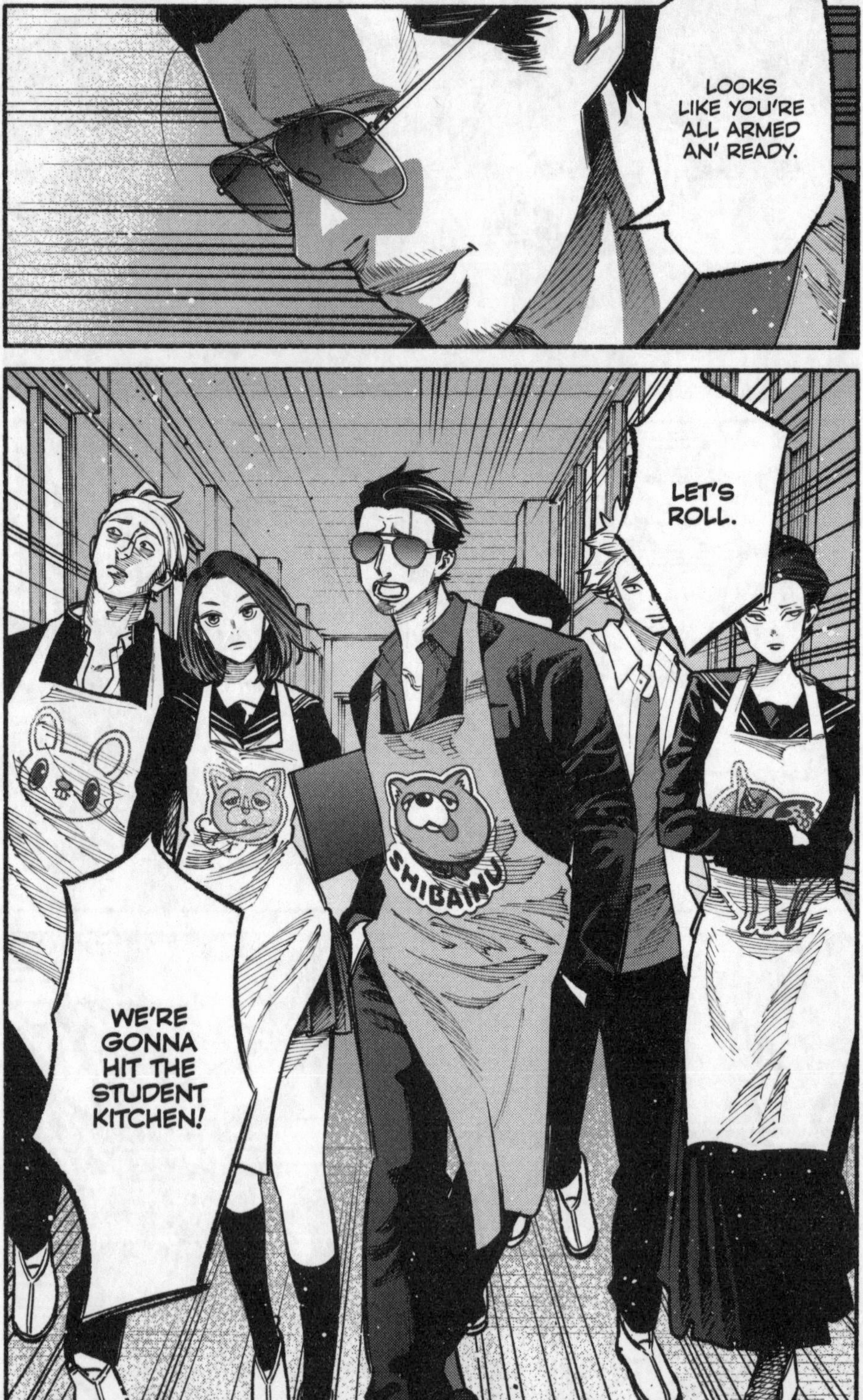
LOOKS LIKE YOU'RE ALL ARMED AN' READY.
LET'S ROLL.
SHIBAINU
WE'RE GONNA HIT THE STUDENT KITCHEN!

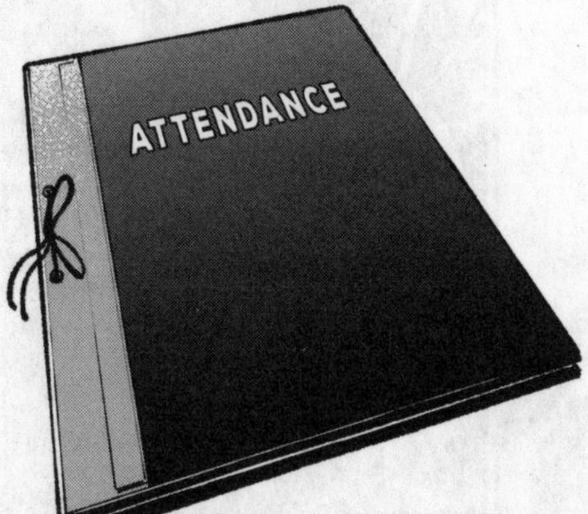
ATTENDANCE

BONUS MANGA ③ TORII & GIN

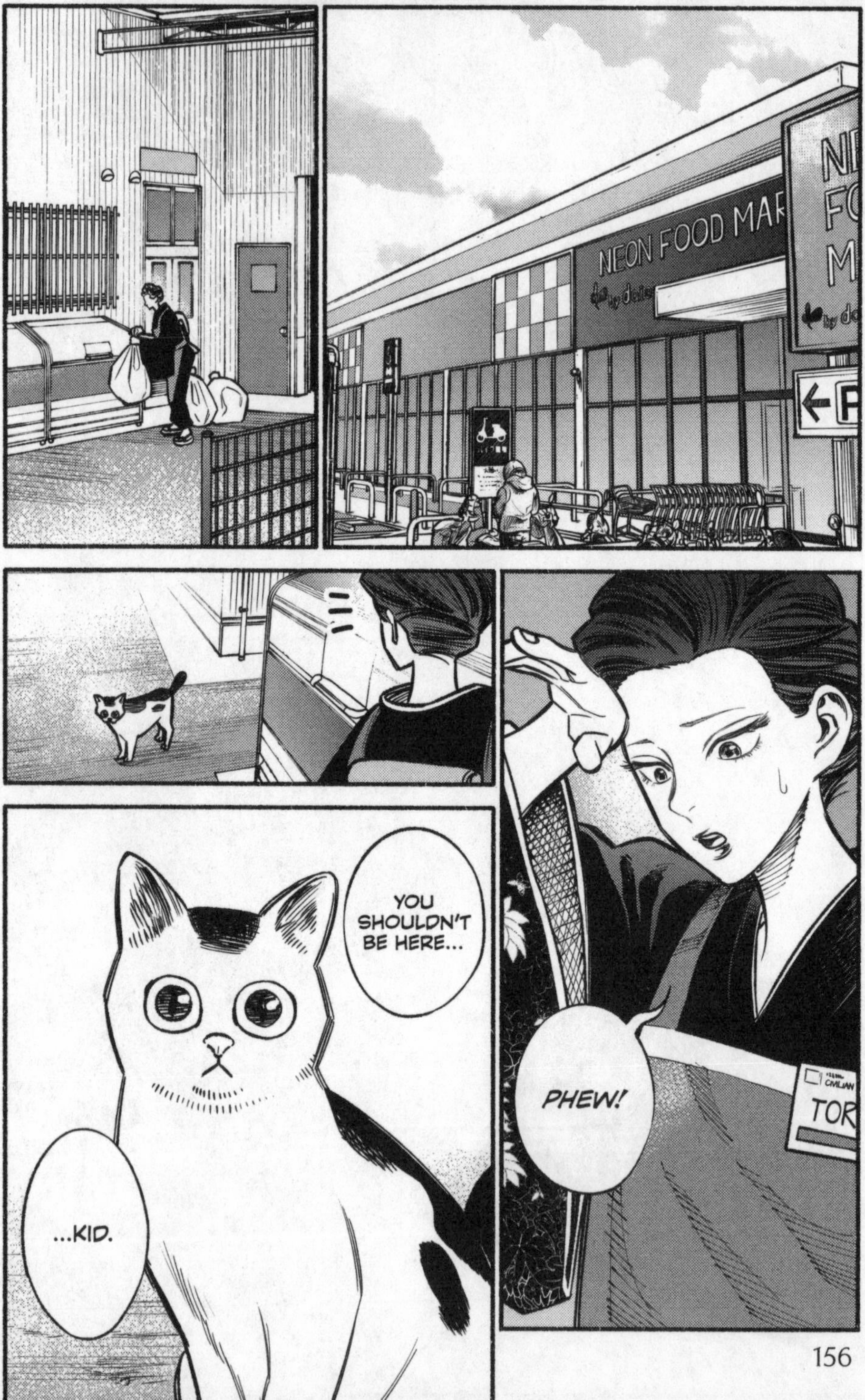
NEON FOOD MAR
PHEW!
TOR
YOU SHOULDN'T BE HERE...
...KID.

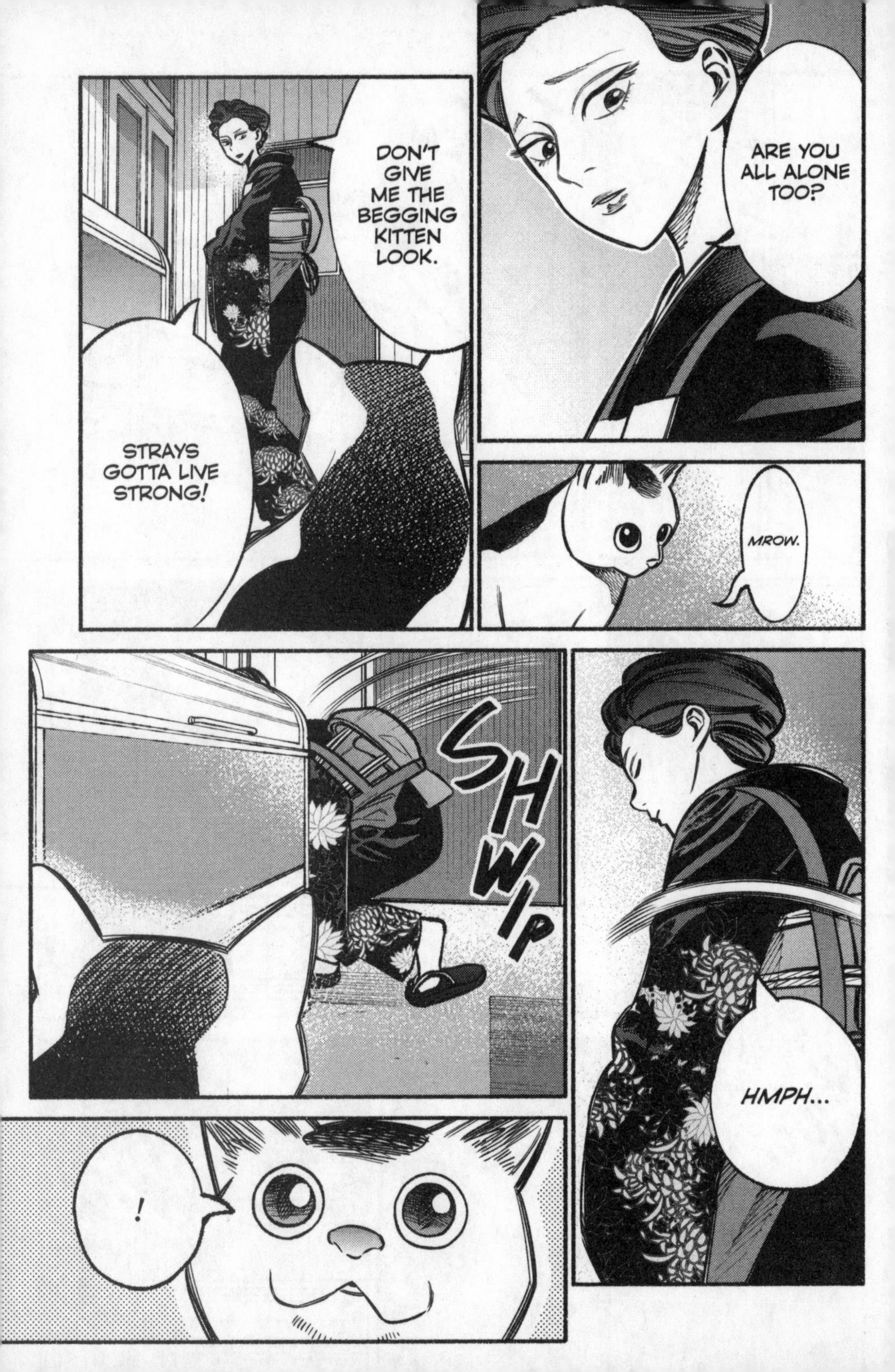
ARE YOU ALL ALONE TOO?
MROW.
DON'T GIVE ME THE BEGGING KITTEN LOOK.
STRAYS GOTTA LIVE STRONG!
HMPH...
SHWIP
!

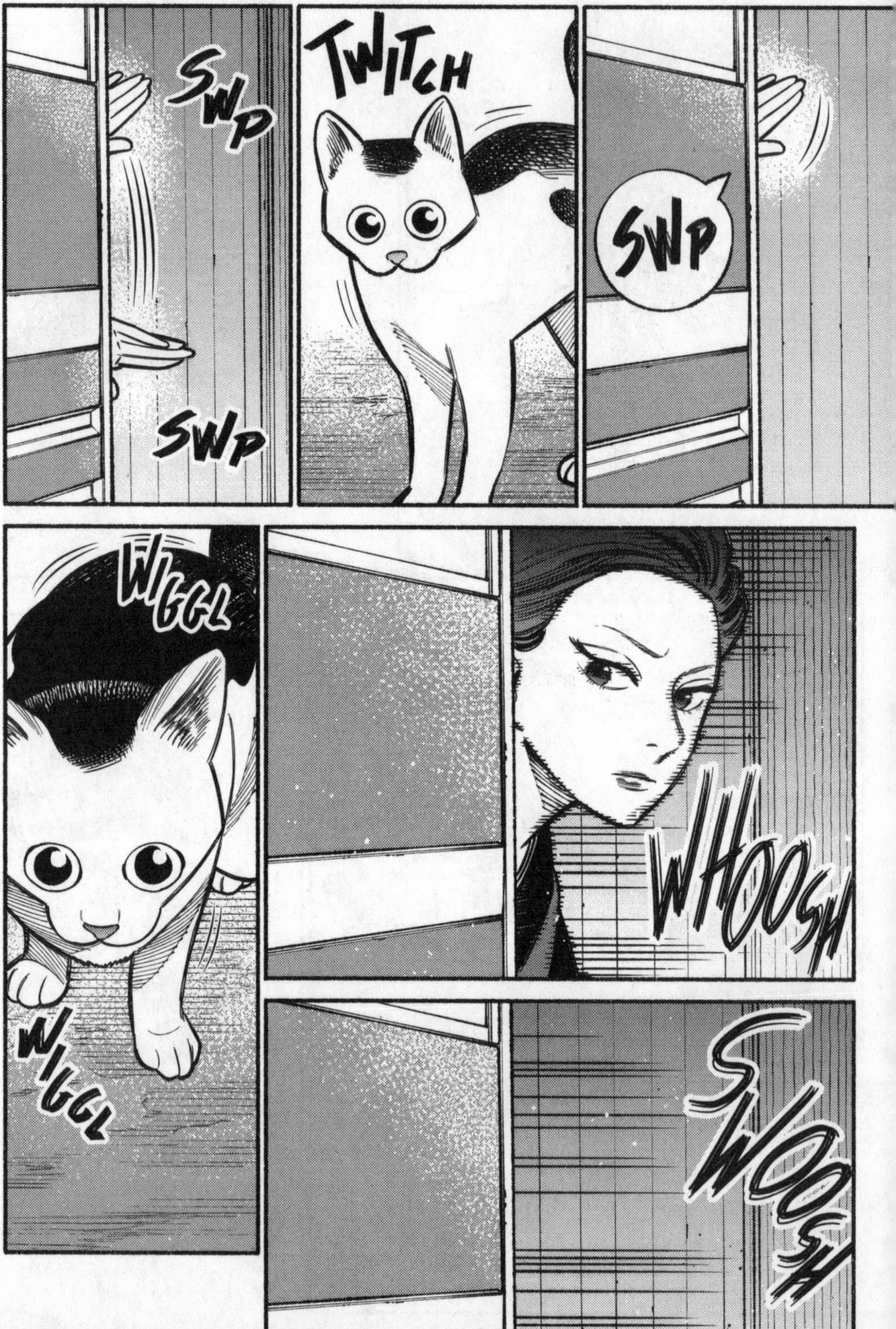
SWP
TWITCH
SWP
SWP
WHOOSH
SWOOSH
WIGGL
WIGGL

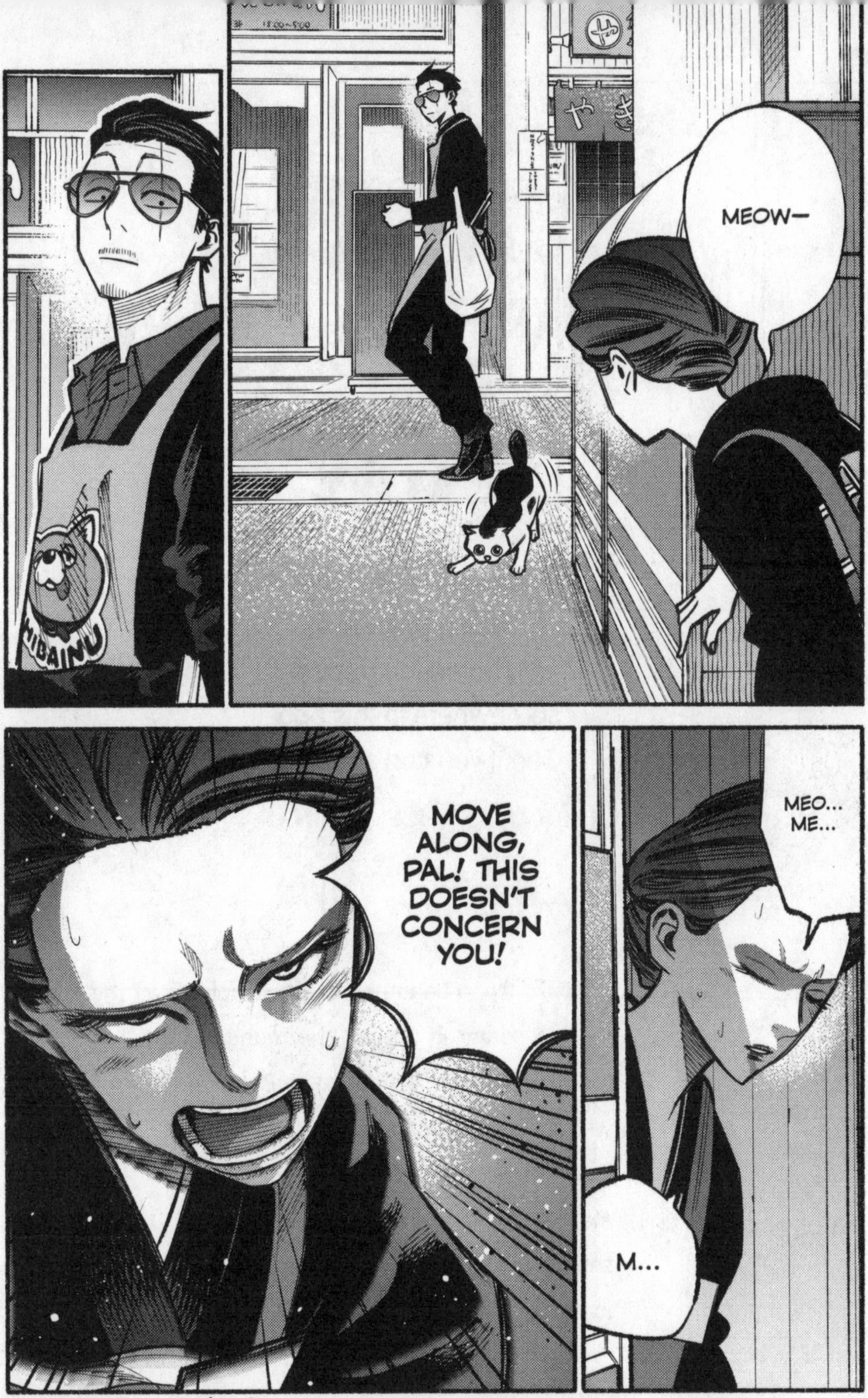
MEOW—
MEO... ME...
M...
MOVE ALONG, PAL! THIS DOESN'T CONCERN YOU!

THANK YOU FOR READING! I'M REALLY HOPING TO GET VOLUME 4 OUT AROUND DECEMBER.

SPECIAL THANKS - KIMU, MIDORINO, HIROE, SECRET SOCIETY FRIEND OF THE HOUSEHUSBAND.

Thanks for waiting.
This is volume 3.
My Shiba Inu appears
somewhere in this book.
See if you can spot him!
KOUSUKE OONO

Kousuke Oono began his professional manga career in 2016 in the manga magazine *Monthly Comics @ Bunch* with the one-shot "Legend of Music." Oono's follow-up series, *The Way of the Househusband,* is the creator's first serialization as well as his first English-language release.

The Way of the House Husband

VOLUME 3

VIZ SIGNATURE EDITION

STORY AND ART BY
KOUSUKE OONO

TRANSLATION: Amanda Haley
ENGLISH ADAPTATION: Jennifer LeBlanc
TOUCH-UP ART & LETTERING: Bianca Pistillo
DESIGN: Alice Lewis
EDITOR: Jennifer LeBlanc

GOKUSHUFUDO volume 3
© Kousuke Oono 2019
All Rights Reserved
English translation rights arranged
with SHINCHOSHA PUBLISHING CO.
through Tuttle-Mori Agency, Inc, Tokyo

Printed in Canada

Published by VIZ Media, LLC
P.O. Box 77010
San Francisco, CA 94107

10 9 8 7 6 5 4 3
First printing, May 2020
Third printing, April 2021

VIZ MEDIA   *VIZ SIGNATURE*

viz.com   vizsignature.com

GANGSTER COOKING RECIPE

JINGI TEI'S FLUFFY RICE OMELET ~GANGSTA STYLE~

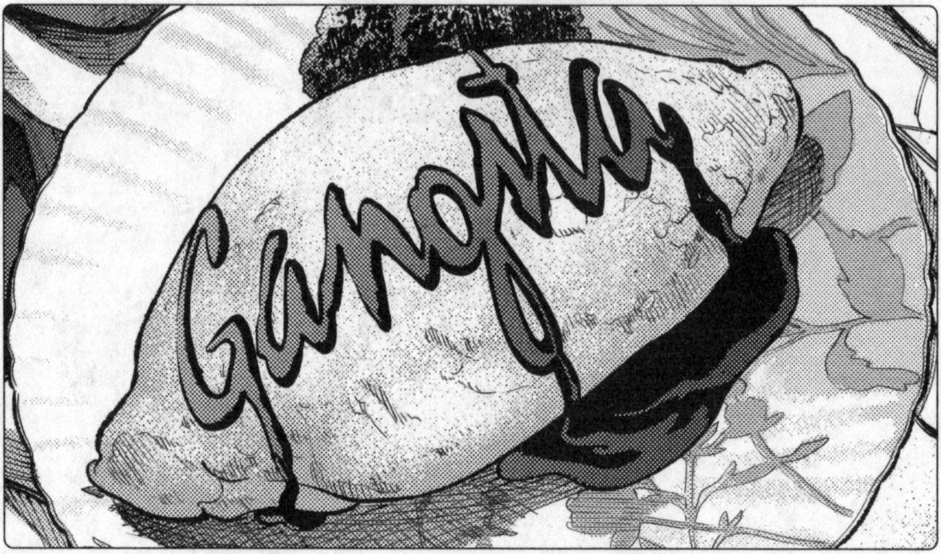
Gangsta

INGREDIENTS (SERVES 1)

- 1 bowl cooked rice (approx. 180g)
- 1/4 medium onion
- 40 grams chicken thighs
- 3 eggs
- 2 tablespoons ketchup
- 1 tablespoon milk
- 1 teaspoon butter
- Salt and pepper

DIRECTIONS

1. Grease a pan with olive oil. Cook chicken that's been cut into one-centimeter pieces.
2. Add salt, pepper and minced onion. Cook until onion is translucent.
3. Add the rice. When no longer clumping, mix in ketchup. Transfer to a bowl once well combined.
4. Melt butter in skillet. Pour mixture of egg and milk into pan and stir constantly until eggs are half done. Remove from heat.
5. Mold ketchup rice from step 3 into an oval shape and place in pan. Gently cover with omelet.
6. Using a spatula to hold the shape, transfer to a plate garnished with parsley, and it's done! If preferred, decorate with the word "Gangsta"!

Made Just for Pups

Chicken and Rice in Clam Broth

WANchan
DOGGY DISHES

BEASTARS

Story & Art by Paru Itagaki

At this high school, instead of jocks and nerds, the students
are divided into carnivores and herbivores.

At a high school where the students are literally divided into
predators and prey, friendships maintain the fragile peace.
Who among them will become a Beastar—a hero destined to
lead in a society naturally rife with mistrust?

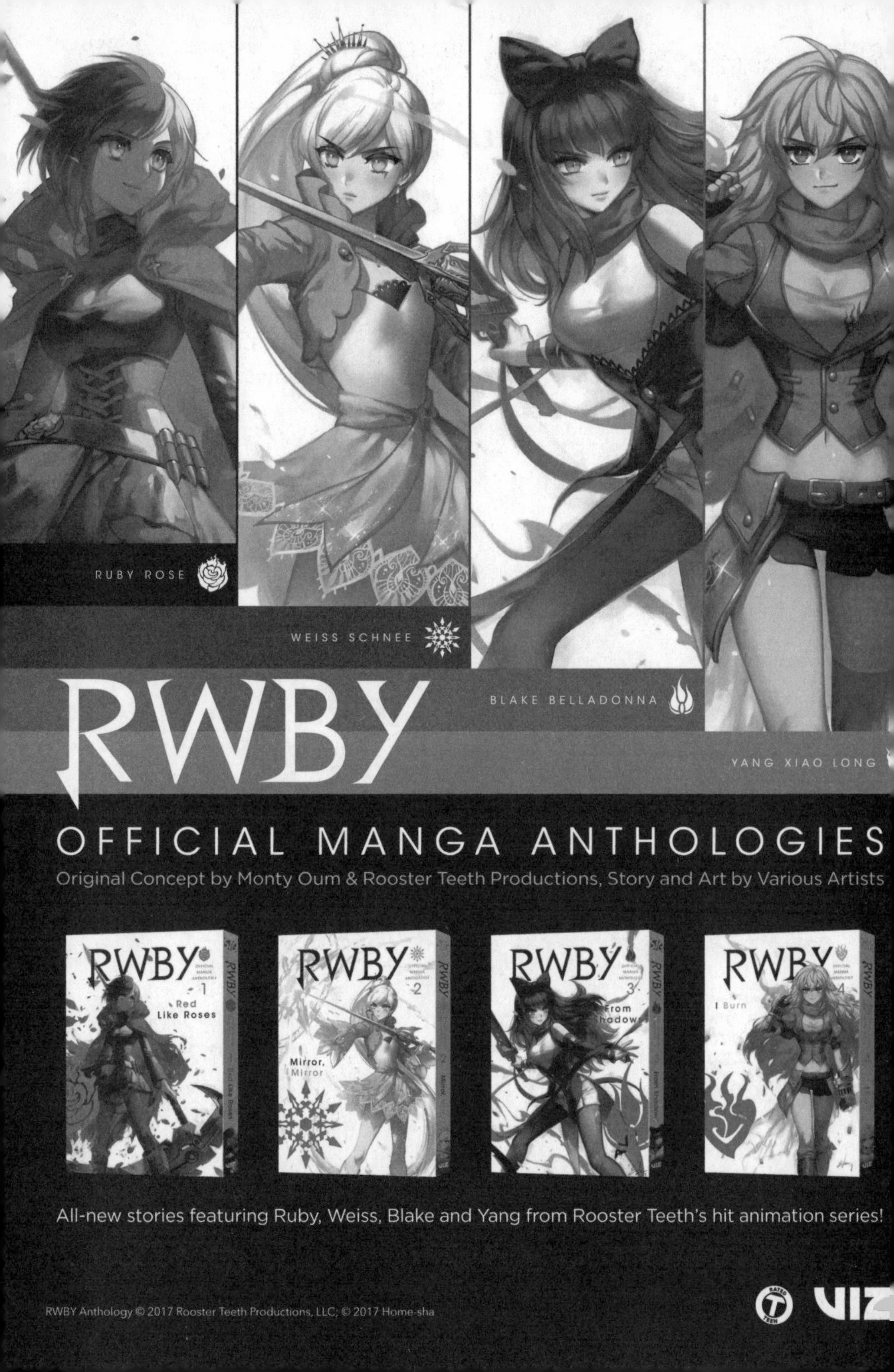
RUBY ROSE
WEISS SCHNEE
BLAKE BELLADONNA
YANG XIAO LONG
RWBY
OFFICIAL MANGA ANTHOLOGIES
Original Concept by Monty Oum & Rooster Teeth Productions, Story and Art by Various Artists
RWBY OFFICIAL MANGA ANTHOLOGY 1 Red Like Roses
RWBY OFFICIAL MANGA ANTHOLOGY 2 Mirror, Mirror
RWBY OFFICIAL MANGA ANTHOLOGY 3 From Shadows
RWBY OFFICIAL MANGA ANTHOLOGY 4 I Burn
All-new stories featuring Ruby, Weiss, Blake and Yang from Rooster Teeth's hit animation series!
RWBY Anthology © 2017 Rooster Teeth Productions, LLC; © 2017 Home-sha
RATED T TEEN
VIZ

20th Century Boys

THE PERFECT EDITION

NAOKI URASAWA